Commodity Market Controls

Commodity Market Controls

A Historical Review

Carmine Nappi
École des Hautes
Études Commerciales
University of Montreal

Lexington Books
D.C. Heath and Company
Lexington, Massachusetts
Toronto

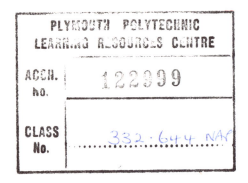
Library of Congress Cataloging in Publication Data

Nappi, Carmine.
 Commodity market controls.

 Bibliography: p.
 Includes index.
 1. Commodity control—History. I. Title.
HF1428.N36   332.6'44'09   78-24715
ISBN 0-669-02812-6

Published simultaneously in Canada.

Printed in the United States of America.

International Standard Book Number: 0-669-02812-6

Library of Congress Catalog Card Number: 78-24715

To my parents

Contents

List of Figures
and Tables

Acknowledgments

Research is a highly time-intensive activity, and in each life, time must be accounted one of the most precious nonrenewable resources. We would therefore like to thank all those who so generously allowed us the use of their time during this study.

Without the extraordinary patience of my wife, Nicole, and my son, Anthony, this work could never have been developed, through several successive manuscripts, into a publishable text. The promises made to them to be more "available" must now be kept.

My very special thanks are addressed to Mr. Pierre Lamy of Montreal's Centre for International Business Studies at École des Hautes Études Commerciales. Our discussions, which always proved stimulating, permitted me to clearly define and delimit the subject of this research.

I am particularly grateful to Ms. Sybil Murray Denis who has most competently translated this book from French and to Ms. Nicole Lamy who was trusted with the thankless task of supplying all the volumes and documents necessary to the writing of this study.

The work of my two research assistants, Messrs. Daniel Depelteau and Fares Khoury is certainly not to be forgotten. This study could not have been completed without their assistance and that of the Centre for International Business Studies. My special thanks to Misses Diane Grenier and Katherine Pan for having typed this long text with such practised skill.

Despite the generosity of these and many other people, I remain, of course, solely responsible for all remaining errors this text may comport.

Montreal
May 1, 1978

1 Introduction

At the end of the sixties, before the creation of the Organization of Petroleum Exporting Countries (OPEC), international trade in commodities (agricultural products, foodstuffs, minerals, and fuels) already accounted for 40% of world trade, 50% of developed countries' imports, and more than 40% of their total exports. Commodities made up 40% of developing countries' imports and 85% of their exports. The production, marketing, and transportation of commodities provided employment for a substantial percentage of the world's labor force. In many cases, commodity shipments furnished most of the export receipts upon which a country's various economic agents counted for the foreign currency necessary to finance imports of equipment and to establish the economic infrastructure. For most developing countries, the taxes and royalties levied on the export sector were the sole source of finance.

Although the creation of OPEC may not have seriously modified the role of commodities in international economic relations nor the structural characteristics mentioned, it did attract added press coverage to questions concerning depletion of nonrenewable resources, government and private controls of commodity markets, and instability of commodity prices. In a certain sense, OPEC may be said to have shaken the foundations of the international economic system and focused attention on developing countries' demands for a more just redistribution of the world's wealth. Several other countries, encouraged by OPEC's lead, abandoned the formula of international agreements sanctioned by the United Nations after the second world war and, through the creation of formal producer cartels, sought to control the international markets for their commodities. What has been made brutally clear with the establishment of OPEC is that "sufficiency" and "accessibility" are not synonymous, and that we are perhaps witnessing a transition from a buyer's to a seller's market.

However, these apprehensions concerning the future availability of commodities and the limits which proliferating producer cartels might impose upon growth in industrial countries are questioned by a large number of other analysts. The statement by the United Nations Conference on Trade and Development (UNCTAD), affirming that the actions of oil-producing countries had finally tipped the balance of economic power in favor of developing countries, now seems of questionable validity. It is thought instead that the phenomenal rise in oil prices has ruined developing countries, increasing their long-term debt and making them even more dependent on industrial countries. Moreover (except perhaps in the case of petroleum, bauxite, chromium, and some tropical foodstuffs), observers maintain that any attempt to control world commodity supply may cause a rise in production and exports in nonmember countries, increased use of secondary supply ("scrap market"), and eventual replacement of commodities by substitutes. After underlining the scarcity of products fulfilling the conditions for a successful cartel (such as control of world production, strong short- and medium-term inelastic demand, absence of appropriate substitutes, and member cohesion and discipline), these authors suggest that there are other means of increasing export receipts and foreign currency or of attracting high value-added plants. They especially propose that developing countries' manufactured and semimanufactured products be given access to industrial markets.

There is nothing new in this divergence of views over the expected effects of the use of controls in international commodity markets. The conflict has been polarizing free traders and interventionists for at least the past sixty years, a period during which controls have come increasingly into use and have become more sophisticated. The present study is situated within the framework of this debate. But contrary to other studies giving a theoretical and empirical analysis of the effects of certain types of control on specific markets, we have preferred to give readers a historical perspective of the use of controls since the first world war. Such a perspective in fact seems essential in order to better situate the recent resurgence of government intervention on world mineral markets; show that these interventions are the fruit of a long development; examine the factors having contributed to the success or failure of certain controls; evaluate their effectiveness and, to some extent, trace the origin of current tensions between producing and consuming countries.

Before proceeding with the historical survey, we examine and evaluate, in chapter 2, a number of statistical tables concerning the place of commodities in world trade; the structure of these exports; market shares by product and region; evolution of average price indexes of certain groups of commodities since the beginning of the sixties; the question of deteriorating terms of trade and the problem of the sufficiency, availability, and accessibility of identified reserves of the major minerals and their hypothetical resources.

The other chapters present a historical survey of the controls used since the beginning of the century and show how they have evolved from private producer cartels to national government controls; to generalized single-product international agreements; to an integrated program of seventeen products (Common Fund) and, finally, to international producing country cartels. Chapter 3 evaluates the types of controls used between 1914 and 1945 for the following markets: rubber, coffee, sugar, copper, tin, tea, and wheat. Chapters 4 and 5 tackle the international agreements based on resolution 30(IV) adopted on March 28, 1947 by the UN Economic and Social Council. This resolution defined the modalities governing all government interventions on international commodity markets. It granted international approval on the following conditions: presence of consumer countries on administrative control boards to moderate producing country demands; supply to come from most efficient sources while discouraging production in countries with relatively high costs; and agreements to be short-term, ending whenever the UN judged problems of excess supply solved. Studying the international agreements signed between 1945 and 1977 for wheat, tin, sugar, coffee, and cocoa, chapters 4 and 5 evaluate the degree to which these conditions have been respected and how, after the start of the sixties, the microeconomic considerations (efficiency in the allocation of resources) underlying UN resolution 30(IV) have been progressively replaced by macroeconomic concerns for development and foreign exchange. In fact, starting with this date, international agreements have been perceived as a normal and acceptable means of transferring resources from rich countries to poor countries and the expressions "international agreements" and "aid to developing countries" have become synonymous for most products (except those from industrial countries).

Chapter 6 is devoted to the Integrated Commodity Program (ICP) adopted at Nairobi in 1976 during the fourth UNCTAD session (resolution 93[IV]). After having enumerated the program's objectives (and pointed out the place of the commodities retained in developing countries' world trade), the means chosen to reach these objectives are evaluated. Special attention is paid to the cost of the international network of buffer stocks to be financed by a common fund and to this fund's capital structure and mode of operation. The fundamental differences in the interpretation of resolution 93(IV) by the Group of 77 and the industrial countries with market economies led to the failure of the second conference on common fund negotiations, held at Geneva, November 7-December 2, 1977. These negotiations are soon to be reconvened and will eventually lead to a compromise formula. We fear that the search for such a compromise will lend more importance to political considerations than to criteria for economic efficiency.

Chapters 7 through 10 evaluate the international producing countries' associations for copper (CIPEC), bauxite (IBA), iron ore (AIEC) and mercury (ASSIMER). (Given the number of existing publications on petroleum, we have preferred to leave aside discussion of this product). In our survey we show how national governments have regulated production, price and marketing for products mentioned; taken control of mineral deposits; regulated their extraction and primary transformation; and established public agencies responsible for their international distribution. Except perhaps for bauxite, these associations have not attained the success recorded by OPEC. The relative success achieved by each of them has been determined by the following variables: cartel's degree of coverage of world production and trade; price-elasticity of short- and medium-term demand; technical possibilities for substitution; size of identified reserves, and discipline of members. The relative importance of these variables will be evaluated through an analysis of the structure of markets that have been the objects of various controls exercised by producing country governments. The last section of the book presents the main conclusions reached by our historical survey. After an evaluation of the difference in the methodology used by economists of the developed and developing world, to analyze the effects of controls, the concluding chapter attempts to determine the possible evolution of controls in the near future.

Our historical survey of course remains incomplete. It does not treat the informal and private cartels established for lead and uranium, the talks being held within UNCTAD on an international tungsten agreement, nor the studies requested to analyze the possibilities of intervening on the international chromium, manganese, phosphate, platinum, potassium and zinc markets. For the moment, we are prevented, by the very complex nature of their markets and the lack of pertinent statistical data, from evaluating the types of controls used or recommended for these products. Moreover, there have been no microeconomic analyses of the effects of export taxes, buffer stocks, buffer funds, and multilateral contracts on price stability, producer revenues, and trade receipts. Finally, the macroeconomic aspects of controls (as underlined by certain producing country governments and economists) have not been examined. Despite these gaps (and many others), we hope our study will permit a better understanding of the past and recent evolution of the international economic order.

2 General Characteristics of International Commodity Markets

For some years now, the specific problems of international commodity markets (such as farm, forestry and fishery products, metals, raw ores) have attracted the attention of economists, governments, financiers, consumers, and other economic agents. The latest statistical data on the evolution of world production are used to evaluate identified commodity reserves, hypothetical resources, and the ever-increasing cost of substitutes. The creation of new producer cartels, and the limits they may impose on control of world inflation are cause for concern. Old theories concerning the historical deterioration of developing countries' terms of trade are being questioned. There is concern over how industrial countries will react to a modified economic environment. One fears they might opt for bilateral exchanges, discard the nondiscrimination clause in tariff negotiations, reduce or modify international capital transfers, or even succumb to pressures from local producers and put up tariff and nontariff barriers. Finally, most observers are wondering to what extent transition from a buyer's to a seller's market will modify economic and political relations among countries.

In the following chapters, some of these problems and apprehensions will be evaluated for certain specific products. For the moment we turn our attention to some of the world commodity markets' general characteristics. The statistical tables presented will help toward a better knowledge of the importance of commodities in international trade, the structure of exports, the evolution of an average price index for certain groups of commodities, terms of trade, identified reserves of major ores and their hypothetical resources.

Evolution of World Trade: 1960-1976

Table 2-1 summarizes the evolution of world trade during the last fifteen years. It indicates that the world export values of developing countries have increased more rapidly than exports from developed countries (684% against 576%). This performance by developing countries' export values must be largely explained by increased prices, since, for the period under study, the increase in the quantum of their international shipments stood at 127% (while the corresponding percentage for developed countries rose to 205%).

It should not be concluded from these data that, since the beginning of the sixties, we have been witnessing a general upheaval in international economic relations; that developing countries are finally receiving what the Group of 77 calls

Table 2-1

Quantum, Value, and Unit-Value International Export Indexes: 1960-1975

Exports	Year	Quantum	Value	Unit Value
Developing countries				
Including oil-exporting countries	1960	52	49	94
	1965	70	65	93
	1970	100	100	100
	1973	131	203	155
	1975	118	384	325
Excluding oil-exporting countries	1960	62	55	88
	1965	77	69	89
	1970	100	100	100
	1973	128	181	141
	1975	124	233	188
Developed countries	1960	44	38	86
	1965	63	57	90
	1970	100	100	100
	1973	131	181	138
	1975	134	257	192

Source: World Bank, *Commodity Trade and Price Trends (1976 edition)*, Washington, 1976, p. 6. Reprinted with permission.

Note: 1970 = 100. Based on trade data in U.S. 1970 dollars. To calculate quantum indexes these weights have been used: developing countries (including oil): 19.8%; developing countries (excluding oil): 16.4%; developed countries: 80.2%.

"just and equitable prices"; or that the lowering of tariff barriers is permitting Third World manufactured goods to seriously penetrate Western markets. In fact, when oil countries are excluded from the group of developing countries, we find that the value of the latter's world exports has increased about 325% while the quantum of their shipments only show a 100% increase. If there has been any redistribution of wealth on a world scale, only a small number of countries (a few members of OPEC) have profited from it and it has occurred mainly toward the end of the period under study.

What is the structure of world trade by economic classes? Table 2-2 reveals that 70% of the developed countries' exports are directed toward other developed countries and only 24% are shipped to developing countries. On the other hand, these latter trade very little among themselves (22.5%), the largest portion of their exports (73%) being absorbed by developed countries. Countries with planned economies are not very important as customers, receiving an average 5% of international shipments. Intrabloc exchanges also characterize the international exports of countries with central planning since 56% of their trade is

Table 2-2
Market Shares of World Trade by Economic Classes: 1960-1975
(*percent*)

Place of Origin	Year	To Developed Countries	To Developing Countries	To Countries with a Planned Economy
Developed	1960	70.5	25.5	3.5
countries	1965	74.7	21.1	3.9
	1970	76.9	18.7	3.7
	1973	76.5	18.1	4.8
	1975	69.6	23.8	6.0
Developing	1960	72.2	22.3	4.5
countries	1965	71.6	21.0	6.5
	1970	74.0	18.4	6.3
	1973	73.3	20.6	4.6
	1975	72.9	22.5	3.9
Countries with a	1960	18.6	9.3	72.0
planned economy	1965	21.5	14.7	63.4
	1970	25.5	16.3	58.0
	1973	27.8	15.2	56.0
	1975	28.1	15.2	55.8

Source: World Bank, *Commodity Trade and Price Trends (1976 edition),* Washington, 1976, p. 12. Reprinted with permission.

Note: Due to errors and omissions, figures do not total 100.

confined within their group, 28% of their shipments are directed toward developed countries and scarcely 15% toward developing countries. Notice, however, that exports from countries with central planning have undergone a certain diversification by economic classes; between 1960 and 1975, the importance of developed countries in their total shipments has increased by 51% while that of developing countries has grown 63%.

What is the composition of world trade according to large product categories and how has each evolved since the start of the sixties? Table 2-3 sheds light on these questions. It indicates that in 1976 agricultural products represented scarcely 17% of world trade, an important drop compared with 1960 when they accounted for 31% of the value of products traded on international markets. Ores and minerals (including fuels and nonferrous metals) have shown the opposite evolution with a 48% increase of their share in world trade, representing close to 25% of this trade in 1976. All the same, it should be noted that between 1960 and 1970 this category's share remained unchanged, implying that the increase mentioned occurred mainly during the first part of the seventies. World trade continues to be dominated by the international shipment of manufactured products. But although their share increased by 22% between

Table 2-3
Composition of World Trade: 1960-1976

	Percent of Value of World Exports			1976 Volume Index[c]		
Product	1960	1970	1976	World Production	World Exports	Export Production Ratio
Agricultural products	31.3	20.5	16.8	147	179	1.22
Ores and minerals[a]	16.4	16.3	24.2	198	221	1.12
Manufactured products	50.0	60.9	56.7	260	403	1.55
Total	100.0[b]	100.0	100.0	220	314	1.43

Source: General Agreement on Tariffs and Trade, *International Trade in 1976/77*, Geneva, 1977, p. 3. Reprinted with permission.

[a]Including fuels and nonferrous metals.

[b]Due to omissions, figures do not total 100.

[c]1960 = 100

1960 and 1970, since then exports have been increasing at a slower pace than that of total shipments, thus causing their relative percentage to weaken.

The second part of table 2-3 corrects the effects of inflation and presents the evolution in quantum of world production and exports compared with 1960. We observe that international shipments of manufactured products have increased fourfold since 1960, while in 1976 the volume index for mineral exports and agricultural products was twice as high as in 1960.

Finally, for the past fifteen years we have been witnessing an intensification of international trade, with world exports increasing much faster than production. This characteristic is especially noticeable for manufactured products whose export/production ratio stood at 1.55 in 1976 as compared with the 1960 hypothetical ratio of 1. For minerals and agricultural products this ratio stood at 1.12 and 1.22 respectively.

The divergencies detected between the ratio for manufactured products and that for commodities can largely be explained by the rise in transportation costs, the General Agreement on Tariffs and Trade (GATT) multilateral negotiations on tariff reductions, and the determination of commodity-producing countries to concentrate as many high value-added activities as possible within their boundaries.

**Structure of World Exports by Products and by Sectors
of Destination and of Origin: 1955-1975**

With this picture of the general evolution and structure of world trade in mind, we now turn our attention more specifically to the destination and origin of international exports of foodstuffs, agricultural products, ores and minerals, fuels, and manufactured products. Tables 2-4 through 2-7 provide specific information on this subject.

In 1975, 66% of total world exports were destined for developed countries, 23% for developing countries, and 10.5% for countries with planned economies. The place of developed countries in international trade becomes even more apparent when we look at percentages by product groups and by sector of destination. One then notices that 66% of the foodstuffs and 72% of the agricultural products exported worldwide are directed towards developed countries; for minerals and fuels the figures are 64% and 76%. The market of developing countries absorbs 22% of the international shipments of foodstuffs and more than 25% of the world exports of manufactured products. Countries with planned economies are of relatively small importance on the international trade scene. However, it is worth noticing that in 1975, despite their policy of self-sufficiency, these countries absorbed close to 16% of world mineral shipments and more than 12% of the agricultural products exported.

Table 2-5 provides the same information as before but by sector of origin. Contrary to popular belief, developed countries remain the leading exporters of foodstuffs, agricultural products, and minerals. In fact, more than 62% of international imports of foodstuffs and agricultural products originate in one of the developed countries; this percentage approaches 75% for ores and minerals. Developing countries mainly specialize in the exportation of fuels, being responsible for 74% of these international shipments. Moreover, while between 1955 and 1975 their percentage for origin of fuels increased from 57% to 74%, that for foodstuffs, agricultural products, and ores fell sharply. Finally, in 1975, 6.6% of the world imports of manufactured products came from developing countries while scarcely more than 9% originated in countries with a planned economy.

Tables 2-6 and 2-7 offer a more detailed study of the export-import product flow as it originates in or is destined for each of the groups of countries under consideration. Table 2-6 indicates that in 1975 commodities (foodstuffs, agricultural products, ores, minerals, and fuels) constituted close to 50% of developed countries' import value as compared to 63.5% in 1955. Manufactured products are gaining an increasingly important place in their total imports while the opposite may be observed for commodities—except fuels, for which the percentage almost doubled between 1973 and 1975. This structural change reflects the effects of two different factors: policies in industrial countries promoting self-sufficiency in food products and increased outlays for mineral exploration; and the level and evolution of world prices favoring manufactured

Table 2-4

Structure of World Exports by Products and by Sectors of Destination: In
Percentage, by Destination (1955-1975)

Export		World	To Developed Countries	To Developing Countries	To Countries with a Planned Economy	
					Europe	Asia
All products	1955	100.0	65.2	24.8	7.8	1.6
	1965	100.0	67.9	20.3	10.2	1.1
	1973	100.0	71.3	18.2	8.7	1.0
	1975	100.0	66.0	22.9	9.5	1.0
Foodstuffs	1955	100.0	72.6	18.9	7.8	0.4
	1965	100.0	69.6	18.8	9.9	1.6
	1973	100.0	71.6	17.8	8.0	1.3
	1975	100.0	65.9	22.4	10.1	0.8
Agricultural products	1955	100.0	76.6	12.0	10.0	1.3
	1965	100.0	74.3	11.2	12.3	2.3
	1973	100.0	74.0	13.8	8.6	2.1
	1975	100.0	71.6	16.0	10.1	2.0
Ores and minerals	1955	100.0	74.1	14.4	9.9	1.2
	1965	100.0	74.8	12.7	11.1	1.0
	1973	100.0	72.5	14.2	10.6	2.1
	1975	100.0	63.5	18.7	13.7	2.2
Fuels	1955	100.0	60.6	26.5	6.7	1.0
	1965	100.0	70.9	18.1	7.4	0.3
	1973	100.0	79.7	13.8	4.6	0.2
	1975	100.0	76.2	17.3	4.5	0.1
Manufactured products	1955	100.0	53.4	32.3	7.2	2.6
	1965	100.0	64.1	23.8	10.5	1.0
	1973	100.0	70.1	19.5	9.2	0.7
	1975	100.0	62.9	25.6	10.1	1.0

Source: United Nations Conference on Trade and Development (UNCTAD), *Handbook of
International Trade and Development Statistics,* Geneva, 1976, p. 82. Reprinted with per-
mission; United Nations, *Monthly Bulletin of Statistics,* New York, May 1977, Special
Table C, pp. XXVIII-LII. Reprinted with permission.

products during most of the period under study. Exports destined for developing
countries are mainly manufactured products—58% in 1975. Although this percentage has proved relatively stable since 1965, the shares of foodstuffs and
agricultural products in their total imports have decreased; this decrease has,

Table 2-5
Structure of World Exports by Products and by Sectors of Origin: In Percentage, by Origin (1955-1975)

Export		World	From Developed Countries	From Developing Countries	From Countries with a Planned Economy	
					Europe	Asia
All products	1955	100.0	64.7	25.4	8.5	1.5
	1965	100.0	68.8	19.6	10.6	1.1
	1973	100.0	71.0	19.0	9.1	0.9
	1975	100.0	66.2	24.1	8.9	0.8
Foodstuffs	1955	100.0	48.7	42.6	5.4	3.3
	1965	100.0	56.7	34.0	7.1	2.1
	1973	100.0	65.1	27.0	6.2	1.7
	1975	100.0	63.3	28.7	5.8	1.8
Agricultural products	1955	100.0	49.4	40.4	7.9	2.4
	1965	100.0	56.2	31.4	10.1	2.3
	1973	100.0	59.7	29.4	8.8	1.9
	1975	100.0	61.3	22.3	11.6	2.9
Ores and minerals	1955	100.0	67.7	21.0	9.1	2.1
	1965	100.0	68.3	18.8	12.0	1.0
	1973	100.0	73.2	15.9	10.3	0.8
	1975	100.0	74.6	14.3	10.4	0.5
Fuels	1955	100.0	31.7	57.4	10.7	0.1
	1965	100.0	24.1	63.1	12.6	0.1
	1973	100.0	22.8	68.2	8.9	0.1
	1975	100.0	17.4	73.9	8.2	0.5
Manufactured products	1955	100.0	85.1	4.7	9.6	0.5
	1965	100.0	83.5	4.6	11.1	0.7
	1973	100.0	83.8	6.9	8.6	0.7
	1975	100.0	84.2	6.6	8.6	0.6

Source: United Nations Conference on Trade and Development (UNCTAD), *Handbook of International Trade and Development Statistics,* Geneva, 1976, p. 80. Reprinted with permission; United Nations, *Monthly Bulletin of Statistics,* New York, May 1977, Special Table C, pp. XXVIII-LII. Reprinted with permission.

however, been counterbalanced by a rise in the percentages for minerals and especially fuels. European countries with planned economies also import more and more manufactured products. On the other hand, the decreased importance of commodities in their imports can only be shown for foodstuffs and

Commodity Market Controls

Table 2-6
Structure of World Exports by Products and by Sectors of Destination: In
Percentage, by Product (1955-1975)

Export		World	To Developed Countries	To Developing Countries	To Countries with a Planned Economy	
					Europe	Asia
Foodstuffs	1955	21.8	24.3	16.6	21.9	4.9
	1965	18.4	18.9	17.0	17.8	25.9
	1973	14.9	15.0	14.7	13.7	20.2
	1975	13.2	13.2	13.0	14.1	11.5
Agricultural products	1955	12.9	15.1	6.2	16.4	10.5
	1965	8.1	8.9	4.5	9.8	16.5
	1973	6.0	6.3	4.6	6.0	12.6
	1975	3.9	4.3	2.8	4.2	8.2
Ores and minerals	1955	12.2	13.9	7.1	15.4	9.5
	1965	12.2	13.4	7.6	13.3	11.1
	1973	10.5	10.7	8.2	12.8	22.9
	1975	9.7	9.4	7.9	14.1	22.4
Fuels	1955	11.0	10.2	11.7	9.4	6.6
	1965	9.6	10.0	8.6	6.9	2.6
	1973	11.0	12.3	8.4	5.9	2.0
	1975	19.3	22.3	14.6	9.1	1.8
Manufactured products	1955	40.5	33.2	52.6	37.3	66.1
	1965	50.1	47.3	58.7	51.6	43.1
	1973	55.5	54.6	59.7	58.4	39.5
	1975	52.0	49.6	58.0	55.6	54.0
All products	1955	100.0	100.0	100.0	100.0	100.0
	1965	100.0	100.0	100.0	100.0	100.0
	1973	100.0	100.0	100.0	100.0	100.0
	1975	100.0	100.0	100.0	100.0	100.0

Source: United Nations Conference on Trade and Development (UNCTAD), *Handbook of International Trade and Development Statistics*, Geneva, 1976, p. 82. Reprinted with permission; United Nations, *Monthly Bulletin of Statistics*, New York, May 1977, Special Table C, pp. XXVIII-LII. Reprinted with permission.

agricultural products, percentages for minerals and fuels having remained stable. Evolution of the composition of imports for Asian countries with planned economies can be summed up as follows: a constant rise in percentages for minerals with a sustained decline in the importance of fuels; between 1955 and

Table 2-7
Structure of World Exports by Products and by Sectors of Origin: In Percentage, by Product (1955-1975)

Export	Year	World	From Developed Countries	From Developing Countries	From Countries with a Planned Economy	
					Europe	Asia
Foodstuffs	1955	21.8	16.5	37.6	14.0	48.0
	1965	18.4	15.2	32.0	12.4	36.1
	1973	14.9	13.7	21.3	10.2	30.4
	1975	13.2	12.7	15.8	8.6	28.8
Agricultural products	1955	12.9	9.8	20.5	11.9	20.0
	1965	8.1	6.6	13.0	7.8	17.2
	1973	6.0	5.1	9.3	5.8	13.7
	1975	3.9	3.6	3.7	5.2	14.1
Ores and minerals	1955	12.2	12.8	10.1	13.2	17.0
	1965	12.2	12.1	11.7	13.8	10.8
	1973	10.5	10.8	8.8	11.8	9.2
	1975	9.7	11.0	5.8	11.5	5.4
Fuels	1955	11.0	5.4	24.9	13.9	0.8
	1965	9.6	3.4	31.0	11.5	1.3
	1973	11.0	3.5	39.6	10.7	1.3
	1975	19.3	5.1	59.3	18.0	11.5
Manufactured products	1955	40.5	53.2	7.6	46.1	14.2
	1965	50.1	60.8	11.7	52.6	33.7
	1973	55.5	65.6	20.0	52.4	44.1
	1975	52.0	66.1	14.3	50.3	38.9
All products	1955	100.0	100.0	100.0	100.0	100.0
	1965	100.0	100.0	100.0	100.0	100.0
	1973	100.0	100.0	100.0	100.0	100.0
	1975	100.0	100.0	100.0	100.0	100.0

Source: United Nations Conference on Trade and Development (UNCTAD), *Handbook of International Trade and Development Statistics*, Geneva, 1976, p. 80. Reprinted with permission; United Nations, *Monthly Bulletin of Statistics*, New York, May 1977, Special Table C, pp. XXVIII-LII. Reprinted with permission.

1965, a rise in percentages for foodstuffs and a decline in those for manufactured products; and between 1965 and 1975, a complete reversal of this trend for the last-named categories.

Table 2-7 provides information on the composition of exports from developed countries, developing countries, and countries with a planned economy. Exports from the developed countries are composed mainly of manufactured products (66% in 1975; 53% in 1955); international shipments of foodstuffs and agricultural products occupy a place of decreasing importance in their total shipments; percentages for minerals and fuels have remained relatively stable. The export structure for developing countries shows the phenomenal rise in the price of bituminous substances. In fact, the share of fuels in their total shipments has more than doubled during the last two decades, going from 25% in 1955 to 59% in 1975. This rise has been sustained over the whole period and the creation of OPEC has been mainly an accelerating factor. On the other hand, the share of agricultural products took a 454% drop, the foodstuffs percentage fell 140% and that of minerals 74%. In 1955 these three groups of products made up more than 63% of developing countries' total exports; in 1975 this ratio stood at 25%. The share of manufactured products continued to increase up to 1973 when they started to decline; in 1975 they constituted 14% of their total shipments. Table 2-7 gives the exact evolution of the export structure of countries with a planned economy. The share of fuels in their international shipments increased; the importance of exports of other commodities decreased. Their trade structure is increasingly characterized by shipments of manufactured products.

Relative Share of Leading Commodities in Trade and Export Receipts of Developing Countries

Up to this point, the role of commodities in international trade relations has been emphasized. They constitute 44% of world export value, 50% of developed countries' imports and 44% of their exports, 42% of developing countries' imports and 85% of their exports. However, among all these statistics, one should not lose sight of the importance of specific commodities in the trade and export receipts of the developing countries.

Table 2-8 shows the relative share in their total commodity exports of the thirty-two leading commodities exported by developing countries. The place of each of these minerals and products in overall world commodity exports (and in world exports of the particular product) is also quantified. These thrity-two products represent 73% of developing countries' total commodity exports. The share of petroleum alone reaches 50.4% while that of sugar, coffee, copper, tropical wood, cotton, rubber, and iron ore, in each case, exceeds 1%. On the other hand, exports of the developing countries' thirty-two major commodities constitute a feeble 25.6% of international commodity trading—14.3% for petroleum, 1.4% for tropical wood, 1.2% for wheat, 1.1% for copper, and 0.9% for sugar. If we now compare developing countries' export levels for each of

Table 2-8
**Relative Share of Leading Commodities in Developing Countries' Trade
and Relative Share of Developing Countries in World Trade of These
Products: 1972-1974**

Commodity	$XDCC/XDC$[a]	$XDCC/WX$[b]	$XDCC/WXC$[c]
Petroleum	50.4%	14.3%	76.5%
Sugar	3.1	0.9	73.4
Coffee	2.9	0.7	94.1
Copper	2.9	1.1	58.5
Tropical wood	1.7	1.4	25.8
Cotton	1.6	0.7	52.1
Rubber	1.3	0.3	97.5
Iron ore	1.0	0.6	37.3
Cocoa	0.8	0.2	98.2
Beef	0.7	0.6	25.5
Tin	0.7	0.2	84.4
Bananas	0.5	0.1	93.1
Rice	0.5	0.4	31.1
Corn	0.5	0.7	15.4
Tea	0.5	0.1	80.8
Phosphate	0.4	0.1	61.1
Tobacco	0.4	0.3	28.9
Palm oil	0.3	0.1	80.3
Bauxite	0.2	0.1	64.5
Peanuts	0.2	0.1	58.6
Coconut oil	0.2	0.1	78.4
Jute	0.2	0.1	48.0
Silver	0.2	0.1	30.7
Zinc	0.2	0.2	18.2
Wool	0.2	0.4	10.3
Copra	0.2	—	99.1
Fish	0.2	0.1	44.8
Furs and skins	0.2	0.3	17.3
Wheat	0.2	1.2	3.7
Manganese	0.1	—	59.3
Lead	0.1	0.1	28.2
Peanut oil	0.1	—	71.7
Total	72.7	25.6	

Source: Derived from World Bank, *Commodity Trade and Price Trends (1976 edition)*, Washington, 1976, pp. 19-22.

[a] Average ratio of exports from developing countries of the commodity under study (*XDCC*) as compared to all commodity exports from developing countries (*XDC*).

[b] Average ratio of exports from developing countries of the commodity under study (*XDCC*) as compared to world exports of all commodities (*WX*).

[c] Average ratio of exports from developing countries of the commodity under study (*XDCC*) as compared to the world exports of the same commodity (*WXC*).

these commodities to those of the international community, we obtain ratios exceeding 90% for coffee, rubber, cocoa, bananas, and copra while the percentage for petroleum, sugar, tin, tea, palm oil, coconut oil, and peanut oil exceeds 70%. Notice the absence from this list of all minerals except tin. In fact, we observe that the trade monopoly of developing countries is not always substantial in ores and minerals: copper (58.5%), iron ore (37.3%), phosphate (61.1%), bauxite (64.5%), silver (30.7%), zinc (18.2%), manganese (59.3%) and lead (28.2%). This characteristic must not be forgotten in considering developing countries' power of negotiation and when the performance of the international copper, bauxite, and iron ore cartels is evaluated.

The weight of eleven leading commodities in the trade and in the export receipts of some developing countries is quantified in table 2-9. This table brings out the degree to which exports of raw materials are concentrated in a limited number of countries and the strong dependence of these countries' export receipts on the international shipments of certain commodities.

In fact, more than 40% of the world exports of sugar, coffee, copper, rubber, cocoa, and tin come in each case from a maximum of three developing countries. We also notice that, for some developing countries, more than 50% of the export receipts flow from the sales of a single commodity. This is the case of Saudi Arabia, Iran, and Libya for petroleum; Cuba for sugar; Colombia for coffee; Chile, Zambia, and Zaire for copper; the Sudan for cotton; Liberia for iron ore and Ghana for cocoa. The same phenomenon can be observed for the other minerals, foodstuffs, and agricultural products not included in our sample.

Since the currency inflow needed to finance imports, level and structure of employment, establishment of economic infrastructure, and elaboration of a planning program are directly related to export receipts, it is easy to understand the interest and determination of developing countries concerning the stabilization of this inflow, and consequently the prices and quantities of commodities exported.

Evolution of Commodity Prices: 1960-1977

Several studies have been published concerning the instability of export receipts in developing countries.[1,2] Some attribute these difficulties to the instability of commodity prices on international markets, others to the instability of quantities or to economic distortions in producing countries. Rather than participating in this debate, this section proposes to give a general presentation of the behavior of prices for tropical foodstuffs and beverages, vegetable oils and seeds, agricultural raw materials, and minerals during the last seventeen years. (In later chapters we will study the evolution of prices and quantities for a large number of specific commodities). Since we are here studying price evolution over such a

Table 2-9

Importance of Leading Commodities in Trade and in Export Receipts of Some Developing Countries: (1972-1974)

Commodity and Country	XDCC/WXC[a]	XRC/XR[b]
Petroleum		
Saudi Arabia	16.9	96.4
Iran	11.5	89.8
Libya	5.8	99.1
Total	34.2	
Sugar		
Cuba	20.6	76.4
West Indies	13.3	22.0
Philippines	7.3	21.4
Total	41.2	
Coffee		
Brazil	25.8	17.1
Colombia	14.7	52.3
Ivory Coast	5.1	23.5
Total	45.6	
Copper		
Chile	16.8	72.7
Zambia	15.6	93.3
Zaire	10.2	67.2
Total	42.6	
Wood		
Malaysia	6.4	20.3
Indonesia	5.6	11.8
Philippines	3.0	13.5
Total	15.0	
Cotton		
Mozambique	5.7	17.8
Sudan	5.2	57.1
Iran	3.4	1.2
Total	14.3	
Rubber		
Malaysia	52.2	27.7
Indonesia	20.8	8.6
Thailand	10.9	11.0
Total	83.9	
Iron Ore		
Brazil	11.1	6.4
Liberia	6.1	67.0
Venezuela	5.5	3.1
Total	22.7	

Table 2-9 — *Continued*

Commodity and Country	XDCC/WXC[a]	XRC/XR[b]
Cocoa		
Ghana	28.9	58.2
Nigeria	17.8	3.9
Ivory Coast	14.6	18.0
Total	61.3	
Beef		
Argentina	10.9	13.2
Brazil	3.9	2.4
Uruguay	3.0	36.1
Total	17.8	
Tin		
Malaysia	41.8	13.7
Bolivia	15.0	45.8
Indonesia	10.5	2.7
Total	67.3	

Source: Derived from World Bank, *Commodity Trade and Price Trends (1976 edition)*, Washington, 1976, pp. 17-20.

[a]Average share of developing countries named (*XDCC*) in world exports of commodity under study (*WXC*).

[b]Average share of export receipts from shipments of commodity under study (*XRC*) in comparison to export receipts from shipments of all commodities from developing countries mentioned (*XR*).

long period, we have modified the available price indexes for the four categories of products. They are now all based on the same year (1960=100), thus permitting an evaluation of their variations as related to the same year of reference. Table 2-10 presents statistical data for the period 1960-1977 and figure 2-1 traces the evolution of these data.

The agricultural raw materials include cotton, wool, jute, sisal, abaca, natural rubber, skins, and tropical wood. The average price index for these products declined steadily between 1960 and 1972. At the end of this period this index was at 74% of the level reached at the beginning of the sixties. The presence of numerous substitutes and the competition from synthetic products prevented any recovery of prices for agricultural raw materials during this period. Prices suddenly increased toward the end of 1972 and the beginning of 1973. A flourishing world economy (industrial production was then recording a 6.5% annual growth, 1.5% more than the trend observed during the preceding decade) stimulated demand both for agricultural raw materials and their substitutes, causing an 80% increase in their price index. This increase proved

Table 2-10
Average Price Index for Certain Commodities on the Open Market: Annually
1960-1975, Quarterly 1976-1977

Year	Tropical Foodstuffs and Beverages	Vegetable Oils and Seeds	Agricultural Raw Materials	Ores and Metals
1960	100	100	100	100
1961	95	94	84	97
1962	93	89	80	95
1963	125	94	79	94
1964	119	99	76	119
1965	97	112	76	142
1966	99	96	75	153
1967	100	98	69	125
1968	99	99	68	130
1969	110	98	76	144
1970	119	113	70	145
1971	114	110	69	127
1972	137	97	74	130
1973	186	182	133	184
1974	337	326	144	256
1975	273	190	116	206
1976				
I	263	153	134	206
II	307	157	149	230
III	310	190	163	235
IV	341	206	164	218
1977				
I	341	236	161	234
II	489	268	158	226
III	432	204	147	221
IV	397	198	147	229

Source: Derived from UNCTAD, *Handbook of International Trade and Development Statistics*, Geneva, 1976, pp. 61-66; UNCTAD, *Monthly Bulletin of Commodity Prices*, Geneva, December 1977, various issues.

Note: 1960 = 100. The price indexes are based on current U.S. dollar prices. Sales under long-term contracts or at preferential prices have been excluded.

particularly strong for skins and wool; for the prices of cotton, jute, and rubber it was more moderate, appearing mainly at the end of 1973. The average price index for agricultural raw materials started a sharp decline towards the end of 1974, reaching a level of 116 in 1975. In order to evaluate the depressed state of the market during this period, the following variables must be taken into account: world recession, production increases brought about by the high prices of 1973, greater competition from synthetic products during a period of deflation, and liquidation of excess stocks. During the first three quarters of 1976 the international market for agricultural raw materials became very active again. This price recovery did not last very long. Although cotton and skin prices

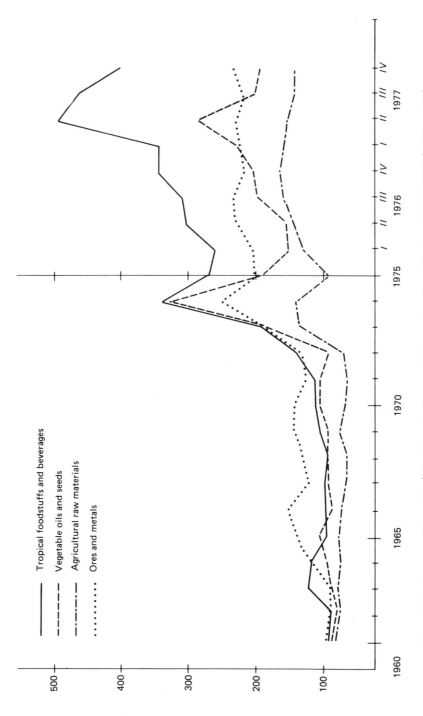

Figure 2-1. Average Price Index for Certain Commodities on the Open Market: 1960-1977 (1960 = 100)

remained high, the decrease in those for wool, jute, and rubber was such that the average index for agricultural raw materials declined by 11.0% between the middle of 1976 and the end of 1977.

The category of tropical foodstuffs and beverages includes products such as wheat, corn, rice, sugar, coffee, cocoa, tea, beef, bananas, and pepper. The average price index for all this produce proved rather stable between 1960 and 1971. The continual rise in productivity observed in these industries and the price support policies applied by most countries resulted in the accumulation of enormous stocks, preventing the average price from showing much of a percentage difference from that recorded at the beginning of the sixties. From 1972-73 on, there was a complete change. Although the 200% rise in the average price index for tropical foodstuffs and beverages is usually attributed to an abnormal growth in world demand (demand for tropical produce being very sensitive to variations in income), there were other factors: the disastrous grain harvests in Russia, the increase of Chinese wheat purchases in Western markets, the cold snap that destroyed a good portion of Brazil's coffee-producing capacity, the bad atmospheric conditions in Colombia, and the drastic decline in sugar's stocks/consumption ratio. Price increases were especially marked for sugar, cocoa, wheat, and coffee. Between 1967 and 1974 the price of sugar was multiplied by 22; during the same period, the prices of the other three products rose 360%, 320%, and 190% respectively. The 1975 recession brought to a close this unprecedented price rise for tropical foodstuffs and beverages. The average price index then fell 23% in a single year, showing a more marked decline for sugar (70%), cocoa (30%) and wheat (25%). However, the price for these products remained high compared to the levels reached toward the end of the sixties. Bad weather slowed down the evolution of supply and largely cancelled the world recession's depressive effect on prices.

Vegetable oils and seeds include soya beans, groundnuts, copra, palm kernels, (their respective oils), sunflower oil, coconut oil, palm oil, olive oil, and linseed oil. Up to the middle of the seventies, the evolution of the average price index for these products followed very much the same path as that for tropical foodstuffs and beverages. But after a 78% increase between 1973 and 1974 and a 113% drop between 1974 and the beginning of 1976, the average price index for vegetable oils and seeds remained clearly below that recorded for tropical foodstuffs and beverages. In the fourth quarter of 1977 this index reached 198, a very modest increase considering the world inflation of the past seventeen years. The previously mentioned cyclical variables have also influenced the price behavior of these products, seconded by weather conditions, technological changes, and marketing problems.

The average price index for minerals (ores and metals) (phosphate, manganese, iron ore, aluminum, copper, lead, zinc, tin, and tungsten) proved very unstable between 1960 and 1972. The difference between the maximum and minimum levels settled at 59, a margin above that for the other commodities.

The average price index rose to 127 in 1971, just as world production was starting to expand. In 1974 it reached 256. A Brookings Institution report underlines the main variables responsible for this increase:

> The most general cause undoubtedly was the world boom of 1972 and 1973 . . . There were, however, special factors that accelerated the pace of price increases for many commodities. For instance, in the case of the metals, a long lead time is needed to install additional mining and processing facilities. The worldwide boom caught the mineral-producing industries with capacity inadequate to meet the sudden surge of demand for consumption and stock building. Environmental require-ments and political uncertainties in a number of locations may have contributed to this deficiency by inhibiting new mining and processing investment recently. Inventory building and speculative purchases in anticipation of further price rises have been an important special factor on the demand side; inflation and exchange rate fluctuations led to a preference for holding commodities rather than currencies. Much of the explanation for the 1973-74 escalation of mineral prices is to be found in the cumulative effect of these conditions.[3]

Price increases on the mineral markets were not uniform. Between March 1973 and March 1974 these increases stood at 81% for copper, 90% for lead, and 115% for tin. There was a faster and more pronounced increase for the price of zinc: it rose by 240% between March and December 1973. The 1975 recession brought this boom to a halt. Although the average price index fell 24% between March 1974 and March 1976, price decreases for nonferrous metals proved much greater: 140% for copper, 120% for zinc, 112% for lead, and 50% for tin. In the fourth quarter of 1977 the average price index for minerals (ores and metals) had not yet regained 1974 levels. A world economic growth below forecasted levels and a sustained increase in supply forced firms to do considerable stockpiling (except tin whose stocks fell 25% in 1977). Prices leveled off at averages close to those for 1976, except for some metals, whose markets were not overstocked, for which prices increased noticeably.

Evolution of Terms of Trade: 1960-1977

Terms of trade, the ratio at which goods are exchanged among nations, can be calculated by several different methods. The net barter terms of trade divides a country's export price index (Px) by its import price index (Pm). The gross barter terms of trade is the quantification of the ratio between the import quantity index (Qm) and the export quantity index (Qx). The income terms of trade, expressing the combined effect of variations in relative prices and export volume, is the ratio $Px\ Qx/Pm$. Factoral terms of trade have the advantage of accounting for the productivity index in the export (Zx) and in the import

(Zm) sectors of a country's trade. These are referred to as either single ($Px\ Zx/ Pm$) or double ($Px\ Zx/Pm\ Zm$) factoral terms of trade.

According to economists such as Prebisch and Myrdal, developing countries' terms of trade have deteriorated continually during the second half of the twentieth century. (This implies that the export price (Px) index increases less rapidly than the import price index (Pm), or that the export volume index increases continually in relation to the import volume index. In both cases, the ratio decreases.) These economists attribute this deterioration to: technological progress causing steady reduction of the percentage of commodities in the total cost of finished products; increased production of synthetic substitutes; subsidizing of industry in developed countries and the protectionism of industrial countries, limiting access of exports from developing countries to their markets. This deterioration of developing countries' terms of trade lowers their real income, restrains economic growth and limits their power to negotiate. Consequently, these authors maintain that Third World countries are now justified in joining producer cartels or the United Nations Conference on Trade and Development (UNCTAD)'s proposed Integrated Commodity Program just as they were in supporting the international agreements signed after the second world war. The actual goal of these interventions on international commodity markets is to stabilize prices, keeping them in the vicinity of objective prices which (with allowances for inflation) would both be compatible with developing countries' development objectives and encourage them to sustain adequate production levels. These authors therefore support the use of quotas, buffer stocks, buffer funds, multilateral contracts, or any of the other techniques used to regulate the supply and demand of these products.

However, this theory of the historical deterioration of developing countries' terms of trade has been strongly contested by Viner, Kindleberger, Ellsworth, Haberler, Meier, Baldwin, and others. They maintain that, due to the relative scarcity of commodities and the trend towards decreasing returns to scale in production, these terms of trade are being continually improved. The results obtained by Prebisch and Myrdal might have been very different had they used factoral or income terms of trade. Deterioration might be due to domestic causes quite unrelated to international trade. Their assessment uses 1950-52 as a starting point, a period during which there was a commodity boom due to the Korean War. Choosing this period as reference point makes the decline in terms of trade seem more pronounced than it really was. These authors consider neither quality changes in products traded nor the importance of transportation costs.

There will be long and continuing debate on these questions, especially if participants continue to consider improvement or deterioration in terms of trade an objective measure of variations in a nation's economic welfare. The choice of the "terms of trade" measure may imply some value judgment.[4]

Despite the debate over the exact meaning of the terms of trade concept, it continues to be extensively used. Table 2-11 (and figure 2-2) traces the evolution of this indicator for developed (North America, Europe, South Africa, Israel, Japan, Australia, and New Zealand) and developing countries between 1965 and the third quarter of 1977. It is based on United Nations data which measure terms of trade by dividing the index of export unit value by that of import unit value. It is apparent from the table that developed countries' terms of trade remained relatively stable between 1965 and 1973; these terms subsequently declined by about 12% before the third quarter of 1977. Developing countries' terms of trade also remained stable between 1965 and 1972 but after this period they started to increase at an unbridled pace. In mid-1977 their terms of trade index stood at 145 (1965=100). Notice, however, that the exclusion of oil-producing countries from their ranks rather tarnishes the performance of the developing countries; the latter's terms of trade then fall 15% below those recorded 10 years earlier.

Table 2-11
Evolution of Terms of Trade Index

		Developing Countries	
Year	Developed Countries	Including Oil-producing Countries	Excluding Oil-producing Countries
1965	100	100	
1966	100	101	
1967	101	100	
1968	101	101	
1969	101	102	
1970	102	101	101
1971	101	105	96
1972	102	103	94
1973	101	113	102
1974	89	158	95
1975	92	140	85
1976			
I	91	147	
II	91	148	
III	91	147	
IV	92	146	
1977			
I	91	146	
II	90	147	
III	90	145	

Source: United Nations, *Monthly Bulletin of Statistics*, New York, January 1978, pp. XXII-XXIII. Reprinted with permission.

Note: 1965 = 100. Unit value index of exports divided by unit value index of imports.

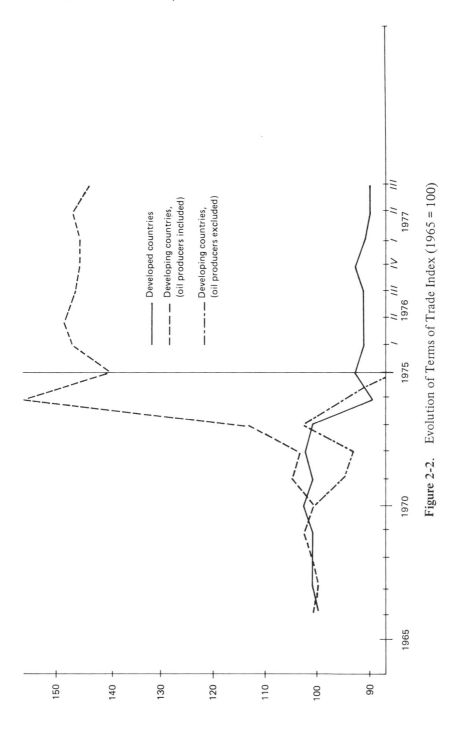

Figure 2-2.   Evolution of Terms of Trade Index (1965 = 100)

International Mineral Reserves and Resources

There was some consternation in the international community over the statement by the Club of Rome maintaining that mineral reserves would soon be
depleted if demand continued its exponential growth. This body counseled that
all nonrenewable resources (no mention was made of specific products) should
be subject to more selective growth and to measures preventing their waste.
What exactly is the truth of the matter? Are available reserves and resources
sufficient to satisfy demand from now to the end of the century? Can excess
demand be forecast for the beginning of the next millenium? If so, for which
products can we expect shortfalls?

An adequate response to these questions requires that we define a certain
number of terms commonly used in discussing these matters. The U.S. Bureau
of Mines defines "total resources" as the entirety of identified and undiscovered
resources. "Undiscovered resources" include hypothetical resources (as yet
undiscovered but which can be reasonably assumed to exist in a known mining
district under known geologic conditions) and speculative resources (as yet
undiscovered but likely to occur either in known types of deposits in a favorable
geologic setting where no discoveries have been made, or in as yet unknown
types of deposits that remain to be recognized). "Identified resources" interest
us most. These include "identified reserves" (that portion of the identified
resources from which a usable mineral or energy commodity can be legally and
economically extracted at the time of determination) and "subeconomic identified resources" (materials that are not reserves but may become so as economic
and legal conditions change. Identified reserves have been either "measured"
(their quality and quantity calculated and analyzed by sampling with a margin
of error less than 20%), "indicated" (their quality and quantity calculated and
analyzed partially by sampling and partially by reasonable geologic projections),
or "inferred" (their quality and quantity estimated on the basis of geologic
evidence and projections). "Subeconomic identified resources" are either "paramarginal" (about to be economically producible or not commercially available
solely because of legal or political circumstances) or "submarginal" resources
(open for consideration as reserves if prices increase more than 150% or if a
technological discovery causes an appreciable decrease in cost). Our discussion
will be mostly limited to the "identified reserves" of twenty-one minerals.

Table 2-12 presents, for these twenty-one minerals: annual production
rates, identified reserves, ratio of identified reserves/1974-75 annual production,
ratio of identified reserves/1974-2000 cumulative demand and finally, ratio of
identified resources/1974-2000 cumulative demand. The following characteristics should be noted.

First, at 1974-75 annual production rates, there are enough reserves of
bauxite, platinum, chromium, iron ore, manganese, columbium, tantalum, and
vanadium to satisfy industrial needs for a very long time. Their identified

reserves/annual production ratios all exceed 100 (except for platinum where it stands at 97). For copper, selenium, nickel, cobalt, molybdenum, tungsten, tin, and lead this ratio exceeds 42, implying that identified reserves will be able to satisfy medium-term needs. The situation is less encouraging for zinc, germanium, mercury, and silver whose identified reserves seem insufficient to sustain current production demands for another twenty-five years. However, the ratio used gives a very static perspective of the sufficiency of world reserves; no allowances are made for the fact that any significant price increase would raise the level of identified reserves nor that, in certain cases, projections are in marked excess of 1974-75 recorded demand.

A more precise sufficiency ratio may be obtained by replacing current production by the cumulative demand for the next twenty-five years and by adding subeconomic identified resources to the numerator. Inclusion of sub-marginal and paramarginal resources implies the hypothesis that prices will increase 150% between now and the year 2000 (or that there will be techno-logical discoveries reducing exploration and mining costs) and that by the same year the legal and political obstacles barring use of paramarginal resources will have been lifted. The last column in table 2-12 reveals that, except for gold, silver, and germanium, identified resources for all twenty-one minerals are twice that of projected cumulative demand from now until the end of the century.

Second, although sufficiency levels for most minerals seem acceptable, this does not mean that they are inexhaustible or that they will be available to in-dustrial countries at the same rate and at the same prices as before. High-grade deposits of tin and tungsten are becoming increasingly rare while deposits of manganese and cobalt must be mined at increasingly lower levels, raising extrac-tion costs. Mineral reserves such as chromium, manganese, columbium, tantalum, tungsten, vanadium, bauxite, tin, and platinum are mostly located in developing countries and countries with planned economies. For all these minerals, the terms "sufficiency" and "accessibility" must not be confused; existing political blocs do not permit their synonymity.

Finally, mention must be made of the creation of formal producer cartels for petroleum, bauxite, copper, iron ore, and mercury. These cartels were created to afford members an increasing share in the profits from mining and refining activities, ensuring that they thus obtain a "just and remunerative" price for their ores. Although the cartels mentioned were not all as successful as OPEC and the International Bauxite Association (IBA), their prevalence will increase unless the deadlock in UNCTAD's negotiations for an Integrated Pro-gram is broken or solutions found for problems raised during the North-South Conference.

Third, sufficiency levels for the twenty-one minerals studied make no allowances for any developments with dynamic impact on international mineral markets. No study has been made of the availability of energy resources per-mitting the development of new mineral resources (or their substitutes) at

Table 2-12
International Mineral Reserves and Resources

Ores	Units[b]	(I) Annual Production 1974/75	(II) Identified Reserves 1975	II/I	Identified Reserves[a] / Cumulative Demand 1974-2000[c]	Identified Resources[a] / Cumulative Demand 1974-2000[d]
Bauxite	thousand LDT	73,995	17,000,000	230	4.0	6.6[d]
Copper	thousand ST metal	7,855	450,000	57	1.3	5.8[d]
Lead	thousand ST metal	3,798	160,000	42	1.2	2.4
Tin	LT metal	220,821	10,200,000	46	1.3	2.7
Zinc	thousand ST metal	6,342	150,000	24	1.1	6.9
Germanium	lbs. metal	250,960	4,000,000	16	.7	1.5
Gold	million troy oz. metal	39.25	1,350	34	1.3	1.8
Mercury	76-lb. flasks metal	258,068	5,250,000	20	.7	2.7[d]
Platinum group	thousand troy oz. metal	5,775	561,000	97	3.1	8.7[d]
Selenium	thousand lbs. metal	5,731	370,000	65	3.0	>10
Silver	million troy oz. metal	291.35	6,100	21	.4	1.7
Chromium	thousand ST gross weight	7,640	1,900,000	249	5.7	>10
Iron ore	million LT ore	877	259,000	295	4.5	9.8
Manganese	thousand ST gross weight	24,488	6,000,000	245	4.9	8.8
Nickel	ST metal	823,612	59,500,000	72	2.1	4.2
Cobalt	ST metal	32,202	2,700,000	84	2.1	3.7
Columbium	thousand lbs. metal	24,753	22,000,000	889	>10	>10
Molybdenum	thousand lbs. metal	181,137	13,200,000	73	1.4	7.0
Tantalum	thousand lbs. metal	1,100	110,000	100	1.1	4.3
Tungsten	thousand lbs. metal	82,979	3,900,000	47	1.2	3.5
Vanadium	thousand lbs. metal	45,749	21,400,000	468	7.5	n.a.

Source: British-North American Committee, *Mineral Development in the Eighties: Prospects and Problems*, British-North American Research Association, National Planning Association, C.D. Howe Research Institute, London-Washington-Montreal, 1976, pp. 32-33 and 40-41. Reprinted with permission.

[a]Estimated on the basis of 1974 prices. Any significant price increase would tend to enlarge them.

[b]LDT = long dry tons; LT = long tons; ST = short tons; n.a. = not available.

[c]The 1974-2000 cumulative demand covers only primary metals; secondary metals ("old scrap") are excluded.

[d]Figures for resources of bauxite, copper and platinum include "hypothetical" and "speculative" resources as well as those presently identified.

acceptable cost levels. No evaluation has been made of the size of nickel, copper, cobalt, and manganese resources in ocean nodules, nor of the availability of secondary metal supplies and the possibility of recycling. Considering the difficulty involved in incorporating these dynamic variables in projections for the supply and demand of minerals, the statistics in table 2-12 must be considered as approximate and tentative. A Brookings Institution study gives a rather satisfactory summary of the limits of these data.[5,6]

Notes

1. The most important are: Robert M. Stern, "World Market Instability in Primary Commodities," *Quarterly Review of Banca Nazionale del Lavoro* (July 1976): 175-195; Marian Radetzki, "Commodity Prices during Two Booms: 1950 and 1973," *Skandinaviska Enskilda Banken Quarterly Review* 4 (1974); United Nations, *Instability in Export Markets of Under-developed Countries* (New York, 1952); United Nations, *International Compensation for Fluctuation in Commodity Trade* (New York, 1961); Klaus E. Knorr, "The Quest for Stabilization Policy in Primary Producing Countries," *Kyklos* 2 (1958); Ragnar Nurkse, "Trade Fluctuations and Buffer Policies of Low Income Countries," *Kyklos* 2 (1958); E.J. Chambers, and D.F. Gordon, "Primary Products and Economic Growth: An Empirical Measurement," *Journal of Political Economy*, no. 4 (August 1966): 315-332; E.M. Brook, and E.R. Grilli, "Commodity Price Stabilization and the Developing World," *Finance and Development* 14 (March 1977): 8-11.

2. For a study of the instability of commodity prices during the first half of the twentieth century, see United Nations, *Instability in Export Markets of Under-developed Countries*. This study shows that the international commodity market was particularly unstable between 1901 and 1950. In fact, the annual fluctuations in average price rose to 20.6% for rubber, 17.2% for coffee, 17.1% for sugar, 16.7% for cocoa, 15.4% for cotton, and 13.3% for tin and copper.

3. The Brookings Institution, *Trade in Primary Commodities: Conflict or Cooperation?* p. 11. Reprinted with permission.

4. An evaluation of this debate can be found in: Gottfried Haberler, *A Survey of International Trade Theory*, Special Papers in International Economics, no. 1, (Princeton University, July 1961), chapter 4. Alton D. Law, *International Commodity Agreements*, chapter 2.

5. The Brookings Institution, *Trade in Primary Commodities*, pp. 15-17.

6. The reader interested in knowing more about the factors influencing the availability of nonfuel minerals is referred to J.E. Tilton, *The Future of Nonfuel Minerals* (Washington, D.C.: The Brookings Institution, 1977).

3 Commodity Market Controls: The Inter-War Period

There has been renewed interest in the control of commodity markets due to the commercial impact of the Organization of Petroleum Exporting Countries (OPEC); export quotas set by the Intergovernmental Council of Copper Exporting Countries (CIPEC); the UN conferences on wheat, tin, sugar, cocoa, and coffee; proliferation of cartels, both formal (bauxite, copper, iron ore, mercury) and informal (lead, uranium); and the North-South Conference of International Economic Cooperation where ministers agreed, in principle, on the creation of a Common Fund. We are interested in finding out what factors contributed to the success or failure of certain controls, what validity such interventions may have, and to what extent they may bring about a new international economic order.

Even though such discussions and negotiations have received good media coverage and have been detailed in books and special journals, much less attention has been paid to the history of controls in the commodities market. In any event, one meets all too often with the tiresome impression that everything started with OPEC, that Third World demands for a more just redistribution of wealth started after the fourth United Nations Conference on Trade and Development (UNCTAD) in Nairobi, or that political will is sufficient to guarantee producing countries the "reasonable" prices they demand.

The following chapters do not pretend to give a detailed and complete history of controls in the commodities market. Our concern is rather to survey the controls used since World War I. More precisely, we want to show how they have evolved from private producer cartels to national government controls, to generalized international one-product agreements, and, finally, to international associations of producing countries. It may well be that these four periods of the development of controls partially coincide. However, we still believe that as a logical device such successive historical divisions make it possible to trace and better understand the conditions governing the success of a control, the evolution of the intervention techniques used, and, in part, the origins of current tensions between consuming and producing countries.

From World War I to the Great Depression: 1914-1930

Although several commodities had been controlled before 1914, outside intervention in commodity markets really came into play following the first world war.[1]

The disruption of war occasioned scarcities and justified the spontaneous need for intervention. The demand for certain commodities was temporarily increased (copper, tin, rubber, wool); governments were encouraged to control the prices of imported raw materials and to ration food products; subsidies were granted to industries affected by the loss of prewar markets. The effect of all this on prices and profits was strongly felt by the producers of raw materials.

From 1917 to the Depression, attempts at controls can be pointed out in these markets:

Rubber. In 1917 Malaysian producers established a voluntary production restraint scheme leading to a 25% cut in production and the lowering of their stock levels. In 1922 Great Britain adopted a scheme of obligatory production and export restraints covering not only Malaysia but Ceylon (the Stevenson Plan). The subsequent drop in production (which in 1924 was at 50% of productive capacity) doubled the price of rubber. This in turn stimulated production in third party countries (Indonesia) and American consumers set up a monopsony. Prices dropped and the Stevenson Plan was abolished in November 1928.

Coffee. Between 1923 and 1925 Brazil's Sao Paulo State returned to its 1907 policy and stockpiled large quantities of coffee in order to regulate the market flow. Coupled with an increasing world demand, this policy had an almost immediate impact on prices. The high prices overstimulated production and Brazil was left with surpluses that had to be destroyed to prevent a further drop in prices. Between 1931 and 1937 Brazil was forced to burn close to 57 million bags of coffee each weighing 132 lbs. The holocaust consumed 78 million bags from 1931 to 1944–five times the average world demand for the interwar period.

Sugar. The war had made Cuba the largest exporter of sugar in the Western Hemisphere, European sugar beet production having been wiped out. These high price levels induced Cuban producers to double their production. However, European production recovered more quickly than expected and, as European countries reduced imports, Cuban producers could only stand by and watch the rapid accumulation of their stocks. Faced with the prospect of a bumper crop for 1926, the producers, with the help of local government, decided to make a 10% cut in production. The effects of this cut were modified by the fact that, as Cuban exports decreased, importing countries increased their own sugar beet production. The Cuban policy thus encouraged them to become self-sufficient.

Copper. The copper market was also hit by this flood of controls. The Association of Copper Exporters came into existence as early as 1918. This association, dominated by American producers and fostered by the Webb-Pomerane Act of

April 10, 1918 allowing the existence of American cartels abroad, favored a policy of production restraints meant to raise the price of copper exports. After a brief period of success, cooperation among members faded quickly and in 1923 the association dissolved. It was replaced in 1926 by the international cartel of Copper Exporters Inc. which brought together foreign (Union Minière of Haut Katanga controlling 15% of world exports) and American producers (controlling at the time 75% of world production). European markets were rationed so as to reduce commercial stocks and production was subsequently cut. These tactics pushed copper prices up from US 13.0¢/lb. in 1926 to US 24.0¢/lb. at the beginning of 1929. As usual, these artificially high prices stimulated production in noncartel countries (especially Zambia) and encouraged technology to discover substitutes. The cartel could not withstand the situation of excess supply and its participants started a price war which brought prices down to US 4.7¢/lb. in 1932.

Other. In the period before the Great Depression there were also quantitative production controls in the lead, petroleum, zinc, tin (started by the 1921 Bandoeng Plan), beef, wood, wool, tea, and camphor markets. Finally in 1928, Canada—deciding to stockpile rather than export an abundant harvest at lower prices—was the first to put controls on wheat exports.

We find, for this period, that a large number of controls were set up by the producers themselves and that governments only intervened when a commodity representing the principal or only source of foreign exchange was in trouble. Most of the products mentioned were characterized by excess supply, which drove their prices down. When controls were difficult to obtain, producers called upon their governments, who were only too happy to step in. Finally, it is noticeable that in all cases control policies were worked out without the participation of commodity consumers or representatives of importing countries. This was not to be the case for the international agreements signed after World War II.

The Great Depression and the Development of Intergovernmental Agreements: 1930-1940

The depression of the 1930s brought commodity prices down to a level comparable only to that of stock market values. It also put an end to controls which had, in any case, already been outdated by a cessation of world demand—although several cartels and associations did continue their existence on paper. The crash also had the effect of increasing the number of commodities suffering from chronic excess supply; reawakening the need for intervention in primary markets; reviving the kinds of controls used in the 1920s and creating others for important products like cotton, tin, and tea. But unlike the preceding period where many controls had been introduced by the producers themselves, governments' role would now become increasingly important—only the copper market would remain totally free of their intervention. Specialists in this matter such as E.S. Mason, J.W.F. Rowe and A.D. Law are very explicit on this subject:

> To date, little has been done by governments, except in the United States, to prevent or in any way obstruct their nationals' participation in international business agreements that restrict and regulate competition in the export trade. On the contrary, governments have joined in directly, as cartel members and supporters of their national firms, and indirectly, through the implementation of commercial policies that stimulated international business understandings.[2]

J.W.F. Rowe points out that it was gradually becoming realized that stable and strong control schemes could only be secured by governments, especially when legislation was important to prevent new additional capacity.[3] A.D. Law adds that this conviction was reached even more fully by governments than by private industry.[4]

It is also worth noting that some attempt was made to profit from the hard lessons learned in the controls period of the 1920s. From now on controls would have a more international scope; they would bring together most foreign countries and producers of the same commodity, thus assuring tighter monopolistic controls capable of countering nonmembers' increased production due to artificially high prices. A few producing countries had the idea of inviting consuming countries to sit on the administrative controls boards. Even if at first this initiative was limited to wheat and rubber agreements, the idea—once launched—spread so quickly as to become general practice by the beginning of the 1950s. Finally, control techniques began to be more diversified, buffer stocks and buffer funds were established in addition to quantitative production restraints.

Here is a summary of the development of controls from the 1930s depression to the start of hostilities in 1940.

International Tin Market

Boliva, Malaysia, and Indonesia were the largest producers of tin. The last two enjoyed a major advantage—surface deposits that could be mined at lower costs. From the beginning of World War I to the middle of the 1920s, tin showed a spectacular price rise—continually increasing production lagged behind the demand. But technological innovations in surface mining techniques and the very high 1926 prices stimulated production to such a degree that the market was soon saturated. The Association of Tin Producers formed in July 1929 suggested production cuts to prevent a still more drastic price drop but this attempt at control was without effect as it was opposed by Indonesia.

The depression brought about greater cooperation among producing countries and in February 1931 an international agreement (the Tin Council) on export restraints was signed by the governments of Malaysia, Indonesia, Bolivia, and Nigeria. When Thailand joined this list, the intergovernmental agreement regrouped the countries responsible for 90% of world tin exports. The commercial restraint rate was set at 78% of the quotas accorded to each member. This rate fluctuated to 33.3% in 1933, to 40% in 1934 (with the signing of the second agreement), 65% in 1935, 90% in 1936 (year of the third agreement), 100% in 1937, 35% in 1938, and 40% in 1939—the rate change being tied to variations in prices and stocks. The successful control of prices during the period under study was largely due to the discipline shown by council members. Its demise was not caused by internal conflicts but rather by the Japanese invasion of the Pacific.

In July 1934 and June 1938 the council set up a buffer stock to stabilize prices. The trial use of this control technique (stocks granted to the council proved clearly inadequate) paved the way for its future use by the International Tin Agreement signed after World War II.

International Sugar Market

Because of the importance of sugar in its economy, Cuba took the initiative in 1930 of sending a delegate, Mr. Chadbourne, to Java and Europe to convince exporting countries to sign an international agreement to stabilize prices through quantitative production controls. The Chadbourne Plan was accepted and signed in May 1931 but the exports of the participating countries represented only a small percentage of world sugar production (not more than 25%) since neither Great Britain, the United States, nor—above all—their colonies signed the agreement. Be that as it may, the participating countries decided to control production so that their total stocks of 4 million tons would be liquidated in four years at the rate of 25% a year. Despite a 50% cut in production (6 million tons), this plan only managed to prevent a still greater drop in prices. Exclusion of the American and British empires, where production increased by 4.5 million tons during the same period, explains in large part the failure of the Chadbourne Plan which was abolished on September 30, 1935.

A second intergovernmental agreement was signed in May 1937, now including the United States, Great Britain, a large part of Europe, and the other largest world sugar producers. Participating countries agreed to respect the export quotas granted and to reduce stock levels to 25% of the quota set. Moreover, consuming countries like Great Britain promised to meet any new increase in consumption by importing equally from its colonies and the participants in the agreement. The effects of the agreement were weak and it was further weakened by the 1938 drop in world consumption and the 1939 excessive stockpiling brought on by fear of an imminent outbreak of hostilities. The agreement was to fall into disuse during World War II. We should point out that the 1931 agreement was signed by associations of producers while that of 1937 was ratified by the governments of the participating countries.

International Tea Market

In 1930 the international tea market was dominated by Great Britain, alone absorbing more than 50% of world shipments, while India, Ceylon, and Indonesia (then a Dutch colony) provided more than 80% of exports. The stockpiling and price drops which had characterized this industry since the mid-1920s were accentuated by the economic crisis of the 1930s. At the end of 1932, in fact, the average price of tea on the London market had fallen to one-half its 1926-1928 level and stocks were equivalent to six months of consumption. The Dutch producers of Indonesia then took the initiative of proposing a five-year production control scheme to their English counterparts in India and Ceylon. An agreement was signed on April 1, 1933. The International Tea Committee then started allotting export and production quotas. By 1938, when the agreement was renewed, East African producers and representatives of the English and Dutch governments had joined the list of committee members. The English and Dutch governments proved to be very cooperative, passing the necessary legislation to assure the success of the controls: granting export licenses transferable among the producers; making it illegal to exceed allotted quotas (quotas which moreover could not be accumulated from year to year) and putting very severe restrictions on new production. In 1933 the commercial restraint rate was set at 85% of allotted quotas and it fluctuated much less than that set for tin, minimum and maximum levels reaching 82.5% (1935-1937) and 92.5% (1938-1939) respectively. On the average, there was very little price fluctuation during the control period and a tendency toward lower stocks; the International Tea Committee was in part responsible for such performance. From the 1938-1939 period on, a rapid rise in prices is noted, but this cannot be credited to the committee. It was rather the political situation just before the second world war which, through stockpiling to meet future consumer needs, caused prices to rise.

International Wheat Market

The first world war and the 1915 interruption of Russian exports to the West had sent wheat prices to such levels that overproduction resulted in the United States, Canada, Argentina, and Australia. This gap between supply and demand was accentuated by return to production by the major European countries, eager to reduce wheat imports at any cost. Consequently, world prices continued to drop until the end of the 1920s because of production surpluses which became obvious from 1926 on. At this point the Canadian and American governments gave in to producer demands to protect domestic prices and set up marketing boards which stockpiled to prevent a continual fall in prices.

These attempts at control were very costly. In 1935 the Canadian government reported stocks of 200 million bushels. The U.S. Federal Farm Relief Board established in 1929 stockpiled 250 million bushels in less than three years. More important, this price support policy had the negative effect of making exports less and less competitive.

Since importing countries were finding their import substitution policy just as costly as the price support policy of producing countries, it was easy to convince them to sign the first International Wheat Agreement in 1933. The signatories (nine exporting countries and thirteen importing) agreed that producing countries were to respect export quotas and reduce crop acreages by 15% for the 1934-1935 period, while importing countries promised not to increase such acreages and to reduce tariffs when world prices reached a certain level.

This agreement lasted only one year due to difficulties in enforcing crop-planting regulations. At the beginning of 1934 Argentina was forced by a rich harvest to exceed her export quota, thus bringing the agreement to an end.

Prices increased slightly during 1934, due more to poor harvests in Canada and the United States than to production restraints. Subsequently, the market slumped back into a situation of excess supply and in 1939 world stocks rose to 700 million bushels. Still, the history of controls considers this agreement important because, as mentioned by J.W.F. Rowe, it was the first commodity control scheme in which so many governments (including the U.S. government) cooperated.[5] Also, this control scheme was a direct forerunner of the international wheat agreement of 1949.

International Rubber Market

We saw earlier that in 1928 price drops and high stock levels had caused the Stevenson Plan to be abolished. Return to a free market situation was no solution to this industry's problems. American demand, representing more than 60% of world demand, vanished with the depression. Moreover, the artificially high prices of 1924 had brought about an overproduction of Indonesian rubber which was now arriving on the market. At the end of 1932 the situation was characterized by a stock of 200,000 tons and a price equivalent to 3% of that recorded for 1925. Dutch authorities (Indonesia) then pressured English authorities (Malaysia and Ceylon) to sign an international rubber agreement.

The International Rubber Regulation went into effect in April 1934. It too included quantitative production and export restraints aimed at reducing stocks and assuring a "just and equitable" price. Unlike most of the other intergovernmental agreements, this agreement admitted three representatives of rubber consumers to the administrative board, although they were not given the right to vote.

Due to the recovery of world demand starting in 1934 and commercial restraint rates reaching 60% (1934-1935), 65% (1936 and start of 1937) and 90% (last half of 1937) of export quotas, producers enjoyed prices five times higher than the average price of 1932. When in 1938 the agreement was renewed, India and Siam joined, giving it almost absolute control of world production. Following the American recession, there was a drop in demand in 1938 and prices fell by 40% not to increase again until 1939 after commercial restraint rates were set at 45% of allotted quotas.

The agreement was rendered void by the Japanese invasion of Southeast Asia in December 1941. Even more important, starting in 1941, rubber producers had to face competition from synthetic rubber. This posed a definite threat to their future.[6]

International Copper Market

The 1930s depression, increased production in countries outside of Copper Exporters Inc., growth of demand for copper substitutes, and the price war among cartel members had driven copper prices down from US 24.0¢/lb. in 1929 to US 4.7¢/lb. in 1932. Wishing to correct the situation, the American government imposed a US 4.0¢/lb. customs duty on imports, making the entire American market the exclusive domain of domestic producers.

From 1932 on, the international copper market was split in two: the American market which became more and more self-sufficient and the world market which remained freer, with its prices determined on the London Metal Exchange.[7]

Although the economic situation of American producers improved very slightly from 1932 to 1935 (things could hardly have become worse), it remained disastrous in the rest of the world.

In April 1935 a few producers outside of the United States decided to influence the market by cutting production. After eight months of negotiations the International Copper Cartel was created and began to operate as early as the start of 1936. This cartel was composed exclusively of private copper ore producers from Chile, Peru, Northern Rhodesia (now Zambia), and the Belgian Congo (now Zaire). American producers judged it wiser not to join the cartel and agreed only to limit their foreign exports. Since the Canadians (largest producers after the United States), Europeans, Russians and Japanese also refused to sign the agreement, the cartel controlled only about 70% of world production—U.S. excluded. The board of directors allotted export quotas to producers and imposed a commercial restraint rate, varying from 75% (1936) to 100% (1937, when prices rose to U.S. 10.0¢/lb.). The war put an end to this cartel which had proven a great deal more stable than Copper Exporters Inc.

Even though, during the period under study, controls were also tried in the cotton and coffee markets, these attempts remained on a national level and were not of sufficient strength to influence production and prices in a tangible way.

Notes

1. Before 1914 attempts to establish controls proved to be either isolated or cyclical and speculative. These were the most important.

a) Towards the end of the 1880s, the French financier, Pierre Secretan, with the complicity of a few banks, managed to manipulate world copper prices through massive purchases at a fixed price. In a matter of months the price of copper doubled on the London market. Then in 1889, when the production stimulated by these artificial prices started to come on the market, the bottom fell out.

b) In 1892, the American Producers' Association, by limiting its production and exports, succeeded in influencing the price of copper. The variation, however, was slight because European producers cut their production by only 5% instead of the 15% demanded.

c) In 1907, the state government of Sao Paulo in Brazil (and not the federal government) managed to increase world coffee prices through the regulation of exports. This stabilization scheme, financed by a handful of European banks, was something of a success since Brazilian exports then made up 80% of the world coffee trade.

d) At the start of the twentieth century, the attempt was also made to control commodities such as sugar and zinc as well as less important metals and ores.

2. E.S. Mason, *Controlling World Trade: Cartels and Commodity Agreements* (New York: McGraw-Hill, 1946), p. 14 Reprinted with permission.

3. John W.F. Rowe, *Primary Commodities in International Trade*, pp. 137-138.

4. Alton D. Law, *International Commodity Agreements*, p. 38.

5. Rowe, *Primary Commodities in International Trade*, p. 152.

6. According to A.D. Law, synthetic rubber production in the United States increased from 8,000 tons in 1941 to 1,000,000 tons in 1944. Law, *International Commodity Agreements*, p. 62.

7. The reader interested in knowing more about the way this bicephalous market works is referred to F.E. Banks, *The World Copper Market: an Economic Analysis* and F.M. Fisher, P.H. Cootner, and M.N. Baily, "An Econometric Model of the World Copper Industry," *Bell Journal of Economics and Management Science*, 3, (Autumn 1972):568-609.

4 International Commodity Agreements: 1945-1964

The second world war not only put an end to most of the agreements discussed, but it also dislocated the entire international commodities market. The impending conflict caused the excessive rise of all commodity stocks. Vast portions of the European market disappeared, leaving excess supplies of cotton, wool, jute, wheat, sugar, coffee, and cocoa. Japanese invasion of production zones caused excess demand for tea, rice, rubber, tin, and sugar. Direct government controls and rationing returned. An important part of production capacity was destroyed and prices fluctuated sharply. One can therefore scarcely be surprised that, at the end of 1945, economic agents showed a strong desire to return to greater stability in production, receipts, and prices.

But how was such stability to be ensured? Although the international commodities agreements signed from 1931 on were not all as successful as hoped, these failures were not attributed to the concept itself but rather to technical shortcomings such as lack of consumer participation and the limited number of control techniques used. Therefore, the use of such controls was still encouraged because, even if the international agreements of the interwar years had limited world production and consumption, it seemed possible to have improved versions of such agreements. Improvements to be made involved replacing quantitative controls by buffer stocks or multilateral contracts; enlarging administrative boards to incorporate the moderating influence of consumers; seeking the blessing of international organizations, such as the UN, capable of defining the framework and methods of control.

Not only did the second world war give new impetus to international agreements but, more important, it brought them a certain measure of respectability and, soon after, international assent. One of the first international conferences on commodities was held at Hot Springs toward the end of the war. The final communique decided that agreements should promote orderly growth of the world economy; their operational guidelines should be made explicit; the principle ensuring real representation of consumer interests on agreement boards should be upheld.

These proposals were taken up again at the Havana Conference of 1947. The goal of this conference was to liberalize international trade by setting up the International Trade Organization. But in order to reach a final compromise on the question, chapter 6 of the Havana Charter granted exemptions to countries participating in intergovernmental commodity agreements as long as certain guidelines were respected. It also provided ways and means to encompass any possible kind of government intervention in commodity markets. Although the Havana Charter was not ratified, chapter 6 was adopted by the United Nations Economic and Social Council—resolution 30(IV)—on March 28, 1947. The statutes of the General Agreement on Trade and Tariff (GATT) even provide in Article XX(h) that these agreements could constitute, under certain conditions, an exception to the general rule of free trade. The principles and procedures governing international commodity control schemes as adopted by the United Nations have been summarized by Rowe.

International Commodity Agreements are permissible under either of two conditions:

1. where a "burdensome surplus," such as would cause serious hardship to the producers, of whom a substantial proportion must be small producers, will not be avodied or prevented from developing by normal market forces, because a substantial reduction in price does not lead to a significant increase in consumption or decrease in production, or

2. where widespread unemployment or underemployment involving undue hardship to the workers has developed, or is expected to develop, and will not be prevented by normal market forces because of the absence of reactions as above to price reduction, and because there is no alternative employment for the workers involved.

Any member country of GATT which considers that one of these conditions is satisfied may ask the United Nations to appoint a study group for the commodity concerned. All members who consider that their country is substantially interested in the production, consumption or trade in that commodity may send a representative to the study group. Nonmembers may also be invited. On the basis of the recommendations of such a study group, or at the request of members whose interest represents a substantial part of world production or consumption, the United Nations shall convene an intergovernmental conference, which can establish a commodity control scheme subject to the following governing principles. These are:

1. All members substantially interested in the production, consumption or trade in the commodity shall be invited to participate in the control scheme, and nonmembers similarly interested may be invited also.

2. Nonparticipating members must receive equitable treatment, and that must in no case be less favourable than the treatment accorded to nonmembers of GATT (in other words a sort of most-favoured-nation principle).

3. An agreement must include consumers as well as producers, and exporters and importers must have equal voting power on the governing body, which is termed a Commodity Council. An escape clause, however, permits unilateral action by exporters in an emergency, but only as a very temporary measure.

4. There must be full publicity of the terms of the agreement.

5. Adequate supplies of the commodity to meet the world demand at reasonable prices must be assured, and any expansion of supplies must come from the most efficient producers.

6. Each participating government must put in hand such internal economic adjustments as should solve the problem within the duration of the agreement.

7. No agreement or renewal shall be for more than five years.

8. The United Nations shall make an official investigation and report every three years at most.

9. The United Nations can call for a revision of the agreement, or its termination, at any time if its operation has failed substantially to conform to the above principles.[1]

As soon as these principles and procedures were adopted by the UN, international study groups were set up for tin, rubber, and wool while those already in operation for sugar, cotton, and wheat studied possibilities of a new international agreement on these products. In all cases, the wish was to reach international agreements different from those experienced before the second world war. In these new agreements importing and exporting countries would have the same number of votes; expansion of world consumption of the controlled commodity would be encouraged; this increase in demand would be met by the most efficient producers; and member nations would agree to take internal corrective measures to ensure elimination of the causes of excess supply or widespread unemployment. Moreover, there was a need to set up short- and medium-term agreements meant solely to solve very specific problems and which could be abolished whenever the UN judged appropriate. Although chapter 6 of the Havana Charter allowed too broad an interpretation of the terms "equal treatment," "adequate supplies of commodities," and "reasonable prices," it had opened a new era for international commodity agreements.

Between 1945 and 1964 international agreements were established for wheat, tin, sugar, coffee, tea, and olive oil, while controls by national governments or by private producers were tried for another twenty commodities. Below, we present the characteristics of the wheat, tin, sugar, and coffee agreements, both because they are important in themselves, and because they are based on chapter 6 of the Havana Charter.

International Wheat Agreements

In 1939 world wheat stocks had reached 700 million bushels or more than nineteen million metric tons (a metric ton [MT] of wheat contains 36.66

bushels). In spite of the war, these stocks remained high, good harvests counterbalancing production cuts due to the outbreak of hostilities. Then in 1942 the second international wheat agreement was signed by the main producing countries (the United States, Canada, Argentina, and Australia) and one of the consuming countries (Great Britain). Besides establishing the International Wheat Council, this agreement imposed production and export controls, gave clear indications for reserve stock limitations and introduced a minimum/ maximum price bracket.

Due to good harvests and the high level of suggested prices, the 1942 agreement had no effect on world wheat stocks which in 1944 climbed to 1.1 billion bushels or 30.5 million metric tons. The international wheat market showed much greater instability during the second half of the 1940s. The strong postwar world demand and the disastrous European harvest of 1947 caused a 20% rise in prices and a drop in world reserves. Producers did not enjoy this favorable situation for very long. The pickup in European production, the excellent weather of 1948-1949 and the larger crop acreages resulting from 1947 prices led to a 10% increase in world production (see table 4-1). Prices fell by 36.0¢/bushel as compared to the record high of US $2.52 reached in 1947. The conjuncture proved favorable to the approval of a third international wheat agreement and it was signed in August 1949 by thirty-three consuming countries and by the principal exporting countries (excluding Argentina and Russia).

The 1949 agreement was remarkably original—no production and export restrictions, no reserve stocks, but the introduction of multilateral contracts as a new control technique. Each producer and consumer was allotted an export or import quota, and a maximum (US $1.80/bushel) and minimum (US $1.50/ bushel) price was established. Producing countries agreed never to charge more than the ceiling price for exports allowed under quota and consuming countries not to pay less than the floor price for allotted imports.

This agreement—for which the sum of quotas granted amounted to nearly 65% of the world wheat trade—was to last four years (1949-1952) during which period the floor price experienced a yearly drop of US 10¢ to reach US $1.20/ bushel in 1952-1953. The ceiling price was raised to US $1.86/bushel in 1951, implying that market forces could cause prices to fluctuate within a relatively broad margin of US 66.0¢. Consuming countries were favored during the first years of the agreement, since the Korean War (1950) had caused strategic stockpiling and forced nonmember consuming countries to pay more than the ceiling price for their wheat.

From 1951 on the International Wheat Council found it harder to control its members. Consuming countries (competing for supplies) accused producing countries (constituting an oligopoly) of stockpiling in order to obtain the ceiling price from member nations, while forcing nonmember consuming countries to pay higher than maximum prices. These complaints were proved to be

Table 4-1
International Wheat Market: 1936-1964

Year	Production (million MT)	Trade (million MT)	Stocks (million MT)	Average Price (US $/Bushel)
1936	122.1[a,b]			
1937	124.7			
1938	144.8			
1939	133.3			
1940	116.5			
1941	113.8			
1942	119.5			
1943	113.9			
1944	119.1			
1945	114.0			
1946	132.9			
1947	129.6			
1948	145.5			
1949	139.3		20.2[e,f]	
1950	144.1		20.6	
1951	142.9	28.6[d]	18.4	2.43[g,h]
1952	160.0	27.5	34.4	2.32
1953	160.0	25.5	52.2	2.27
1954	152.3	23.9	54.8	2.37
1955	157.5	25.7	55.1	2.18
1956	226.5[c]	31.9	55.5	2.21
1957	221.6	29.9	51.2	2.15
1958	257.7	26.1	61.5	1.94
1959	249.4	30.0	61.3	2.00
1960	245.3	32.2	63.7	1.94
1961	237.1	38.8	54.5	2.05
1962	263.6	37.1	56.2	2.25
1963	245.2	42.5	47.7	2.00
1964	277.3	50.4	47.4	1.57

Source: Derived from Commodity Research Bureau Inc., *Commodity Year Book*, New York, 1964 and 1977; International Wheat Council, *World Wheat Statistics,* London, 1977; United Nations, *Statistical Year Book,* Economic and Social Affairs Commission, New York, 1956, 1965, 1969, 1976; Food and Agriculture Organization (FAO), *Production Year Book*, Rome, various issues; Food and Agriculture Organization (FAO), *Trade Year Book*, Rome, various issues.

Note: there are 36.66 bushels in a metric ton.

[a]World production excluding Russia from 1936 to 1955.

[b]Civil years (July to June), not farm years.

[c]Including Russia from here on.

[d]The arithmetic average of wheat and wheat flour exports and imports.

[e]Statistics on stocks are given in farm years (July to June). Also, data show stocks brought forward at commercial closing and exclude those from new harvests.

[f]These are stocks from seven exporting countries (or group of exporting countries): Argentina, Australia, Canada, European Economic Community, United States, Spain, and Sweden.

(Table notes continued on next page)

Table 4-1 – *Continued*

[g]Farm years (July to June).

[h]1951/1952-1963/1964: No. 2, Hard and Dark Winter, Kansas City. 1964/1965-1977/ 1978: No. 1, Hard Red, ordinary proteins, Kansas City.

justified with the publication, in early 1952, of wheat statistics which revealed that producing countries' stocks had climbed 86% in the preceding year in spite of very high prices. The outlook was not bright for negotiations to renew the agreement.

However, the agreement was renewed in 1953 for another four-year period with a ceiling price of US $2.05 and a floor price of US $1.55. Great Britain refused to sign, demanding that the maximum price not exceed US $2.00. Between 1953 and 1956 other consuming countries followed Britain's lead, which left the agreement with quotas representing only 25% of the 1956 world trade.

The fourth international agreement had only a slight effect. World stock levels continued to rise because of good crops in both producing and consuming countries which, of course, led the latter to reduce their imports. Despite this rise, the prices of the major producers fluctuated between US $1.70 and US $2.00 with the United States and Canada pursuing their policy of stockpiling in order to prevent a further fall in prices.

In the fifth agreement signed in 1956, the maximum price was reduced to US $2.00 and Argentina returned to the club of producing countries, but world stocks continued to increase due to good American crops. In 1959 they rose to more than 2.2 billion bushels or 61 million MT. Average price declined somewhat but clearly not enough to effect a balance between production and consumption.

Negotiations leading to the signing of the sixth agreement in 1959 were at once more serious and more conciliatory. In addition to lowering the ceiling price to US $1.90 and thus facilitating Great Britain's participation in the agreement, the terms of multilateral contracts were modified. Instead of producing countries being required to export only quota-allotted quantities at or below a ceiling price, these countries would respond collectively to average total consumer demand when market price was at maximum. In exchange, consuming countries agreed to buy from exporting members of the agreement a fixed percentage of their average imports so long as the price remained within the limits set. Quotas thus became inoperative and a larger portion of member countries' trade was brought under controls, both within and at either extreme of the established price bracket. During the three years of this agreement's existence, the international wheat market showed some recovery. For the first time in ten years world wheat stocks declined, due to massive purchases by continental China, production restraint policies in the main exporting countries, poor European crops and growth of extraagreement sales to developing countries. In 1962 these stocks measured 2.06 billion bushels or 56.2 million MT. This drop in stocks made possible a stabilization of export prices which varied less than 5% between 1959 and 1962. It is difficult to determine how much the agreement contributed to this market stability since it then covered only 60% of world trade. However, it was apparently a significant part of the fortunate circumstances which characterized the wheat market between 1959 and 1962.

The seventh international agreement, concluded in 1962, retained the principal elements of the 1959 agreement. The price bracket was adjusted to US $2.025-US $1.625. The principal consuming countries of Europe raised the percentage of their average imports to be furnished by producing countries and Russia signed the agreement as an "exporter." The 1962-1964 period proved fruitful for American and Canadian producers since poor crops in Europe (1963-1964) and especially in Russia pushed their exports up by about 35%. Moreover, world stocks having fallen to 47.4 million MT, a certain stabilization of export prices was made possible. This situation did not last very long since world production increased by 30% between 1964 and 1966. Negotiators charged with the renewal of the agreement (which had expired in 1965) were reminded that a permanent solution had not yet been found for the problem of excess supply. Moreover, considering the market's evolution since 1949, one wonders if an international multilateral agreement was useful and possible, given a situation of confrontation between the oligopolistic character of producing countries and the strong competition among consuming countries anxious to secure supplies.

International Tin Agreements

The Tin Council—which since February 1931 had guaranteed relatively stable prices for this product—disappeared with World War II. Production picked up slowly in the countries of the Pacific and up to 1948 the tin market was characterized by excess demand which raised prices from US 56.0¢/lb. in 1946 to US $1.019/lb. in 1948 (see table 4-2). The market subsequently slid back into its usual vice of excess supply: 22,000 MT excess in 1948; 48,000 in 1949; 32,000 in 1950; and 62,000 in 1951. The high prices of the postwar period had once again overstimulated production. At the same time, demand could not keep pace because of the practice, begun during the war, of replacing tin with other metals and the introduction of a new electrolytic process for producing tin plates. The price fell to US 98.0¢/lb. in 1950. When this happened, some thought was given to controlling the market by reactivating the Tin Council but this talk of intervention faded with the outbreak of the Korean War in 1950. A large portion of world stocks then became strategic stocks, and prices climbed to a record high of US $1.317/lb. in 1951. Between 1951 and 1954,

Table 4-2
International Tin Market: 1946-1964

Year	Production (thousands MT)	Consumption (thousands MT)	Δ Stocks (thousands MT)	Price (US ¢/lb.)
1946	87[a]	111[a]	−24[b]	56.0[c]
1947	108	121	−13	80.0
1948	146	124	22	101.9
1949	157	109	48	102.0
1950	162	130	32	98.1
1951	162	100	62	131.7
1952	165	125	40	123.7
1953	174	126	48	98.3
1954	177	134	43	94.3
1955	170	144	26	97.3
1956	167	150	17	104.0
1957	158	143	15	98.8
1958	121	136	−15	97.6
1959	114	148	−34	104.8
1960	146	162	−16	104.1
1961	139	159	−20	116.3
1962	144	159	−15	117.7
1963	141	160	−19	116.7
1964	147	166	−19	157.8

Source: A.D. Law, *International Commodity Agreements*, (Lexington Mass.: Lexington Books, D.C. Heath and Company, 1975), p. 59. Reprinted with permission of the publisher.

[a]"World" production and consumption of tin, excluding Albania, North Korea, Mongolia, the German Democratic Republic, the People's Republic of China, North Vietnam, and the USSR.

[b]Time series: the difference between production and consumption for each year.

[c]The average tin price "prompt delivery straits ex-docks" on the New York market.

world stocks increased on the average by 44,000 MT a year with world demand running down as the United States neared the strategic stock levels desired. In 1954 the price reached US 94.3¢/lb. Negotiations were then resumed for the establishment of an international tin agreement which would respect the guidelines advanced by the United Nations.

The agreement was ratified in June 1954 by the most important of the tin producing and consuming countries, except for the United States (which refused to participate although granted 45% of consumer votes) and Indonesia. However, this last country joined the producers in July 1956, making it possible for the Tin Council to start operations.

This first international metal agreement was characterized by the following traits. The producing and consuming countries held the same number of votes on the council—each member's exact vote varied according to its percentage in the total exports and imports covered by the agreement. On questions concerning market control, a majority in each of the two groups (importers and exporters) was required. The council could rule on export restraints only so long as buffer stocks amounted to at least 10,000 MT of tin. A buffer stock of 25,000 MT was amassed through contributions, either in kind or in cash (most choosing the latter) or both, from the major producing members: Bolivia, Indonesia, Malaysia, Nigeria, Thailand, and Zaire. The buffer stock was to be controlled by a director whose market intervention would be regulated by a price grid. This meant that, after ceiling and floor prices were determined, the difference between the two extremes was divided into three parts: the lower, middle and upper thirds. If the price rose to the predetermined maximum, the director "must intervene" by putting all available tin on the market to prevent the ceiling being overshot. If the price stood in the upper third, he or she "could sell" the tin necessary to reverse the bullish tendency, if in the lower third, he or she "could buy" to reverse the bearish tendency. If the price stood in the middle third, the director "could neither buy nor sell." Finally, if prices fell to minimum level, he or she "was obliged to buy" all the tin available on the market, making full use of all the financial resources at his disposal, to prevent the floor falling out.

The stock director's first interventions were made in the second trimester of 1957 when prices fell from the level reached during the 1956 Suez crisis. It became more and more necessary to support the floor price as Russia and a few European countries liquidated their strategic stocks and the United States stopped the stockpiling begun during the Korean War. The stock director bought up large quantities of tin (thus decreasing its financial resources) to justify the establishment of three-year quantitative export controls. During that period production decreased from 158,000 MT (1957) to 114,000 MT (1959). Despite this drop in production, continuing Soviet sales forced the stock director to exhaust his financial resources (during the first part of 1958) to keep prices from sliding below the minimum. By September this capital was exhausted and prices dropped suddenly to 14% below floor price. Consuming countries then helped the council meet the crisis by imposing quotas on their Russian imports, an extraordinary move in the history of controls. This move along with the first effects of export cuts and the recovery in world demand (end 1958, beginning 1959) sent prices up by 22%. The stock director could at last begin to dispose of the 23,500 MT of tin he had been forced to accumulate during the period of excess supply.

The year 1958 was an important one for the tin market because from this year to 1966 world demand would exceed production by about 18,000 MT on the average. Buffer stock sales prevented the price from overshooting the ceiling until, in mid-1961, these stocks were depleted. Prices rose above the preestablished maximum thus terminating the control. In any case, the first agreement was to end on June 30, 1961 and negotiations were already under way for the signing of a second International Tin Agreement. With excess demand at 20,000 MT (in 1961) and price at US $1.163/lb. (US $0.976/lb. in 1958), consuming countries seemed eager to conclude an agreement on the tin market without delay.

The second international agreement was ratified on July 1, 1961 and went into operation in February 1962 for a five-year period. Its goals were the same as before: to prevent the underemployment of human resources in the tin industry, to avoid exaggerated price fluctuations and to ensure "adequate" supplies at "reasonable" prices. The council's members were practically the same as before, Russia and the United States still refusing to participate in any way whatsoever. The buffer stock remained the market's principal line of defense, backed up if necessary by quantitative export controls. These latter could now be used as soon as the stock reached 5,000 MT whereas, under the first agreement, 10,000 were needed. Finally, the price grid used to regulate the stock director's market interventions was also retained. But this grid was continually revised upward to reflect the substantial price increase characterizing the market between 1961 and 1966.

This second agreement was in fact signed during a period of excess demand caused, among other things, by intensification of the Vietnam War. Prices rose from US $1.041 in 1960 to US $1.763 in 1965. Despite the stock director's intervention, the council was incapable of holding prices down, since by September 1963 its stocks were already exhausted. It was rather the United States General Services Administration which ensured the control of tin prices by deciding—toward the end of the 1950s—to liquidate strategic stocks. By partially filling the gap between world production and consumption (the United States remained the world's largest consumer although it was not a member of the council), this organization prevented tin prices from reaching as yet unrecorded levels. The Administration's intervention force was enormous; at the beginning of 1962, its strategic stocks had reached 349,000 long tons (LT)—164,000 of which were considered superfluous to military needs. These strategic stocks were fifteen times greater than the buffer stock and two and a half times that of 1962 world production. An estimated 92,500 LT of these stocks were liquidated between 1962 and 1966.[2] In 1966 the tin market began to be characterized by excess supply, production having finally responded to the high prices of the preceding years.

International Sugar Agreements

Through the scarcities it created, World War II modified the traits which had characterized the sugar industry since the 1931 Chadbourne Plan. World supply became insufficient and a still greater jump in prices was only prevented by the establishment of a ceiling in consuming countries. These controls were removed at the end of the war and, in 1946-47, prices climbed to US 5.0¢/lb, tripling the average level reached between 1934 and 1938. These inflated prices so stimulated production that, despite an ever-increasing demand, the sugar market was characterized by excess supply up to 1955. In that year prices were at US 3.24¢/lb. (table 4-3). Although the Korean War momentarily reversed the tendency of prices to drop, it actually worsened the overall situation by creating artificially high prices and stimulating production even more.

Given this situation, the major producing countries succeeded in convincing consuming countries of the necessity of an international sugar agreement based on chapter 6 of the Havana Charter. The agreement was signed on January 1, 1954 for a five-year period and a Sugar Council, bringing together the major sugar exporting and importing countries, was set up immediately. Each of the two groups was given the same number of votes but the weight of each country's vote within the group remained dependent on its percentage in the exports and imports covered by the agreement. Adoption of important measures required a simultaneous majority in each group. However, although there seemed to be a large number of participating countries, the agreement covered only 15% of world production. This was—as Law so clearly explains—because:

> Exports normally constitute less than one-third of total world production. Of that sugar which is imported, the United States accounts for more than 30 percent and Britain another 20 percent. Since both of these economies have usually maintained special trading agreements with a number of countries, less than 50 percent of exported sugar constitutes the free market even when an international agreement isn't in force. World price, then, and world market are based upon roughly 15 percent of total world production. This contributes greatly to the instability of that segment of trade.[3]

Despite this drawback, the council developed a rather original control technique to stabilize sugar prices in "world" trade. After having fixed a ceiling (US 4.35¢/lb.) and a floor price (US 3.25¢/lb.), the council allotted export quotas admitting of variation according to market tendencies. This was done to ensure that market price would fluctuate within the two suggested limits. Rowe explains the exact method of intervention.

> If the price fell below the minimum for fifteen consecutive days, the Sugar Council, the administrative body, was to reduce the export quotas, but if the amount of the reduction could not be agreed within ten days, quotas were to be automatically reduced by 5%. The opposite procedure was to be followed if the price rose above the maximum, the automatic increase in this case being 7½%. The Council, however, was not permitted to reduce export quotas below 80%, or in the case of very small exporters 90%. The exporting countries also undertook so to regulate production in their countries as to limit carry-over stocks to 20% of their basic tonnages, but to hold minimum stocks of 10%. The Council had limited powers to vary these percentages.[4]

Table 4-3
International Sugar Market: 1947-1964

				Prices (US ¢/lb.)	
				World	U.S.
	Production	Stocks as Percent of	Trade	Gross Price	Preferential Price
Year	(thousand MT)	Consumption	(thousand MT)		
1947	27,500[a]		10,165[d]	5.03[f]	5.10[g]
1948	29,000		12,100	4.22	5.08
1949	31,300		12,175	4.16	5.09
1950	31,200		13,525	4.98	5.09
1951	34,900		13,225	5.70	5.77
1952	36,300[b]		13,000	4.17	5.35
1953	33,800[b]		15,200	3.41	5.43
1954	37,500		14,175	3.26	5.21
1955	37,990	27.5[c]%	14,404[e]	3.24	4.99
1956	39,200	24.5	14,035	3.47	5.10
1957	41,500	22.0	15,125	5.16	5.30
1958	44,410	22.0	15,350	3.50	5.41
1959	50,080	26.5	14,695	2.97	5.35
1960	49,850	28.0	17,095	3.14	5.35
1961	56,670	31.0	20,265	2.70	5.36
1962	51,890	28.0	18,740	2.78	5.56
1963	50,570	21.5	17,570	8.34	7.28
1964	54,380	22.0	17,250	5.77	5.98

Source: Derived from Commodity Research Bureau Inc., *Commodity Year Book 1977*, New York, 1977; FAO, *Production Year Book*, Rome, various issues; FAO, *Trade Year Book*, Rome, various issues; FAO, *FAO Commodity Review and Outlook 1976-1977*, Rome, 1977; L. Myers, "Analyzing Sugar Price Trends," *Commodity Year Book 1977*, Commodity Research Bureau, Inc., New York, 1977, pp. 21-30; United Nations, *Statistical Year Book*, New York, 1977; World Bank, *Commodity Trade and Price Trends (1976 edition)*, Washington, pp. 64-65.

[a]All production data are given in farm years, indicating production for the agricultural season ending with the year quoted. From 1947 to 1952, the data concern centrifugalized and noncentrifugalized beet and cane sugar expressed in raw sugar equivalents.

[b]From 1953 to 1971, the data are also given in farm years but they relate only to centrifugalized beet and cane sugar expressed in raw sugar equivalents. Official figures provided by countries for refined sugar production have thus been converted into raw sugar weight on the basis of a 92% refining rate.

[c]World sugar stocks at annual closing as compared to world consumption. Usually, when this ratio declines, world prices increase and vice versa.

[d]From 1947 to 1954, data indicate the arithmetical average of world imports and exports of both raw and refined beet and cane sugar. World trade includes the trade between the United States and Hawaii, Puerto Rico and the Virgin Islands.

[e]From 1955 to 1964, data show the arithmetical average of world imports and exports in raw sugar equivalents. As before, this world trade includes the exchanges between the U.S. and Hawaii, Puerto Rico, and the Virgin Islands.

[f]From 1947 to 1960, prices correspond to World Contract No. 4—New York f.a.s. Cuba; from 1961 on, they correspond to the daily "world" price of the International Sugar Council, f.o.b., stowage in West Indian ports.

(Table notes continued on next page)

Table 4-3 – *Continued*

[g]The American sugar industry has always been protected from international competition by specific tariffs. As set out in the various Sugar Acts, these tariff barriers keep domestic prices above the world price by a margin combining amount of import tariff plus cost of shipping to the U.S. The time series gives the American market price for bagged sugar imports stowed in West Indian ports.

Moreover, consuming countries had to promise not to increase their imports from nonmembers.

During the first two years of the agreement, the price of sugar was especially stable—slight reductions of export quotas keeping prices close to the floor level. Starting in 1956-1957—when the Suez Crisis pushed prices up to about US 5.2¢/lb.—consuming countries expressed less satisfaction with the agreement. Prices remained above the ceiling until the beginning of 1958 when the production stimulated by 1956-1957 prices started to come on the market. The price then fell about 50% and finally in 1959 dropped below the floor price when producing countries recorded larger than average crops.

A second international sugar agreement was ratified towards the end of 1958 for the 1959-64 period. The terms of agreement remained essentially the same; the only important modification was the allotment of quotas for a three-year period—meaning they had to be renegotiated before the beginning of 1962. It is also worth noting that the price bracket was pushed down slightly and that Brazil and Peru joined the list of producing countries. This period was characterized by great instability, not only because of the market's structural difficulties but also because sugar was then being used as a political weapon. Following the overthrow of the Cuban regime, the United States decided in 1960 to reduce by 700,000 tons the preferential access formerly granted to this country's sugar exports. Moreover, after having, at the end of 1960, placed an embargo against all imports from Cuba, the United States provided economic incentives for local sugar production and decided to satisfy its excess demand by increasing imports from other producing countries. The American market for Cuban exports was replaced by mainland China and Russia. Between 1960 and 1962 these political upheavals had little effect on the price of sugar which remained below the floor price—good crops continually counterbalancing the effect of quota reduction.

Since the 1958 agreement only fixed quotas for three years, signatories began negotiations in 1961 for their 1962-64 allotments. It was at this point that Cuba asked the council for an export quota of 7.3 million tons: a 2.4 million basic quota plus 4.9 million for its contracts with communist countries. This request was considered obviously exaggerated since the sum of quotas for other producing countries was less than 7.3 million tons. Finding it impossible to reach any agreement, the International Sugar Agreement was suspended on

December 31, 1961. The "world" sugar market returned to its characteristic instability with prices increasing by more than 500% between 1962 and 1963 before returning to their initial level of US 2.0¢/lb. for the 1964-1968 period.

The First International Coffee Agreement

Unlike other products which from 1930 on were controlled by inter-governmental organisms, control of the international coffee market was exercised by local (Sao Paulo State as early as 1907) or national (the Brazilian federal government from 1923 on) boards. In the interwar period, these organizations piled up enormous stocks to prevent a price collapse. This defense of the coffee market also forced Brazil between 1931 and 1944 to burn not less than 78 million bags or about 10.3 billion pounds of coffee (a bag of coffee weighs 132 lbs.).

World War II did not change the situation. The disappearance of European markets and the lack of ships for transport to the United States caused increase in world coffee stocks and further destruction of the excess supply. Toward the end of 1945, the economic situation began to look up. As the United States had frozen coffee prices at US 13.4¢/lb. on local market since the beginning of the war, Brazilian producers started reducing their production. In 1946 this production was only at 60% of the level reached at the beginning of the thirties. Given a growing world demand and no reporting stocks (overproduction having been burned since 1931), the price increased by 68%.

From 1946 to 1950 world production remained stable, Brazilian production cuts counterbalancing the rapid rise in African output. Since demand continued to grow, the price climbed to US 50.5¢/lb. in 1950 (table 4-4), compared with US 11.1¢/lb. between 1934 and 1938. In July 1954 the price rose to US 88.0¢/lb., the Korean War and the destruction by frost of a part of Brazilian production contributing to the price increase. Circumstances thus seemed especially favorable to Brazil, Colombia, and a dozen other Latin-American countries which had been showing signs of better cooperation since 1945.

But as cooperation among producers was not a sufficient condition for success, the rapid rise in prices stopped abruptly in July 1954. Prices then started a long plunge, falling to the level of US 34.0¢/lb. in 1962, scarcely higher than the price recorded in 1949.

Several elements explain this 158% drop in the price of coffee. First of all, the high prices of 1950 had encouraged the planting of new trees in Africa, Central America, and, above all, in Brazil's Parana State. Coffee trees give their first yield after four or five years, so this new production started coming on the market just as demand was slowing down. Even more important, since the trees increase in productivity between their fifth and twelfth years, the production capacity implanted in 1950 would go on increasing supply until 1962.

Table 4-4
International Coffee Market: 1947-1964
(*thousands of metric tons*)

Year	Opening Stock	Pro- duction	Supply	Net Exports	Closing Stock	Stock Variation	Santos Price (US ¢/lb.)
1948[a]	1,023[b]	2,078	3,101[c]	1,851[d]	752	−271	26.8
1949	752	2,346	3,098	1,936	602	−150	31.8
1950	602	2,257	2,859	1,876	488	−144	50.5
1951	488	2,290	2,778	1,896	392	−96	54.2
1952	392	2,312	2,704	1,929	316	−76	54.0
1953	316	2,491	2,807	1,976	337	21	57.9
1954	337	2,640	2,977	2,008	390	53	78.7
1955	390	2,531	2,921	1,753	672	282	57.1
1956	672	3,021	3,693	2,298	991	319	58.1
1957	991	2,725	3,716	2,172	898	−93	56.9
1958	898	3,301	4,199	2,240	1,431	533	48.4
1959	1,431	3,700	5,131	2,339	2,212	781	37.0
1960	2,212	4,735	6,947	2,541	3,656	1,444	36.6
1961	3,656	3,946	7,602	2,653	3,992[e]	336	36.0
1962	3,992	4,323	8,315	2,722	4,347[f]	355	34.0
1963	3,669	4,044	7,713	2,992	4,266[g]	597	34.1
1964	4,266	4,260	8,526	2,962	4,278	12	46.7

Source: Derived from Pan American Coffee Bureau, *Annual Coffee Statistics*, no. 36, New York, 1973; International Coffee Organization, various publications.

Note: Bags have been converted to metric tons; a bag contains 60 kg of green coffee.

[a]Marketing year, usually ending Sept. 30 of the year indicated.

[b]Stocks in producing countries.

[c]The sum of net exports (an approximation of world demand), closing stock and domestic consumption in exporting countries. Domestic consumption can be obtained by subtraction.

[d]Consumption and working stocks of importing countries.

[e]Reduced by 180,000 MT allotted for "industrial" use in Brazil.

[f]Reduced by 420,000 MT destroyed in Brazil in 1961.

[g]The 1962-63 to 1976-77 stock series represents data at end of harvest as compiled by the International Coffee Organization (the end of March, for Brazil, to the end of September); not data for end-of-September stocks.

With world production rising from 2.6 to 4.73 million MT between 1954 and 1960, the negative effect on prices can come as no surprise.

Second, the high prices recorded between 1950 and 1954 weakened American demand by 23%; this is a significant drop if one considers that American imports were at the time more than 60% of world imports. American consumers reacted in much the same way as they did at the beginning of 1977, and by using coffee substitutes they caused coffee prices to fall. Although we do not know the price-elasticity of American demand for coffee (the impression being that it is rather important at high prices), we do point out that a recent econometric study has revealed that the price-elasticity of the per capita demand for coffee in industrialized countries is higher than that calculated for tea, cocoa, sugar, or rice.[5]

Third, it is important to notice that the July 1954 record price (US 88.0¢/lb.) was also caused by the rumor that a "substantial" part of Brazilian production had been destroyed by frost. The price fell back to US 70.0¢/lb. toward the end of 1954 when consumers learned that the damage had been grossly exaggerated. This implies that although between 1954 and 1962 there was an important fall in prices, it was less than the 158% mentioned previously.

Faced with this fall in prices, a few Latin-American producers decided— at Mexico in 1957—to sign an agreement limiting exports through quota allotments. In 1958, the Mexico agreement became the Latin-American Coffee Agreement which regrouped the fifteen largest coffee producers of the continent. In 1959, France and Portugal joined the agreement as representatives of their colonies. When in 1960 Great Britain and its colonies followed this lead, the agreement covered the countries responsible for 90% of world production. Export restrictions (applied mainly by Brazil and Colombia) had only moderate influence on the price of coffee, scarcely slowing its fall. The year 1962 found these two countries with 60 million bags in stock (54 million in Brazil alone) and an annual average production of more than 30 million bags. They were, moreover, faced with an annual average world demand of scarcely more than 40 million bags.

In July 1962 a United Nations Conference was called to study the problems inherent in the world coffee market. Negotiations reached an accord in September 1963 and the first International Coffee Agreement was signed at that time.

This agreement, which the United States had pushed for at the 1961 Organization of American States (OAS) meeting for reasons of political strategy, regrouped thirty-six exporting countries, twenty-two importing countries and representatives of thirteen other nations. The agreement covered 95% of world coffee trade. Unlike most of the other agreements studied, the industrial countries participating in this agreement were all members of the consuming bloc, which was not the case for the wheat and sugar agreements. Following the Havana Charter, exporting and importing countries were granted the same number of votes on the council; two-thirds of the votes of each group were needed to ratify council decisions. Although the weight of each member's vote still depended on its percentage of world imports or exports, it is important to note that no country could hold more than 40% of the votes in either group. Brazil (with 36.2% of the producers' votes) and the United States (with 40% of the consumers' votes) were the mainstays of this new control scheme.

The goals of the agreement did not differ from those set for the other products studied: to balance world supply and demand; ensure "equitable" coffee prices without "excessive" fluctuations (the price was not to fall below the prevailing 1962 price, chosen, despite that year's high stock levels, as the equilibrium long-term price); encourage world coffee consumption; and contribute to the economic development of member nations. It was also decided that these goals could be reached by control techniques based on export quotas. So quotas amounting to 45.6 million bags were allotted to the thirty-six exporting countries: 33 million bags to Latin-American countries and about 13 million to African countries. Each country's basic quota and the total quota were both subject to an annual review. Thus in 1963-64 the annual quota was set at 99% of the total quota. Importing countries participated directly in the controls by limiting imports from nonmember nations and by requiring a contract of origin issued by the producing council member.

Between 1962 and 1964, the price of "Brazil Santos 4" coffee rose by US 12.7¢/lb. and reached US 46.7¢/lb. During the same period the African coffee, "Uganda W&C No. 10", recorded a rise of US 14.7¢/lb. Although coffee prices returned to an average level of US 40.0¢/lb. between 1965 and 1969, criticism of the agreement grew and became sharper starting in 1964. Irving B. Kravis and Alton D. Law underline certain important weaknesses of the agreement.

The operation of the export quota system nevertheless encountered difficulties largely attributable to the fact that the prevailing prices paid to producers made coffee production profitable relative to other crops in most of the exporting countries. No international mechanism was in operation which would reduce the incentives that the maintenance of prices provides coffee farmers to continue or even expand coffee production. The result was to encourage persistent excess production (relative to requirements for allotted exports and domestic consumption) in amounts and locations which have varied from one coffee-year to another. Since few Central American or African producing countries find it easy to finance the holding of stocks or even possess the physical facilities for storage, excess production created almost irresistible pressures to export coffee in excess of the quota. Under these circumstances, considerable quantities of above-quota coffee were exported, some through loopholes in the ICA certificate system, some through formal waivers obtained from the Council, and some in simple violation of the agreement.[6]

The intervening period had witnessed transfers of over $600 millions per year from the coffee-consuming nations to the coffee producers. This had been in part the deliberate effort of the consuming nations for political more than economic motives. No effort will be made here to measure or evaluate any political or diplomatic gain which may have occurred. Furthermore, the intervening period had witnessed a dispute over soluble coffee in which the U.S. argued for a higher tax on Brazilian ground soluble coffee than the exporters wanted. Both of these issues hold adequate proof that the inclusion of importing nations holds no concrete hope for representation of the final consumer. It is a fact that for the bulk of the period of the coffee agreement (1963-72) the price of coffee was appreciably higher with U.S. participation than it would have been without.[7]

J.W.F. Rowe's criticisms are more specific, direct, and go straight to the essence and validity of the agreement. After making the following points (the minimum price proposed by the agreement was well in excess of the long-term equilibrium price; the agreement froze the industry's structure through the use of quotas which both prevented the adjustment of supply to demand for different qualities of coffee and forbade the increase of exports from countries with low production costs; the agreement provided no mechanism to encourage the destruction of production capacity in countries with relatively high costs), he concludes that this agreement was admittedly a political move, a move to maintain the price of coffee at an artificially high level as a form of aid, thus divorcing it from the costs of production.[8] We will discuss later the evolution of the international coffee market between 1965 and 1977 and the marginal adjustments made by the council in response to the criticisms mentioned.

Conclusion

So the 1945-1964 period was characterized by an acceleration of controls in commodity markets. Contrary to the preceding period, these controls were now sanctioned by the United Nations. However, this blessing from international authorities came with certain conditions. These were that consuming countries belong to administrative control boards in order to moderate producer demands; that supply come from the most efficient sources and that production in countries with relatively high costs be discouraged; and that agreements be on a short-term basis, dissolving whenever the United Nations considered the problem of excess supply solved.

Were these conditions respected by the international agreements signed during the period under study? Although it would be foolhardy to offer a global answer to that question, we can say that anyone risking an affirmative answer would need to weigh his words. In fact, despite the equal participation of importing countries on administrative boards, their moderating role has either been mocked by the oligopolistic character of producers (in the case of wheat) or handicapped by the monopsonic power of certain consuming countries to prevent prices from finding their equilibrium (for political reasons in the case of coffee and ideological ones in the case of sugar). By putting off necessary economic adjustments, international agreements have very often increased the price instability already characteristic of these products. Moreover, having importing countries join control boards has not always benefited the product's final consumer, evolution of the sugar and coffee markets may be cited in illustration of this point.

As concerns the condition of efficiency contained in resolution 30(IV) of the UN Economic and Social Council, this was in general respected (to a certain extent) by agreements trying to control international markets by means other than quantitative production restraints. In fact, although the Tin Council used no special measures to discourage production in countries with relatively high costs such as Bolivia, Nigeria, and Zaire, at least its buffer stock did not freeze the industrial structure by allotting quotas on the basis of past commercial performance. The same applies to the International Wheat Agreement where multilateral contracts were used instead of the pre-World War II imposition of quotas. The presence of enormous stocks in the wheat sector was far more the result of American and Canadian stockpiling policies than of multilateral contracts. By ensuring that producers received artificially high prices, the control policy of these two countries caused a much greater transfer of physical and human resources than that required by the equilibrium long-term wheat price. The international coffee market was also characterized by poor resource allocation caused by the refusal to tie product price to production costs. In fact, the imposition of export quotas and the council's promise to prevent prices falling below the 1962 recorded price encouraged producers to abandon food crops for coffee, slowed production in countries with relatively low costs, such as Kenya, and handicapped the international transmission of technological discoveries in this sector.

Finally, what can be said about the condition governing the length of the agreements? Although none of the four agreements studied ever lasted more than five years, they were continually renewed in the hope of ending problems of excess supply and underemployment of resources. Study of the 1965-1977 period indicates that, far from fading, these problems have grown to proportions more directly disturbing for the international economic order. Reality has contradicted the United Nations hypothesis that the problem of excess supply was of a temporary nature and could be rapidly solved by the creation of certain kinds of controls. Not only would most post-World War II agreements be renewed but other controls such as formal and informal cartels and an integrated program would be introduced. From 1964 on, these controls would develop in a completely new context. Although they remained as means for stabilizing some commodity markets, it became more and more a question of how controls could be used as elements of a general development policy or as a mainstay in new North-South relations. The United Nations Conference on Trade and Development (UNCTAD) founded in 1964 would become thereafter the defender of this new conception of controls.

Notes

1. J.W.F. Rowe, *Primary Commodities in International Trade,* pp. 159-160 Reprinted with permission.

2. K.W. Clarfield et al., *Eight Mineral Cartels: The New Challenge to Industrialized Nations*, pp. 34-37.

3. Alton D. Law, *International Commodity Agreements*, p. 48. Reprinted with permission of the publisher.

4. J.W.F. Rowe, *Primary Commodities in International Trade*, p. 175 Reprinted with permission.

5. Francis G. Adams and Jere R. Behrman, *Econometric Models of World Agricultural Commodity Markets*, pp. 15-19.

6. Irving B. Kravis, "International Commodity Agreements to Promote Aid and Efficiency: the Case of Coffee," *Canadian Journal of Economics*, I (1968), p. 305. Reprinted with permission.

7. Law, *International Commodity Agreements*, p. 45. Reprinted with permission of the publisher.

8. Rowe, *Primary Commodities in International Trade*, pp. 181-182.

5 International Commodity Agreements: 1964–1977

From 1964 on, the renewal of post-World War II international commodity agreements has taken place in a context where the existence of controls no longer needed to be justified. These controls were rather perceived by several international groups (such as the United Nations Conference on Trade and Development and the Group of 77) as normal means of transferring resources from rich to poor countries. The microeconomic concern for efficiency in resource allocation underlying resolution 30(IV) (adopted in 1947 by the United Nations Economic and Social Council) was now replaced by macroeconomic concern for development and growth of foreign exchange. The expressions "international agreements" and "aid to developing countries" came to be synonymous for most products (except those originating in industrial countries). The economist, C.D. Rogers, states that explicitly.

> Throughout the 1960s there has been a gradual widening of the scope of commodity agreements with the tacit emergence of their new role as a means of economic aid. It has been accepted that, in certain circumstances, agreements may be a useful form of providing international economic assistance, especially when incorporated into a general programme of help to less-developed countries and combined with other measures as part of an over-all trade strategy.[1]

Since international commodity agreements were then seen as one of the numerous means (the Integrated Commodity Program was already under discussion) suited to accelerate this transfer of resources, we will attempt to evaluate their importance during the 1964-1977 period.

International Wheat Agreements

Since 1949 the international wheat market had been characterized by international agreements based on multilateral contracts. According to certain countries signing these agreements, this control technique permitted a high degree of price stabilization. We argued earlier that this stabilization was accomplished at a high cost when the stock levels for that period are considered. What is more, we found that international agreements had made a relatively modest contribution to this stability in comparison to that of the producing countries. By accepting the piling up of enormous stocks, the producers prevented prices from diverging by too large a percentage from the ceiling price set by the agreements.

The 1963 production was below the average recorded for the 1958-1962 period and there was a distinct growth of world demand (see table 5-1). Although these circumstances would have justified an increase in prices, the growth in world demand was met instead by liquidation of stocks which decreased from 47.4 to 37.6 million metric tons (MT) between 1964 and 1966. So the international wheat market seemed to be on the right path when the 1962 agreement came up for renegotiation in 1966. However, these talks were slowed down when it was announced that the 1966 crop would attain 308.9 million MT (a 15% increase over the 1965 production) and that world demand was showing a marked decline. Given the forecasted increase in stocks, it was decided to extend

Table 5-1
International Wheat Market: 1963-1977
(millions of metric tons)

Year	Production	Trade	Stocks	Average Price (US $/bushel)[d]
1963	245.2	42.5	47.7	2.00
1964	277.3	50.4	47.4	1.57
1965	266.5	50.0	35.7	1.61
1966	308.9	67.1	37.6	1.85
1967	299.1	57.3	45.5	1.59
1968	331.5	57.5	64.7	1.46
1969	314.4	53.3	67.2	1.45
1970	319.1	60.7	51.5	1.58
1971	353.8	58.0	51.2	1.60
1972	346.9	63.0	30.4	2.33
1973	376.6	79.1	28.4	4.62
1974	359.8	65.6	31.2	4.13
1975	355.8	77.1	38.6	3.74
1976	416.8[a]	69.3[b]	59.0[c]	2.88
1977				2.59[e]

Source: Derived from Commodity Research Bureau Inc., *Commodity Year Book*, New York, various issues; International Wheat Council, *World Wheat Statistics*, London, 1977; United Nations, *Statistical Year Book*, New York, various issues; FAO, *Production Year Book*, Rome, various issues; FAO, *Trade Year Book*, Rome, various issues; FAO, *FAO Commodity Review and Outlook 1976-1977*, Rome, 1977, pp. 43-45.

Note: See notes to table 4-1.

[a]Estimated.

[b]Estimated data for world wheat and flour trade during the 1976-1977 farm year.

[c]Closing stocks for Argentina, Australia, Canada, EEC, and the United States.

[d]There are 36.66 bushels in a metric ton.

[e]Estimated average price between July 1977 and January 1978.

the 1962 agreement for another year and to work out solutions for the market's excess supply by 1967.

In 1967 it was suggested that the controls cover not only wheat but all other grains as well; the first International Grain Agreement (the eighth wheat agreement) was then signed for a four-year period. This agreement was much like the preceding one except for the creation of a food aid program, better coverage of world grain markets and a slight "upward" revision of the price bracket. Study of the 1967-1971 period indicates that it had a rather moderate impact. Despite a very weak growth in world production up to the end of the sixties, wheat prices could not rise beyond an average level (US $1.58/bushel between 1964 and 1970) which was the lowest recorded since the end of World War II. A world demand in decline up to the beginning of 1970 largely explains the evolution of prices and the accumulation of stocks during that period.

Things were looking decidedly better for wheat producers at the beginning of the seventies. From the end of 1969 on, prices would increase at a very rapid rate, even exceeding US $5.00/bushel in 1973. World demand had finally managed to outstrip wheat supplies in spite of record crops. We would like to determine the fortunate play of events which caused such improvement in this market's economic conditions between the beginning of 1970 and the middle of 1974.

As the 1967 International Grain Agreement was to end on June 30, 1971, sixty-nine countries were called to Geneva in January of that year in order to negotiate a new one. After five weeks of discussion, the decision was made to abolish the international grain scheme and to return to an agreement only on wheat. Study of this agreement discovers the following characteristics.[2]

There was to be elimination of all price arrangements as well as the rights and obligations concerned therewith. The Food Aid Convention would be continued and within its terms nine donor countries (Argentina, Australia, Canada, European Economic Community, United States, Finland, Japan, Sweden, and Switzerland) agreed to make annual contributions of wheat and other cereals totaling 4 million MT (about 150 million bushels). The International Wheat Council would be maintained in existence as a center for international cooperation and consultation on wheat-related questions and also for the world-wide gathering and diffusion of precise information on wheat prices, sales, and freight rates. Consultations among members would be structured through the establishment of a consulting subcommittee responsible for watching the current market situation and giving immediate warning when market instability is either actual or imminent. Finally, the council is instructed by the agreement to keep a timely watch on the question of prices and their concomitant rights and obligations. When these questions seem open to fruitful negotiations leading to measures applicable during the agreement's mandate, the Secretary General of UNCTAD should be asked to call a negotiating conference.

From 1971 on, the International Wheat Agreement became largely a purely administrative arrangement and all its market interventions ceased. This agreement came to term on June 30, 1974. In the absence of any consensus on the best means of influencing the market, the agreement was given three extensions, carrying it up to June 30, 1978. The 1971 agreement may be judged even less effective than the other different agreements signed since 1949 which, despite their interventions, had little influence on market evolution. (However, we do point out that market forces had, for six years, been easier to read and that the agreement's clauses on food aid had allowed some liquidation of stocks.)

But what were the other events contributing to the tripling of prices between 1970 and 1974? This spectacular rise in prices was caused above all by an unprecedented increase in world demand which grew by more than 40% between 1969/70 and 1972/73. This rise in demand can be explained by an average growth rate of 6.5% (1.5% above the normal trend) for the world economy between 1971 and 1973; disastrous crops in Russia causing an increase in American and Canadian exports; increase of Chinese purchases on Canadian markets; production below forecasted levels in India; serious flooding in Afghanistan, Pakistan, and the Philippines; beginnings of drought in the Sahel and elsewhere; and bad crops in cereals other than wheat. The "providential" (for wheat producers in industrial countries) combination of all these elements for the 1970–1974 period sent the average wheat price up from US $1.45/bushel in 1969/70 to a summit of US $4.62/bushel in 1973/74 (even climbing to US $6.00 in February 1974). This price increase was possible despite the three record crops from 1971 to 1973, during which period average world production was 12% above the level recorded in 1970. This situation of excess demand carried world stocks down by 80% between 1971/72 and 1973/74 before they stabilized at 30 million MT between 1973 and 1975.

The 1974-1977 period was characterized by a reversal on the world wheat market—supply went from insufficient to overabundant, prices rolled back from their very high level but remained above those recorded for 1969. Recovery of production in the USSR; good crops in Argentina, Canada, India, and Turkey; stabilization of American production; and the settling of world demand all contributed to the doubling of stock levels. The Food and Agriculture Organization (FAO) thus evaluates the present conjuncture on the world wheat market:

> Following two years of stagnation, world wheat production in 1976 increased by 17 percent to a record 417 million tons. All economic regions participated in this growth though the main contribution came from a recovery in the USSR crops. Stocks at the opening of the 1976/77 season were high, and wheat supplies for the crop year exceeded effective demand. Due to improved supplies in importing countries, world trade declined by 10 percent. Consequently, stocks of wheat are expected to rise substantially, and by the end of 1976/77 they may well reach 86 million tons. Prices in international markets declined throughout the marketing year and by mid-May 1977 they were approximately 31 percent below their levels in July 1976.[3]

International Tin Agreements

From 1958 to 1966, the international tin market was characterized by an excess demand averaging 18,000 MT. So it is not surprising that prices rose appreciably, going from US $0.976/lb. in 1958 to US $1.763/lb. in 1965 before falling back to US $1.64/lb. in 1966. But, as we have already mentioned, prices would have been higher if it had not been for liquidation of American strategic stocks. This implies that the commercial sales of the General Services Administration (GSA) did more than the International Tin Council's buffer stock to prevent, during that period, tin prices from overshooting the ceiling. (In any case, the council's intervention stocks had been exhausted since September 1963, thus crippling its capacity to bring prices back within the preestablished bracket.)

Producers were not to profit from such a favorable situation indefinitely; the high prices attracted new producers while discouraging consumption. From 1964 to 1968, the consumption growth rate scarcely exceeded 8% while production increased by 28%. During these five years, there was an even greater growth in supply due to GSA commercial sales amounting to 80,000 long tons (LT) and the fact that secondary tin was being increasingly used to satisfy consumer needs. In 1966 this conjuncture triggered a price drop which was to last until 1968; during this period the international tin market, for the first time in ten years, experienced a situation of excess supply.

Producers then rushed to sign the third International Tin Agreement which on July 1, 1966 went into effect for a five-year period. This agreement went back to the intervention mechanisms negotiated in 1961: variable export restraints, establishment of a buffer stock and determination of a price bracket (ceiling at US $1.81/lb. and floor at US $1.43/lb.). Although the anticipated effect of this third agreement on the international tin market was hobbled by the failure to convince the U.S. to join and by the fact that intervention stock levels were clearly insufficient in periods of scarcity, the buffer stock's purchases of 11,500 MT of tin did prevent the price from falling below the floor between 1966 and 1968. (Table 5-2)

The 1969-1972 period turned out to be relatively stable for the international tin market. A consumption rise just slightly in excess of production caused very moderate variations in world stock levels. The market stability was maintained by the discontinuation of all GSA commercial sales between June 30, 1968 and June 7, 1973. At the same time, buffer stock interventions (purchases of 10,200 MT in 1969-1970) neutralized the effects of secondary tin production and the liquidation of certain European strategic stocks. Prices increased slightly between 1969 and 1972 but remained generally lower than those recorded in 1965. Moreover, the stability of the situation made possible the signing of the fourth international tin agreement on July 1, 1971.

Here are the most important characteristics of that fourth tin agreement. The agreement was administered by the International Tin Council (ITC)

Table 5-2
International Tin Market: 1964-1977

Year	Production (thousands MT)	Consumption (thousands MT)	Δ Stocks (thousands MT)	Price (US¢/lb)	Stocks (thousands MT)	Buffer Stock[e] (thousands MT)		GSA Sales (thousands LT)	Trade (thousands MT)
1964	147[a]	166[a]	-19[b]	157.8[c]	42.2[d]	—		31.15[f]	124.7[h]
1965	151	173	-22	176.3	44.7	—		21.73	132.9
1966	157	176	-19	164.0	41.6	+0.036	(0.036)	16.28	136.2
1967	177	175	2	153.4	45.5	+4.795	(4.831)	6.15	147.2
1968	188	180	8	148.1	55.2	+6.640	(11.471)	3.49	160.5
1969	183	187	-4	164.4	42.1	-6.807	(4.664)	2.05	165.4
1970	184	185	-1	174.1	35.1	-3.432	(1.232)	3.04	161.7
1971	186	189	-3	167.4	39.1	+5.405	(6.637)	1.74	159.5
1972	191	192	-1	177.5	41.2	+5.842	(12.479)	0.36	165.6
1973	185	213	-28	227.2	37.9	-11.478	(1.001)	19.95[g]	159.0
1974	179	199	-20	395.8	34.4	-0.859	(0.142)	23.14	151.1
1975	177	177	0	339.8	—	+20.000[i]		0.60[k]	119.4[i]
1976	—	—	—	383.3	—	-17.000[j]		3.05[k]	—
1977	—	—	—	538.8	—	—		—	—

Source: Derived from Commodity Research Bureau Inc., *Commodity Year Book*, New York, various issues; International Tin Council, *Tin Statistics: 1964-1974*, London, 1976; International Monetary Fund, *IMF Survey*, October 11, 1976, pp. 290-293.

[a] "World" production and consumption of tin metal excluding Albania, North Korea, Mongolia, German Democratic Republic, People's Republic of China, North Vietnam, and USSR.

[b] The difference between annual production and consumption.

[c] Tin price "prompt delivery, straits ex-docks" on the New York market.

[d] Unlike the first four series, this represents "primary and secondary" tin stocks for the end of each period mentioned; stocks in transit and in the countries.

[e] The lefthand figure indicates net purchases (+) and sales (−) made by the Buffer Stock Director; the figure in parentheses indicates the tin metal level (cumulative position) contained in the buffer stock at the end of the period mentioned.

[f] Sales of tin metal by the GSA from U.S. strategic stocks in long tons. The GSA's commercial sales of tin began in September 1962 (1.4 LT). In 1963, they rose to 10.626 LT. No commercial sales took place between June 30, 1968 and June 7, 1973; the decrease in strategic stocks during this period were due to other than commercial reasons.

[g] Between September and December, 1973, there were intragovernmental transfers amounting to 687 LT.

[h] The arithmetic average of exports and imports in primary and secondary tin by the major trading countries, excluding reexportations as much as possible.

[i] IMF estimate.

[j] January to June 1976.

[k] Janaury to November 1976.

composed of seven producing countries (Malaysia being the largest member of the group with 47% of its votes) and of twenty-two consuming countries (Japan remaining the most important with 24% of the votes); the two groups had the same weight on the Council. The executive president, elected by a two-thirds majority, personally chose the council secretary and the director of the buffer stock. He could also suspend intervention activities if prices reached established limits or if this move were justified by exchange rates. The 1971 agreement allowed for the establishment of a 20,000 MT buffer stock or its equivalent in currency; the stock was to be financed by producing countries in proportion to the percentage of their respective votes within their group. The International Monetary Fund (IMF) also helped to finance the buffer stock established by the fourth agreement. Moreover, France and Holland made symbolic voluntary contributions in 1972 to make the point that, since they profited from stable prices, consuming countries ought also to bear some of the financial burden. The principle of a price grid regulating the stock director's interventions between floor ($900 in Malaysian currency by picul) and ceiling ($1,100 in Malaysian currency by picul) prices was retained.

Among the important modifications made over previous agreements, the two following may be emphasized. First, the International Council could, by a two-thirds majority, institute export controls regardless of the quantity of tin in the buffer stock (the 1961 agreement only allowed application of export controls if the buffer stock contained at least 5,000 MT). Second, the 1971 agreement foresaw situations of excess demand and granted the council the power to pressure producers in case of scarcity (the council could also recommend a system for distributing available supply to the consuming countries that had signed the agreement). Finally, the United States continued to refuse membership in the agreement because of the size of its strategic stockpile and the need to use it to protect U.S. industry from shortages or high prices.[4]

Despite the modifications, the 1971 international agreement was not successful in moderating the excessive rise in prices which would characterize the world tin market until mid-1974. After having increased from US $1.79/lb. to US $3.01/lb. between January and December 1973, the price of tin climbed to a record high of US $4.628/lb. in June 1974. How is such a performance to be explained? Like most of the other metals, world tin consumption (which has a high revenue-elasticity) had been stimulated between 1970 and 1973 by an annual 6.5% growth rate in the world economy, 1.5% above the average trend.[5] Since there was even greater growth of gross national product in developed economies, the world consumption of tin increased by 15% in this period. The growth rate of tin supply available on the market was much lower. One of the reasons for this was stockpiling by producers who counted on a continued rise in prices. This divergence of growth rates widened from January 1973 to June 1974, with excess demand reaching 28,000 MT in 1973 and 20,000 MT in 1974.

The advent of world inflation and two devaluations of the American dollar gave even greater impetus to the price rise initiated by the imbalance of world consumption and production. The net result of all these pressures was a 68% price increase between January and December 1973 and a 54% increase between December 1973 and June 1974. Resumption of the liquidation of American strategic stocks on June 7, 1973 came too late to prevent the boom in tin prices, and only sales of 11,500 MT by the buffer stock prevented an even greater rise in prices. Although GSA sales amounted to 23,140 LT in 1974, they were made mostly towards the end of the second semester during the phase of decreasing tin prices. This lack of coordination between the interventions of the GSA and the buffer stock, has often been pointed out.

On June 7, 1973, GSA resumed sales initially offering 1,500 LT until July 1 and an additional 5,000 LT for the first six months of fiscal 1974. However, much to the dismay of producer members of the ITC, GSA sold the entire 5,000 LT by July 11—selling as much as 1,600 LT in one day at prices well below market levels. However, on September 10, 1973, GSA announced a program to sell over 25,000 LT of stockpile tin; this program is still running. However, the present program's success has tapered off in recent months, with sales sparse at the beginning of 1975.[6]

Starting in July 1974, tin prices subsided, quoting an annual average (US $3.963/lb.) distinctly lower than the level reached in June. The buffer stock director did not have to buy much tin during the second semester of 1974 since as early as May the International Tin Council raised the floor price by 34% and the ceiling price by 38%. In 1975 the situation deteriorated. Despite an approximate 1% decrease in world production, prices declined by 16% compared with 1974 levels. Tin consumption recorded a 12% drop (such tin substitutes as aluminum, glass, plastic, steel, and various alloys having increased their market share) and tin exports showed a 21% decline. The Tin Council then decided to intervene. On April 15, 1975, it adopted a program of export controls to reduce the quantities offered by producers during each quarter by 18% compared with the average quarterly exports of the period preceding controls. Moreover, in 1975, the buffer stock bought 20,000 MT of tin, equivalent to 12% of annual world consumption. The effects of these interventions were not hurt by GSA sales because the liquidation of strategic stocks amounted only to 600 LT as compared to 23,140 in 1974. This cooperation between GSA and the council can be explained by the fact that the fifth International Tin Agreement was being negotiated in 1975 and the American government had decided—upon congressional approval—to join the agreement which was to take effect on July 1, 1976.

The fifth International Tin Agreement was signed by the negotiators on

June 21, 1975. It reiterated the goals of previous agreements: to prevent excessive fluctuation of tin prices; contribute to the increase of export receipts provided by tin; and ensure a sufficient supply of tin at prices that are "fair" to the consumer and "profitable" for the producers.

It also retained the previous operational mechanisms, two major ones being a buffer stock and export controls. The buffer stock operates following a margin between floor price and ceiling price (£3,030 and £3,690 by MT at London);the margin is divided into three parts. Export controls, to adjust supply to demand, can under certain conditions be used to back up buffer stock action.

The agreement also contained the following modifications. Producing countries were required to contribute the equivalent of 20,000 MT to the buffer stock (in tin, currency, or both, according to the council's decision). Currency contributions made after the agreement went into effect would be calculated as equivalent to the then existing floor price and not—as with the fourth agreement—according to the floor price envisaged when the agreement went into effect. This was done in order to slow down the decrease in volume of the buffer stock which could result from increase in the floor price during the agreement mandate.

The fifth agreement also imposed on all countries invited to the conference, additional contributions equivalent to 20,000 MT of tin metal at the maximum. This, of course, included consuming countries. (The agreement even stipulated that after two and a half years, the council should check results obtained for additional contributions and if necessary call a meeting to renegotiate the agreement.)

The council was not only allowed to support the buffer stock by borrowing on its reserves but could also solicit the help of those consuming countries which did not contribute to the stock in meeting payment of debts occasioned by loans or other transactions. The council was also charged to study other means of complementing or replacing the means already used to finance the buffer stock.

The council could revise the price margin at any of its sessions, revision being based on factors such as production costs. The council was also to encourage closer relations with research organizations engaged in finding more efficient means of prospecting, producing, transforming, and using tin.

In case of scarcity, the council could recommend that producing countries favor consuming countries belonging to the agreement, giving them preferential access to available supplies.

Finally, the fifth agreement was expected to be more effective in controlling price fluctuations, not only because the buffer stock volume had theoretically doubled but also because the United States (with 25% of world consumption) had joined the agreement with 25.9% of the votes allotted to the twenty-eight consuming countries.

The price support measures adopted by ITC at the start of 1975 and the signing of the fifth agreement occasioned a remarkable improvement in the international tin market for 1976. The commodities section of the IMF gave the following evaluation of the market's new conjuncture:

> The market for tin improved dramatically in the first seven months of 1976. The Penang (ITA) price in July, in terms of U.S. dollars, was back at the last level in the third quarter of 1974, and the LME spot price was at a similar high figure. Much of the demand has been speculative, but the improving industrial climate has led to stock replenishment as well as increased consumption. The ITA export controls were substantially relaxed for the second quarter of the year and were lifted on June 30. Sales of tin from the buffer stock by the ITC during the second quarter of 1976 reached 17,000 tons, more than during any single quarter since the ITA came into operation in 1956. When the low level of ITC buffer stock holdings of 2,820 tons on June 30 was announced, market demand and prices strengthened so sharply that the price rose above the ITA ceiling and remained above it until the second week of August. Average prices in August were 5 percent below the July level, but a slight decline is not unusual during the summer business lull.
>
> During the remainder of 1976, tin prices and demand seem likely to remain buoyant, although price rises are unlikely to be as sharp as at mid-year.[7]

International Sugar Agreements

On December 31, 1961, the 1958 international sugar agreement was suspended when no agreement could be reached concerning the Cuban demand for an export quota of 7.3 million MT. At the start of 1962, prices were already on the upswing and, in 1963, climbed to US 8.34¢/lb. This sudden rise cannot be explained by the lifting of controls since their influence had proved relatively modest from 1954 on. It was more likely a reflection of the fact that world production had shown a 12% drop since the 1961 period of low prices and that the ratio of stocks to world consumption (at 21.5%) was at its lowest level since 1955. Producers did not profit from this favorable situation for very long because by 1966 prices had already fallen to US 1.81¢/lb. (table 5-3). Production and the stock-consumption ratio had increased by more than 25% since 1963.

The attempt was then made to negotiate a third International Sugar Agreement which would establish a floor price for this product and a more effective coordination of production and consumption plans. But 1966 could scarcely be termed the year for international cooperation. Acceleration of the Vietnam War and increased east-west tensions disrupted negotiations on this product for which western demand is so inelastic to price variations. Alton D. Law gives a good description of that era's political atmosphere.

Table 5-3
International Sugar Market: 1964-1977

Year	Production (thousands MT)	Stocks, (Percent of Consumption)	Trade (thousands MT)	World Gross Price (US ¢/lb.)	Preferential U.S. Price (US ¢/lb.)
1964	54,380[a]	22.0	17,250	5.77	5.98
1965	66,084	28.0	19,075	2.02	5.80
1966	63,292	28.5	18,985	1.81	6.04
1967	64,627	30.0	20,195	1.92	6.32
1968	66,441	31.0	20,200	1.90	6.54
1969	68,497	29.0	19,295	3.20	6.75
1970	72,704	28.5	22,075	3.68	6.94
1971	72,121	25.0	21,320	4.50	7.39
1972	74,251	21.5	21,950	7.27	7.98
1973	78,342	20.0	23,205	9.45	8.91
1974	78,717[b]	17.0	23,075	29.70	27.85
1975	81,691[b]	21.5	21,810	20.43	20.50
1976	81,853[b]	25.5	22,700[b]	11.58	14.02[e]
1977	87,390[c]	–	–	8.22[d]	10.09[b]

Source: Derived from Commodity Research Bureau, Inc., *Commodity Year Book 1977*, New York, 1977; FAO, *Production Year Book*, Rome, various issues; FAO, *Trade Year Book*, Rome, various issues; FAO, *FAO Commodity Review and Outlook 1976-1977*, Rome, 1977; L. Myers, "Analyzing Sugar Price Trends," *Commodity Year Book 1977*, Commodity Research Bureau, Inc., New York, 1977, pp. 21-30; United Nations, *Statistical Year Book*, New York, 1977; World Bank, *Commodity Trade and Price Trends* (1976 ed.), Washington, pp. 64-65.

Note: See notes to table 4-3.

[a]From 1964 to 1971, farm years. (Centrifugalized beet and cane sugar expressed in raw sugar equivalents.) From 1972 to 1977, data correspond to the civil year during which the largest part of the harvest was made.

[b]Provisional.

[c]Estimated.

[d]January to October 1977.

[e]January to June 1977.

The extent of political influence can easily be seen. As an illustration, in 1966 the world price of sugar was at 1.5¢ per pound, yet the sub-sidized price in New York was 7¢. U.S. sugar beet allotments were being increased, while world sugar stocks were over 20 million tons— of which nearly 10 million tons were in excess of demand, with a good 1966-67 crop in prospect. The Soviet Union was under long term contract for sugar from Cuba at 6¢ a pound despite the low world price and her occasional resale over the preceding years. Cuba was suffering a variety of problems due to the low world price but still spurned even "gentlemen's agreements" to put a floor under price.

Once a new International Sugar Agreement was reached in 1968, Castro staked the "honor of the revolution" on reaching an output of 10 million tons in 1970.[8]

The mid-sixties were thus characterized by significant economic distortions; a substantial difference between the world gross price and the U.S. preferential price (an average difference of about US 4.0¢/lb. between 1965 and 1970); a revival of distrust between political blocs, as well as erratic fluctuations in exports from the world's largest producer. (From 1961 to 1966, the level of Cuban exports in million MT was 6, 5, 3.5, 4, 5 and close to 6.) These events gave rise to a climate of uncertainty, prompting consuming countries to strive for self-sufficiency through increased support for local sugar industries or for research and development of substitutes such as dextrose, corn syrup and all other forms of artificial sweeteners. Not surprisingly, the 1965-1968 period was marked by an average price scarcely exceeding US 1.9¢/lb., a zero growth rate for world production and an increase of the stock-consumption ratio from 22.0% (1964) to 31.0% (1968).

In 1967, after several unfruitful attempts and continued market stagnation, the main producing and consuming countries were finally brought together in order to negotiate a third International Sugar Agreement. These talks led to an agreement covering the 1968-1973 period. The text ratified at that time contained nine outstanding objectives.

1. To raise the level of international sugar trade, especially in order to increase the export receipts of Third World exporters.
2. To maintain stable sugar prices and ensure producers reasonable incomes while not encouraging further expansion of production in developed countries.
3. To ensure sugar supplies adequate to meet—at fair and re____ _ _rices— the needs of importing countries.
4. To increase sugar consumption, with special emphasi┊   ⌐asures likely to encourage this consumption in countries where the per ⌐⌐   ⌐ ·mr. tion level is low.
5. To improve the balance between world consumption and production.
6. To facilitate coordination of sugar commercialization policies and market organization.
7. To guarantee sugar from developing countries adequate participation in the markets of developed countries and better access to these markets.
8. To keep a close watch on the evolution of use for all forms of sugar substitutes, including the artificial sweeteners.
9. To promote international cooperation in the sugar trade.

The International Sugar Organization (ISO) was delegated powers to establish basic export tonnage and determine a price bracket likely to help attain the objectives.[9] These powers saw relatively little use, since between 1968 and 1973 the international sugar market was to experience sustained price increase and a major fall of the stock-consumption ratio, despite an 18% increase in world production.[10]

Although it would seem that the 1968 agreement allowed for a certain re-alignment of production and consumption plans and contributed to a 390% rise in world sugar prices between 1968 and 1973, market forces also appeared to play a strong role. Prompted by prices below US 2.0¢/lb., world consumers abandoned sugar substitutes and stimulated a 22% increase in the world sugar trade. The consumption increase of that period must in fact have been even larger since, despite an 18% production increase, the 1973 stock-consumption ratio reached the very low level of 20%. Faced with this high level of market activity which called for the enlargement of acceptable fluctuation margins and a redistribution of basic export tonnages, negotiations for ratification of the fourth International Sugar Agreement would prove difficult.

In May 1973 an international conference was called for the purpose of negotiating a new agreement to take effect on January 1, 1974 after expiration (on December 31, 1973) of the 1968 agreement. Although this conference did result in an agreement, a reading of the text reveals that it not only repeats the objectives of the preceding agreement but also fails to take up economic questions.[11] Since the future evolution of production and prices on the free market was uncertain (given the new conditions of supply and demand which had characterized the last three years), the adopted text acknowledges that the conference was not able to resolve all the following important problems of general policy: basic export tonnage; prices, including the problems of inflation and exchange rates; reciprocal rights and duties of exporters and importers, especially those concerning contracts of delivery and supply; the International Sugar Agreement statute relative to special arrangements; the redistribution of deficits and other elements of the quota system intended to balance supply and demand and stabilize market rates within a price bracket. It concludes therefore that it was impossible to negotiate an agreement including economic provisions.

The 1973 agreement was concerned only with very broad administrative questions: financing the ISO's expenses; general commitments of members; setting up committees to study means of promoting sugar consumption or to keep close watch on the evolution of sugar substitute markets; role of the International Council (charged with gathering statistical or other information on sugar) and, above all, preparations for a new agreement. As concerns economic questions, no majority vote could be obtained; the conference even rejected a proposition providing for a bracket price (US 5.4¢/lb. to US 7.9¢/lb.) and a delivery commitment price of US 8.9¢/lb. The thirty-eight exporting and twenty-eight importing countries left Geneva convinced that they would be recalled only when the market showed signs of stagnation.

The year 1974 upheld the judgment of sugar producers who, the preceding year, had refused to make medium-term economic commitments. In June 1974, the U.S. Congress decided not to ratify the Sugar Act, opening the American market to imports of foreign sugar. This free-trade decision provoked a 50% increase in the quantity of sugar to be bought on the "world" market, lessening the negative effect on the market of Britain's joining the EEC. Great Britain had pulled out of the British Commonwealth Sugar Agreement in 1973. This agreement committed Britain to buy most of the sugar exported by Commonwealth countries. This decision had caused increased sugar supply on the "free" or "world" market and somewhat slowed the rise of prices.

World total imports increased by 2 million metric tons compared with the 1968-72 average—import demand being especially strong in the United States, Eastern Europe, and Japan. Total demand showed a rate of growth greater than that of production, causing the stock-consumption ratio to drop further to 17% —its lowest level since 1954. These events caused the world gross price to climb to US 29.7¢/lb., a 1,460% increase compared with 1968.

The international sugar market went through important changes during the next two and a half years.

> In response to the extremely high prices of 1974 and 1975, world sugar output increased by 7.5 percent in 1976/77, compared with an annual average growth rate of only 2.3 percent over the preceding decade. Consumption in 1976 recovered by 3.8 percent from the depressed level of 1975, when a slight decline interrupted a steady long-term growth averaging 3.8 percent per annum during the ten-year period ending in 1974. The prospect of large carry-over stocks at the end of the 1976/77 season has maintained a depressing impact on world markets since August 1976, and free market prices have apparently been below production costs in many sugar producing countries. Due to lower prices, the terms of trade for sugar exporting countries deteriorated in 1976, and overall export values are estimated to have fallen by 32 percent, although export volume rose by 7 percent.[12]

Given this state of affairs, it is not surprising that there were pressures to ratify a new International Sugar Agreement. These were particularly strong in the U.S., where sugar beet producers begged the Carter administration to increase the customs duties on sugar imports (they had already been increased by the Ford administration from US 62.5¢/100 lbs. to US $1.875/100 lbs. in September 1976). In May 1977 President Carter refused to make such a duty increase and to establish import quotas. He suggested instead that an effective International Sugar Agreement be negotiated, stimulating world prices and thus protecting American domestic prices.

President Carter's suggestion coupled with the fall of prices to 1972 levels facilitated the adoption of a new International Sugar Agreement on October 7,

1977. This agreement, unlike the one of 1973, foresees the use of export quotas and a system of buffer stocks (under international control but held independently by various exporting countries) to stabilize the sugar market. This new agreement is applicable for a period of five years, renewable in 1982 for a maximum of two years.

From a reading of the text adopted by the United Nations Conference on Sugar, the following three characteristics appear:

1. The agreement's goal is to stabilize sugar prices on the free or world market at a level between US 11¢/lb. and US 21¢/lb. by using export quotas and buffer stocks.[13] Thus, when prices fall below 14¢/lb., the volume of sugar exportable toward the free market must be reduced through application of export quotas and the constitution of special stocks. On the other hand, when prices reach the upper limit of the stabilization margin—19¢/lb., the volume of sugar exportable to free markets must be increased by progressively releasing the special stocks built up when export quotas were in force. Member responsibility for establishing export quotas and buffer stocks is based on the Basic Export Tonnage (BET) assigned to each of the fifty-one producing countries having signed the agreement.[14]

2. Floor and ceiling prices are defended by export quotas. Thus, if the market price is falling and lies between US 13¢/lb. and US 14¢/lb., producing countries can export toward free markets only 95% of their respective BETs. This percentage gradually decreases by 5% when prices fluctuate between US 12¢/lb. and US 13¢/lb. reaching 85% if the price lies between US 11¢/lb. and US 11.5¢/lb. If prices fall below the floor price for seventy-five consecutive days, the Sugar Council may set quotas at 82.5% of assigned BETs. The reverse strategy is used for rising prices. Also the new agreement strengthens the support of the floor price by supplementary measures.[15]

3. The agreement proposes to start applying quotas as early as 1978 in order to increase stocks held by member countries and thus raise prices. Each exporting country must build up a minimum volume of special stocks and maintain these stocks under the control of the International Sugar Organization until they are needed to support the ceiling price. The agreement sets the maximum level of special stocks at 2.5 million tons, stocking obligations being ascribed to producing countries according to their BET share. These buffer stocks serve as the second line of defense since they are built up only when export quotas are in force—when prices are below US 14¢/lb. (for falling prices) or US 15¢/lb. (for rising prices). These stocks are released in three equal portions when prices reach US 19¢, 20¢, 21¢/lb., respectively. The cost of holding stocks will be shared among importing and exporting countries through a stock financing fund supported by agreement members.

Although it is still too soon to evaluate the new agreement's influence on the world sugar market, we would like to point out that never in the history of this market has there existed between consuming and producing countries an agreement which was more precise or better endowed with means of intervention.

International Coffee Agreements

As a result of the first International Coffee Agreement signed in September 1963 and a very slight variation in stocks, 1964 saw the first price rise in ten years. This agreement was to attract very bitter criticism. It was accused of defending a floor price well above the long-term equilibrium price; of freezing the industry's structure through the allotment of export rights and of not providing any mechanism to encourage destruction of relatively high cost production capacity. The data in table 5-4 justify these criticisms since, as early as 1966, carry-over stocks were at 5,328,000 MT, a level exceeding that period's production by more than 400,000 MT, while net exports reached 3,099,000 MT.

Although the market situation improved somewhat between 1966 and 1968 (19% production drop and 4% net export rise), prices continued to fall because of the size of stocks. Prices reached US 37.4¢/lb. in 1968, a level clearly below the average prices of the fifties. The reasons for such failure cannot be blamed entirely on the 1963 agreement. But it did become obvious that any new agreement would have to solve the problem of chronic excess supply characterizing this market and find effective methods for aligning production to demand. The International Coffee Agreement signed in 1968 between forty-one producing and twenty-one consuming countries came just in time since it made a frontal attack on these problems.

In fact, articles 30 to 39 of the 1968 Agreement permitted the International Coffee Council to establish quarterly and annual export quotas for all member countries. Thus, it was adopted that immediately following the fixing of the annual export quotas, the council shall fix quarterly export quotas for each exporting member for the purpose of keeping supply in reasonable balance with estimated demand throughout the coffee year. Moreover, these quotas shall be, as nearly as possible, 25% of the annual export quota of each member during the coffee year. No member shall be allowed to export more than 30% in the first quarter, 60% in the first two quarters, and 80% in the first three quarters of the coffee year. If exports by any member in one quarter are less than its quota for that quarter the outstanding balance shall be added to its quota for the following quarter of the coffee year.[16]

Besides controlling world supply, the council was charged with stimulating demand in countries with low per capita consumption. Article 40 provides that the council should set up marketing programs; facilitate commercial agreements; ensure a continued flow toward new markets and prevent reexportation by requiring contracts of origin and final destination.

The 1968 agreement thus retained and reworked more vigorously those of

Table 5-4
International Coffee Market: 1964-1977
(thousands of metric tons)

Year	Opening Stock	Production	Supply	Net Exports	Closing Stock	Stock Variation	Santos Price (US ¢/lb.)
1964[a]	4,266[b]	4,260	8,526[c]	2,962[d]	4,278	12	46.7
1965	4,278	3,037	7,315	2,607	4,182	−96	44.7
1966	4,182	4,897	9,079	3,099	5,328	1,146	40.8
1967	5,328	3,635	8,963	3,026	4,968	−360	37.8
1968	4,968	4,117	9,085	3,220	4,728	−240	37.4
1969	4,728	3,664	8,392	3,181	4,152	−576	40.8
1970	4,152	3,998[e]	8,150	3,231[e]	3,918	−234	54.6
1971	3,918	3,498	7,416	3,138	3,276	−642	44.8
1972	3,276	4,308	7,584	3,450	3,294	18	51.0
1973	3,294[f]	4,290	7,584	3,192	3,360	66	66.9
1974	3,360[f]	4,524[g]	7,884	3,495	2,454	−906	68.1
1975	2,454	4,900	7,354	3,493[h]	2,940[h]	486	78.0
1976	2,940	4,473[h]	7,413	3,598[h]	2,166[h]	−774	149.4
1977	2,166	3,620[i]	5,786	−	−	−	308.0

Sources: Derived from Pan American Coffee Bureau, *Annual Coffee Statistics,* no. 36, New York, 1973; International Coffee Organization, various publications.

Note: Bags have been converted to metric tons; a bag contains 60 kg of green coffee.

[a]Marketing year, usually ending Sept. 30 of the year indicated.

[b]Stocks in producing countries.

[c]The sum of net exports (an approximation of world demand), closing stock and domestic consumption in exporting countries. Domestic consumption can be obtained by subtraction.

[d]Consumption and working stocks of importing countries.

[e]Data estimated by Pan American Coffee Bureau, using U.S. Department of Agriculture data.

[f]From 1973-74 to 1974-75, the data are given in farm years for production and net exports.

[g]The 1973-74 production was calculated from a 1972-74 production average, using 1971-72 and 1972-73 as known data.

[h]Preliminary.

[i]Estimated.

the 1963 articles having economic repercussions. Producing countries were therefore expecting a positive response from the international coffee market. Their expectations were not contradicted by reality, since, starting in 1969, this market was characterized by a strong drop in supply and significant stock liquidation. Although it remains difficult to distinguish the agreement's effects from the influence of the climatic disasters which struck Brazilian production at the end of 1969, they combined to cause an 18% drop in production between 1968 and 1971. Despite a certain stagnation of net exports, opening stocks decreased by 27%, causing a US 7.0¢/lb. rise in prices. The price increase proves much larger when we consider that 1971 represented a year of decreased demand for inventories. In fact, the 1972 price shows a US 13.0¢/lb. difference compared with the 1968 price.

The International Coffee Agreement ended in September 30, 1972, not to be renewed before November 1975. The absence of any International Coffee Agreement between 1973 and the end of 1975 can be largely explained by disagreement among producers concerning export allotments and the quota grid; discord between producing and consuming countries concerning floor and ceiling prices and the climatic difficulties in Brazil and Colombia, rendering production controls useless. During this period, production increased at an average annual rate of 7.0% while net exports showed a 9.5% rise between 1973 and 1974 and no increase from 1974 to 1975. Coffee prices increased by US 10.0¢/lb. between 1974 and 1975. This increase resulted from consumer and producer reaction to a galloping international inflationary trend. Producing countries, wishing to profit from future prices, accumulated their stocks while consuming countries, wishing to profit from current prices, increased their inventory demand. This price rise may also be explained by the November 1974 meeting in Caracas of nineteen producing countries controlling 85% of world exports. They met to form the Cafe Suaves Centrales S.A. Company whose goal it is to coordinate national programs aimed at setting coffee export quotas in order to increase prices.

The Caracas meeting shows how exporting countries were willing to use all means, including a cartel composed only of producers, to ensure continued currency inflow. They were ready to negotiate a new International Coffee Agreement providing it contained clauses guaranteeing periodic price adjustments and, therefore, export receipts having some stability in real terms. Consuming countries, wishing to ensure uninterrupted supply and less volatile prices, also pressured for the signing of a new agreement. The position of the two parties being very clear, the International Coffee Council called them to London toward the end of 1975.

In November, forty-two producing and twenty consuming countries ratified the third International Coffee Agreement. This agreement went into effect on October 1, 1976 for a period of six years. It was characterized by a system of export quotas, essentially like that of preceding agreements. A proposal aimed at including a buffer stock as a control mechanism was abandoned as unrealistic, considering the uncertainty of supply. The quotas will be applied only if prices fall below the current level. In order to protect consuming countries against interruption in supply and price rises, it has been provided that production deficits will be declared and shared and that measures will be taken to prevent shipments inferior to quotas. Both export quotas for each exporting countries and global quotas will include a constant representing 70% of quotas and a variable dependent on market results—for example, actual exports and stocks. By virtue of a provision added to the basic agreement at the last minute, the coffee-producing countries are called upon to spend about US $25 million, in a two-year period, on promoting coffee consumption in importing countries.

Since the third International Coffee Agreement went into effect the clause concerning export quotas has never been applied because prices have remained clearly above those recorded in November 1975. In fact, the International Coffee Council's composite price went from US 94.97¢/lb. in January 1976 to US 206.82¢/lb. in December of the same year. On April 15, 1977 it climbed to US 340.0¢/lb. before beginning an important downturn. The average price level of Santos coffee between January and June 1978 has been US 182.0¢/lb. on the New York spot market.

There are several factors explaining this 335% increase in the price of coffee between 1975 and the first quarter of 1977. First, world production dropped 35% during the period under study. The very low 1976-77 production levels may be largely explained by the July 1975 frost in Brazil destroying, according to official sources, 50% of its production capacity; bad atmospheric conditions in Columbia (second largest producer after Brazil); the Angolan civil war and marketing problems experienced by Ugandan producers. Second, despite the rise in prices, import demand increased by 3%; this increase was caused by high forward market prices and uncertainty concerning the availability of coffee in the medium term. Third, opening stocks fell 55% between 1974 and 1977 (for the 1967-77 period the decline grew to 145%). Table 5-4 shows that never before in its modern history had the international coffee market's stock/net export ratio been so low.

Even if the recent conjuncture has permitted an important increase in export receipts, producing countries look pessimistically ahead to the beginning of the eighties. The American consumers' boycott and the rise in demand for coffee substitutes have already led to a 25% decline in coffee prices on the forward market. Producing countries are worried about this situation and realize that the US $25 million to be spent on promoting consumption in coffee importing countries will be clearly insufficient.

The Other International Agreements: The Case of Cocoa

In addition to the international agreements on wheat, tin, sugar, and coffee, other agreements have been signed or proposed for cocoa, olive oil, jute, hard fibres, wool, rubber, tea, tropical wood, meat, phosphate, tungsten, copper, bauxite, and iron ore. Some of the mineral and metal markets mentioned will be taken up later. Here, as an example of agricultural and tropical produce we give very briefly the characteristic traits of the product for which there have been the most precise international controls—cocoa.

As with coffee, cocoa's supply is not price-elastic because it takes about seven years from planting to harvest of the first crop. The international cocoa demand does however appear rather sensitive to price variations since the manufactured products using cocoa as an ingredient, such as drinks, chocolate, cosmetics, and pharmaceutical products, are not essential. These economic characteristics usually give rise to great price instability and cocoa has not been an exception to this rule since the end of World War II.

Ghana, Ivory Coast, Brazil and Nigeria are the principal cocoa-producing countries while the United States and the EEC absorb more than 70% of its international trade.

The first International Cocoa Agreement was signed in October 1972. It comprised export quotas and a buffer stock which was to maintain prices between a floor level (US 23.0¢/lb.) and a ceiling level (US 32.0¢/lb.). This agreement (coupled with the double devaluation of the American dollar and a fast-growing world demand) caused cocoa prices to triple, going from US 31.1¢/lb. in 1971-72 to US 100.0¢/lb. in April 1974. The fact that prices broke through the ceiling can be largely explained by the fact that quotas produce a rapid decrease in supply while demand reacts only after a certain time lag. Demand began to decrease toward the middle of 1974, automatically causing an important price drop.

The price of cocoa again exceeded the ceiling price in 1975, leveling off to an average of US 34.09¢/lb. following a slight improvement in world demand. The market took off again in 1976 when the International Cocoa Council announced that crops would fall below the 1975 level by 33,000 MT (heavy rains, cold, and epidemics having caused a production drop in Nigeria, Ivory Coast, and Ghana). The market price then rose to US 49.68¢/lb. As this was clearly above the ceiling price it rendered the 1972 agreement inoperative and obsolete. Consuming countries demanded and obtained a revision of the 1972 agreement for the purpose of regulating the stock administrator's market interventions more closely and thus promote greater price stability than had been recorded during the four preceding years.

The second agreement was ratified by sixty-three nations in November 1975. It went into effect for a three-year period on October 1, 1976, the expiration data of the 1972 agreement. Its principal characteristics may be summarized as follows: 1. The new International Cocoa Agreement provides for a US 30-55¢ price bracket and an average price of 47 cents for a pound of cocoa. 2. Within a 47-53¢ price bracket, cocoa prices will fluctuate according to supply and demand, without intervention. 3. Prices applicable to export quotas—(which are the same as those in the 1972 agreement)—spread out between 45 and 47 cents. Quotas falling within the 42-45 cent bracket will be reduced by 3% in favor of the buffer stock. In the 39-42 cent price bracket, the buffer stock could also buy a volume equivalent, at most, to 4% of total export quotas. 4. Below minimum price, the buffer stock would continue to buy a maximum volume of 250,000 tons of cocoa, about one-sixth of total annual production. 5. In the upper bracket, going from 53 to 55 cents, the stock administrator could sell a maximum of 7% of total quotas. 6. If cocoa prices outstripped the 55 cent maximum—and so long as they remained outside the established bracket—cocoa sales could continue, provided they did not decrease the stock below a given volume.[17]

The effects of this new agreement on the international cocoa market cannot be evaluated because as early as October 1976 the market price rose to US 100.0¢/lb., almost double the ceiling price. Not only was it impossible to bring prices back within the negotiated bracket but the gap between the market and ceiling price also widened, the former rising to US 170.0¢/lb. in April 1977. An 8% drop in world production and the absence of carry-over stocks explain why the 1976 agreement is now inapplicable.

The international cocoa market is not the only one where stabilization mechanisms could not be put into practice, making the agreements practically inoperative. As current prices are clearly above the specified ceiling, the economic provisions contained in the last coffee agreement have not yet been applied. The same applies to the tin market where the buffer stock has been non-existent since January 1977. Nor does the International Wheat Agreement have any influence on that market, since it includes no provisions for setting a bracket price or regulating supplies. Finally, the same remark applies to the International Olive Oil Agreement created in 1955; actually this agreement is not intended to stabilize prices or income but only to provide for exchange of information and adoption of common quality norms among producers.

Notes

1. C.D. Rogers, "International Commodity Agreements," *Lloyds Bank Review*, no. 108 (April 1973), p. 38. Reprinted with permission.

2. United Nations, *United Nations Conference on Wheat, 1971*, pp. 1-31.

3. Food and Agriculture Organization of the United Nations. *FAO Commodity Review and Outlook 1976-1977*, p. 42. Reprinted with permission.

4. Other reasons are given by Kenneth W. Clarfield et al., *Eight Mineral Cartels*, p. 37.

5. In the U.S.—the largest consumer—the use of tin was concentrated in the following sectors: cans and containers (37%), electrical products (16%), transport (13%), construction (12%), machinery (10%), and the chemical industry (8%). The interested reader may consult various issues of *Commodity Year Book*.

6. Clarfield, et al., *Eight Mineral Cartels* p. 37. Reprinted with permission.

7. G.I. Brown, *IMF Survey*, International Monetary Fund, vol. 5, no. 19, October 4, 1976, p. 295. Reprinted with permission. The reader interested in

the history and the exact working of the international tin agreement is referred to William A. Fox, *Tin: the Working of a Commodity Agreement*.

8. Alton D. Law, *International Commodity Agreements*, p. 50. Reprinted with permission of the publisher.

9. None of the exporting countries (including Cuba) could hold more than 20% of the votes allotted to its group within the International Sugar Council. Moreover, the distribution of votes among exporting countries was proportionate to the weighted average of their net exports on "free" or "world" markets, their total net exports and their total production—the coefficients of weighting were 50% for the first factor and 25% for each of the other two. To the extent that this technique of distributing votes among the exporting countries influenced the establishment of basic export tonnages, it solved the problem responsible for the 1958 dissolution of the agreement.

10. The "world" or "free" sugar market is a relatively modest one. In fact, until 1973-74, between 85 and 90% of world sugar was either consumed in the producing country or exported to the mother countries of producing colonies or sent to countries granting preferential treatment. The size of the "free" market thus scarcely exceeded 15% of world production and consumption. Since this market was used by world consumers mostly in periods of scarcity (and producers in periods of surplus), it was strongly marked by instability. The nature and size of this market were greatly modified when Great Britain joined the EEC (1973) and the U.S. suspended its Sugar Acts (1974).

11. United Nations, *United Nations Conference on Sugar, 1973*.

12. Food and Agriculture Organization of the United Nations, *FAO Commodity Review and Outlook 1976-1977*, p. 17. Reprinted with permission.

13. The size of the "world" market had been modified in 1974 by expiration of the U.S. Sugar Act and Great Britain's pulling out of the Commonwealth Sugar Agreement. This latter agreement was replaced by the Lomé Convention signed by forty-six African, Caribbean and Pacific countries (ACP) and the EEC. From 1974 on, the "world" market was thus composed of total net imports minus those resulting from application of special arrangements (sugar exports from ACP countries toward the EEC and Cuban exports toward countries with centrally planned economies).

14. The 1977 Agreement assigns Basic Export Tonnages (BETs) amounting to 17,445,000 MT (2,500,000 to Cuba and 2,350,000 to Australia and Brazil respectively). Since these BETs exceed total demand forecast for 1978 and 1979 at the US 11¢/lb. floor price, the agreement provides for limiting them to 82.5% of the total for the next two years and to a minimum of 85% for the 1980-82 period. Moreover, to avoid the freezing of market shares, the agreement provides that the BETs be renegotiated during the first quarter of its third year of application.

15. The first of these concerns the redistribution of export deficits as related to quotas; this will only take place if the price exceeds US 12¢/lb. unless

the council decides otherwise. It is inevitable that such deficits should occur, considering that members will not all be able to export a volume equal to their total export rights. The other measure will consist of the imposition by member countries of tougher restrictions on sugar imports from nonmember countries when prices fall below US 11¢/lb.

16. The interested reader is referred to: United Nations, *United Nations Conference on Coffee, 1968*, Articles 30-39.

17. Information derived from International Monetary Fund, *IMF Survey*, vol. 4, no. 21, November 10, 1975.

6 The UNCTAD Integrated Commodity Program (ICP) and the Common Fund

The idea for an integrated commodity program was discussed at the very first session of the United Nations Conference on Trade and Development (UNCTAD), held in Geneva in 1964. Developing countries then declared that any attempt to study the stabilization problem product by product was bound to fail and that it must be approached through a general integrated program. The industrialized countries were not in agreement, most of them alleging that a global solution of commodity problems must take into account the specific characteristics of each product. The conference then adopted a compromise text stipulating that both approaches could be used to stabilize the prices and incomes involved in international commodity trade. However, as we have seen, up to the present all agreements have been negotiated product by product.

The small number of agreements signed and their very limited success encouraged developing countries to push even harder for general income redistribution during the period under study. They convinced the United Nations that an integrated program for commodities was still one of the principal means of restructuring the world economy. In May and December of 1974, the General Assembly adopted resolutions 3201(S-VI) and 3202(S-VI) which provided for the preparation of a global integrated program to ensure more reliable markets and more stable prices for a wide range of commodities whose exportation involves the interests of developing countries.

The General Assembly then entrusted the UNCTAD Secretariat with the task of defining the ICP's general objectives and techniques.

During its fourth session held in Nairobi in 1976, UNCTAD adopted resolution 93(IV) defining the objectives, means, procedures, and schedule for an integrated commodity program.

Objectives

Resolution 93(IV) stipulates that in order to improve the terms of trade of developing countries, counter the effects of inflation on their real incomes and thus eliminate North-South economic disparities, the international trade of developing countries must be diversified; their production capacity improved; their productivity and their export receipts increased. Consequently, the ICP set out seven objectives.

1. To achieve stable conditions in commodity trade, including avoidance of excessive price fluctuations, at levels which would: (a) be remunerative and just to producers and equitable to consumers; (b) take account of world inflation and changes in the world economic and monetary situations; (c) promote equilibrium between supply and demand within expanding world commodity trade.
2. To improve and sustain the real income of individual developing countries through increased export earnings and to protect them from fluctuations in export earnings, especially from commodities.
3. To seek to improve market access and reliability of supply for primary products and the processed products thereof, bearing in mind the needs and interests of developing countries.
4. To diversify production in developing countries, including food production, and to expand processing of primary products in developing countries with a view to promoting their industrialization and increasing their export earnings.
5. To improve the competitiveness of, and to encourage research and development on the problems of, natural products competing with synthetics and substitutes, and to consider the harmonization, where appropriate, of the production of synthetics and substitutes in developed countries with the supply of natural products produced in developing countries.
6. To improve market structures in the field of raw materials and commodities of export interest to developing countries.
7. To improve marketing, distribution and transport systems for commodity exports of developing countries, including an increase in their participation in these activities and their earnings from them.[1]

Products Covered by the ICP and Their
Importance in World Trade

These objectives—price stabilization, improved terms of trade and redistribution of world income—were retained for eighteen commodities, ten of which termed "core" commodities were well suited to constituting international stocks. These were coffee, tea, cocoa, sugar, rubber, jute (fibre and manufactures), hard fibres, cotton (fibre and yarn), copper, and tin. More appropriate measures such as multilateral contracts, a compensatory finance scheme, or international aid for diversifying exports would be applied for eight "other" commodities: manganese, phosphates, iron ore, bauxite, tropical timber, vegetable oils, meat, and bananas. The list of other commodities has been frequently revised. The most recent version included iron ore, bauxite, meat, bananas, wool, cereals, and rice; resolution 93(IV) foresees the addition of other products as negotiations progress.

Table 6-1 shows that the eighteen products included in the ICP represent a value of US $25 billion in exports for developing countries, their share in the international trade of these products amounting to 53.5%. Although metals comprise 25% of the exports covered by the integrated program, only copper and tin have been included among the products considered suitable for the constitution of international stocks to be eventually financed by the projected Common Fund. UNCTAD does not judge that this procedure is any real solution to the difficulties which the other metals face on the market. With the exception of cotton, copper, and sugar, the international exports of the seven other "core"

Table 6-1
Developing Countries' Exports of the Eighteen Nairobi Commodities, and
Their Share in the Total Exports of these Commodities: Average, 1970-75

Commodity	Exports (US$ million)	Percent of World Exports
Ten core commodities		
Coffee	3,052	84.6
Tea	626	78.8
Cocoa	1,247	84.7
Sugar	4,040	70.7
Rubber	1,428	97.5
Jute fibre	184	95.8
Jute manufactures	462	92.0
Hard fibres	160	100.0
Hard fibre manufactures	69	100.0
Cotton fibre	2,165	71.2
Cotton yarn	369	44.9
Copper	2,881	48.6
Tin	838	80.9
Total	17,521	69.9
Eight other commodities		
Manganese	184	69.2
Rock phosphates	558	51.3
Iron Ore	1,317	37.8
Bauxite	258	71.1
Non-coniferous timber	1,203	52.7
Vegetable oils	1,322	45.8
Vegetable oilseeds	959	24.7
Meat	1,095	16.2
Bananas	536	90.5
Total	7,432	34.4
Total of eighteen products	24,953	53.5

Source: Commonwealth Secretariat, *The Common Fund: Report of the Commonwealth Technical Group,* London, September 1977, p. 77. (Published by Commonwealth Secretariat, Marlborough House, London SW1). Reprinted with permission.

commodities come mainly (more than 80%) from developing countries. Among the "other" commodities, developing countries hold monopolistic power only for bananas (90.5%) and to a lesser degree for bauxite (71.1%) and manganese (69.2%).

Means for Attaining Objectives

In order to reach the seven objectives enumerated above, resolution 93(IV) provides for an international system of commodity stocks financed by a common fund. The resolution calls for the convocation of a negotiating conference in March 1977 by the UNCTAD Secretary-General. In the meantime, the Secretary-General is to prepare working papers defining the common fund's objectives and stipulating its financial needs, structure, sources of finance, operating conditions and administration. These elements, which are essential to the integrated program's proper operation, will be examined later.

Besides constituting international buffer stocks financed by a common fund, resolution 93(IV) enumerates a series of measures intended to back up, consolidate or second this first means of market intervention.

It is also agreed to take the following measures, to be applied singly or in combination, including action in the context of international commodity arrangements between producers and consumers, in the light of the characteristics and problems of each commodity and the special needs of developing countries:

a. Setting up of international commodity stocking arrangements;

b. Harmonization of stocking policies and setting up of co-ordinated national stocks;

c. Establishment of pricing arrangements, in particular negotiated price ranges, which would be periodically reviewed and appropriately revised, taking into account, inter alia, movements in prices of imported manufactured goods, exchange rates, production costs and world inflation, and levels of production and consumption;

d. Internationally agreed supply management measures, including export quotas and production policies and, where appropriate, multilateral long-term supply and purchase commitments;

e. Improvement of procedures for information and consultation on market conditions;

f. Improvement and enlargement of compensatory financing facilities for the stabilization, around a growing trend, of export earnings of developing countries;

g. Improvement of market access for the primary and processed products of developing countries through multilateral trade measures in the multilateral trade negotiations, improvement of schemes of generalized preferences and their extension beyond the period originally envisaged, and trade promotion measures;

h. International measures to improve the infrastructure and industrial capacity of developing countries, extending from the production of primary commodities to their processing, transport and marketing, as well as to the production of finished manufactured goods, their transport, distribution and exchange, including the establishment of financial, exchange and other institutions for the remunerative management of trade transactions;

i. Measures to encourage research and development on the problems of natural products competing with synthetics and consideration of the harmonization where appropriate, of the production of synthetics and substitutes in developed countries with the supply of natural products produced in developing countries;

j. Consideration of special measures for commodities whose problems cannot be adequately solved by stocking and which experience a persistent price decline.[2]

Although this arsenal of suggested measures is very complete (with its compensatory financing mechanism, multilateral contracts system, and recommended international aid to diversify exports by opening markets or financing research and development to stimulate both the supply and demand of commodities), the most important measure taken to attain the objectives set still remains the establishment of the buffer stock system financed by a common fund. In fact, the UNCTAD Secretariat seems to judge that failure of international agreements on individual products was mainly due to lack of adequate financing of stocks. It was then estimated that this problem could be solved by a common fund of about $6 billion. A fund of this size would have greater borrowing power and require less financing than several individual funds since the prices of the various products stocked would not be likely to move simultaneously in the same direction.

Resolution 93(IV) establishing the integrated program was quite different from resolution 30(IV) adopted on March 18, 1947 by the United Nations Economic and Social Council, which encouraged the signing of international agreements between commodity producing and consuming countries. In fact, instead of making each International Council responsible for defining market intervention objectives, techniques and financial needs for its own commodity, the ICP proposed a common set of principles and control methods, a common source of finance and a universal program based on a calendar established by a central organism responsible for supervising its application. Moreover, controls went beyond the establishment of quotas and buffer stocks to include recommendation of complementary measures concerning commercialization, promotion, treatment, diversification, and access to markets. But the most important

difference between the two resolutions is revealed by Jack P. Barnouin, Assistant
Director of the IMF's Geneva headquarters.

> In contrast to previous commodity programs, which were designed
> only to prevent excessive short-term price fluctuations, the new pro-
> gram would pursue four main objectives: (1) stabilizing commodity
> prices around targets which, taking inflation into account, would pro-
> vide incentives for the maintenance of adequate production and would
> be consistent with the development objectives of the developing coun-
> tries; (2) improving access to world markets for exporting countries
> and securing supplies for importing countries; (3) diversifying and ex-
> panding the processing of commodities in developing countries; and
> (4) modernizing marketing and distribution systems for commodities.[3]

Schedule and Chronology of Negotiations
on the Integrated Program

In May and December 1974 the UN General Assembly adopted resolutions
3201(S-VI) and 3202(S-VI) projecting a global integrated program for a wide
range of commodities; following this, negotiations to establish the program were
begun within the UNCTAD Commodities Commission. This commission was to
present clear proposals on the objectives and operational methods of an integrated commodities program to the 1976 Nairobi Conference. However, as it
turned out, all three regional groups composing this commission (the Group of
77 composed of developing countries; Group B composed of industrialized
countries with market economies and Group D composed of the Eastern
European socialists countries) presented minority reports at Nairobi, revealing
serious divergencies concerning both the ICP's objectives and the measures
required to attain them on the international level.

Therefore, resolution 93(IV) which was adopted at Nairobi represents a
compromise proposition. What is more, although it was accepted without
modification by the full assembly, the three groups interpret certain of its
clauses very differently. In fact, we previously noticed that the resolution
calls for separate but parallel discussions and negotiations concerning international agreements for specific products, on the one hand, and on the other, the
creation of a common fund to finance a network of buffer stocks. Consequently, while the Group of 77 takes this clause to be an official consecration
of the common fund as one of the program's central and integral elements,
Group B interprets it as a proposition which does not exclude international
agreements based on stabilization techniques other than buffer stocks or means
of finance other than the common fund.

Such diverging views will no doubt modify the Nairobi schedule for setting
up the integrated program, which foresaw that: 1. the UNCTAD Secretary-

General would immediately call preliminary meetings concerning ICP objectives and the Common Fund's financial needs, financial structure, sources of finance, operating conditions and administrative structure; the reports issued by these research groups would be used at the negotiating conference on the Common Fund to be called before March 1977 by the Secretary-General; 2. starting on September 1, 1976, preliminary assemblies would be held concerning international negotiations on specific commodities; the role of these assemblies would be to propose the appropriate means of carrying out the ICP's objectives, to determine the financial needs arising from the measures suggested and to prepare complete proposals on international agreements likely to be discussed during commodity negotiations; these preliminary assemblies must complete their work as soon as possible but no later than February 1978; and 3. the Secretary-General was responsible for calling negotiating conferences on specific international commodity agreements as soon as the preliminary assemblies turned in their proposals; all these negotiations were to be finished by the end of 1978.

According to this schedule, two series of parallel talks—one on the Common Fund, the other on agreements by product—were begun within UNCTAD after the Nairobi Conference.

As scheduled, a conference was called in March-April 1977 to negotiate on the Common Fund. The conference was unable to reach a compromise agreement acceptable to all participants. In addition to their differing interpretation of resolution 93(IV), the Group of 77 and Group B also held diverging views on the type of common fund to be set up for financing buffer stocks. The UNCTAD Secretariat and the Group of 77 took position that two distinct accounts must be created within the Common Fund. (Both were to apply to the ten core commodities listed in table 6-1 plus iron ore, bauxite, meat, bananas, wool, cereal, and rice.) A general account would finance short-term operations of buffer stocks ($4.5-$5 billion, based on certain hypotheses about support price levels for the ten core commodities) and a special account to finance long-term projects for improving productivity and diversifying exports (temporarily evaluated at $1-$1.5 billion). Group B countries contended rather that the Common Fund must be used only to finance the constitution of stocks and that using its resources for other activities would be incompatible with the principle according to which the fund was not to become an aid organism. Furthermore, they emphasized having made no agreement concerning the kind of fund to be set up. For them, the Common Fund might take any of the following five forms.

The *principal source of funds* structure of a Common Fund envisages that all funding will be arranged by one centralized fund, which will lend funds to the Individual Commodity Organizations (ICOs) associated with it. It seems to be universally accepted that this form of Common Fund would lend funds to ICOs for buffer stock activities at a uniform rate of interest, but that the Common Fund would have some discretion over the interest rate that it charged on lending for non-buffer stock activities. . .

The *pool of finance* approach proposes that the individual commodity organizations, bound together by agreements between producers and consumers, will raise their own funds. The liquid element of these will then be pooled in a Common Fund, which will supervise and control subsequent lending to the ICOs linked to the Common Fund. . .

The *clearing house* version of a Common Fund, relegates the role of the Fund to that of assisting in bilateral loan negotiations between ICOs. The Common Fund would aim to marry the financial requirements of one ICO to the excess liquidity of another, and would not possess any funds entirely under its own control.

As *guarantor of loans* a Common Fund would collect together a range of governmental guarantees, including possibly guarantees from intergovernmental organizations such as the IMF. These could be then used as security by ICOs when they raise loans. A possible precedent for this particular structure would be the various export credit guarantee schemes that governments operate, providing security against which exporters can arrange commercial borrowing.

In addition, there is the *pooling plus source* version. . . , although there is little agreement about the relative importance to be attached to the two functions.[4]

For the Group of 77, the Common Fund was meant only as a source of finance. Moreover, the fund must also finance measures other than the buffer stocks, especially those concerning perishable produce or storable commodities threatened by synthetic replacements or chronic overproduction.

The gap between the positions of developing and industrialized countries was somewhat narrowed on May 7 and 8, 1977, when the United States formally accepted the principle of having *a* Common Fund at the London summit on international cooperation. But although its move was followed by the industrial countries participating in the July 1977 Paris Conference on International Economic Cooperation (referred to usually as the "North-South Dialogue"), the problems concerning the choice of a type of common fund, the financing of activities other than buffer stocks and the importance to be accorded to Individual Commodity Organizations within the integrated program, remained intact. There was agreement on the necessity of a common fund but none on the form it should take. These differences of opinion were not smoothed out at the second round of negotiations held in Geneva in November 1977. The deadline for the creation of a common fund previously set for February 1978 was thus postponed.

Parallel to the Common Fund debate, talks took place within UNCTAD on stabilization programs for five commodities among the eighteen enumerated in Resolution 93(IV): copper, jute and jute manufactures, hard fibres, rubber, and tropical timber. Although these negotiations have so far led to no concrete results, some progress seems to be noticeable for rubber.

> Of all the preparatory meetings held, the most fruitful was that on rubber, where consumer countries expressed interest in the buffer stock scheme suggested by producer countries. The participants agreed to decide on the convening of a negotiating conference on rubber later in the year.

> In the preparatory meetings on jute and hard fibers, the producer countries presented action programs designed to stabilize prices at levels remunerative to producers and equitable to consumers and to improve the export earnings of producer countries in real terms. These programs called for, inter alia, the establishment of buffer stocks; multilateral supply and purchase commitments; comprehensive programs of research and development; and harmonization of the production of synthetic substitutes in developed countries with the supply of hard fibers by developing countries.[5]

Participants in the talks on copper and tropical timber came up against very complex political, statistical, or economic problems and thus recommended that the means for reaching an international agreement on these two commodities be studied by experts. The deadline set for the end of negotiations (fourth quarter of 1978) was here again postponed.

Evaluation of Some Points in the Integrated Program

The integrated program has already undergone a number of evaluations concerning its cost, capital structure, organization and institutional operation.[6] In the following section the essential elements for the program's successful operation will be presented and evaluated.

Cost of the Integrated Commodity Program

The cost of the ICP has been estimated at about US $7 billion. US $5.5 billion of this would go for the short-term financing of some ten buffer stocks and US $1.5 billion for financing long-term projects involving the improvement of productivity and the diversification of exports (through measures such as research and development, improvement of the economic infrastructure, and of industrial capacity of less developed countries). These are clearly approximate figures since the exact level will depend on the following hypotheses.

1. the exact number and size of "other measures" to be financed by the Common Fund. (This part of the ICP is of chief concern to industrial countries. To the extent   these projects are at present rather vague, industrial

countries fear they will occasion a waste of resources, and suggest that the World Bank continue to finance these long-term programs.)

2. general price evolution (It has proven easier for a buffer stock to make a profit when prices are rising since sales are then made at increasingly higher prices while it takes the purchase price some time to catch up with the trend. The UNCTAD Secretariat therefore hypothesizes that the inflationary pressures experienced during recent years will continue to exist in the near future.)

3. length of price cycle (Since the constitution of stocks involves storage costs and interest payments, the longer the storage period, the higher the costs accumulated by the buffer stock. Now, the chances of having to hold large stocks for long periods of time are proportionate to the length of the price cycle—the shorter the cycle, the greater the possibilities of selling at a profit. The US $5.5 billion estimate is based on the hypothesis that three years would be the maximum length of storage for any of the ten selected products. However, the history of the international coffee, cotton, and tin markets shows that storage will be much longer unless production and export quotas are established, along with buffer stocks, to prevent the accumulation of surpluses over extended periods of time.)

4. price covariance of the ten selected products (The UNCTAD Secretariat estimates the cost of constituting the stocks could reach a maximum level of US $6 billion if the Common Fund was obliged to stock simultaneously the proposed maximum quantity of all commodities covered by the program. They hasten to add that this situation is unlikely to occur since commodity prices have a negative covariance, implying that the cost of buying a low-priced commodity will be counterbalanced by profits from selling a high-priced commodity. The secretariat thus estimates that the financial resources actually required by the fund should not exceed US $3 billion; the other US $3 billion would only be used as a contingency fund. We do not share such optimism since a recent economic study shows the possibility of finding commodities with prices having negative covariance to be relatively slim.[7]

5. storage expenses, cost of financing and purchase/sales price margins (Storage expenses cover the renting of warehouses, insurances, stock renewal costs and various other expenses; according to provisional estimates, they amount to an annual average of 3.2% of value for the core commodities.[8] These expenses are added to the fixed interest payments which constitute the main element of operating expenditures. These two costs determine what the margin between the purchase and sales price of stocked commodities must be in order to prevent losses. If the margin is lower than the normal recorded fluctuation of a nonregulated commodity market, then the market is being stabilized by the buffer stock. If the reverse were true, it would be better not to have any buffer stock at all.[9] Moreover, the wider the gap between required prices, the greater the risk of not being able to sell and of having to accumulate supplementary storage and financing expenses. The secretariat is acutely aware of this risk and

has suggested a set of means to reduce fixed interest payments to 3.6% a year.[10] If this were the case, interest payments (3.6% a year) and storage expenses (3.2% a year) would amount to slightly more than 20% for a three-year period. There is no lack of imagination and ingenuity in the conditions and sources of financing enumerated by the secretariat. We simply hope its expectations are not contradicted by reality and the Common Fund forced to borrow on Euro-currency markets on conditions and at rates less generous than foreseen.)

6. the existence and effectiveness of a mechanism aimed at limiting supply in case of acute overproduction (Adequate operation of a buffer stock requires that commodity quantities produced and demanded be sensitive to price variations; this means that consumers will increase their demand as prices approach the floor, with purchases of buffer stocks then intervening to accelerate this adjustment mechanism. The reverse must also be true when prices approach the ceiling. But there are some commodities which—because of a long production cycle, because of a lag between investments and production or a sluggish demand slow to react to price evolution—require massive purchases by the buffer stock to prevent a below-floor price. These interventions are necessary since in these cases the decline of prices is not sufficient to eliminate excess supply. The whole stabilization effort then depends on the support of the buffer stock whose funds often prove insufficient. Moreover, the storage expenses and interest rates generated in such circumstances seriously interfere with the stock's profitability. To prevent these circumstances it is imperative that the buffer stock be seconded by export quotas; that provisions be made within the stabilization program for an annual reexamination of the price bracket; and that financial resources be set aside for the diversification of exports. Such measures are foreseen for the ICP proposed by the UNCTAD secretariat and have even been made requisite conditions to obtain financing for a commodity stock. In another respect, we reproach the secretariat for neglecting to consider the effects of international price stabilization on welfare and income distribution when selecting the commodities for its program. It has in fact been demonstrated that under certain conditions, if variations in demand are at the root of price instability, stabilizing prices will actually reduce the total receipts of commodity-exporting countries and also their welfare.[11] The reverse effects are obtained if price instability is caused by variations in supply.)

As we have seen, the ICP's exact cost depends on the hypotheses proposed concerning the number and scope of the "other measures" to be financed by the Common Fund; the general evolution of prices; the length of the price cycle; the price covariance sign; the level of expenses for storage and loan financing; the gap between the floor and ceiling price; as well as the existence and effectiveness of a mechanism purporting to limit supply in case of acute overproduction. The number of commodities selected, the volume of stocks, and the degree of substitution among the commodities chosen will also influence the ICP's final cost. Considering the number of hypotheses to be worked out with regard to the buffer stock's operation and considering that financing the "other measures" may easily cost more than foreseen, we find the US $6-7 billion requested to be a very rough estimate. The exact level probably hovers around the upper portion of the bracket mentioned.

When we consider the size of the sums involved, it seems imperative to compare the cost of the ICP with that of other measures capable of stabilizing the export receipts of developing countries. This objective, which was accepted by the international community at the London summit and during the North-South Dialogue, can be attained by other means: a program of compensatory finance generally comparable to the IMF's; a greater trade liberalization in favor of developing countries; or a system of direct support to countries suffering from a drop in commercial receipts. The cost and profits of these other measures must also be known if one desires to choose rationally a stabilization policy. We feel that the refusal to consider the whole set of possible solutions has been the principal cause of failure of the second conference for negotiations on the Common Fund held at Geneva, November 7-December 2, 1977.

Capital Structure

The UNCTAD Secretariat's working papers suggest that two or three groups of countries could subscribe to the Common Fund's capital: commodity exporting countries enjoying the fund's support; importing countries and eventually third-party countries (mainly the petroleum-exporting countries). This general principle accepted, a capital structure acceptable to all parties concerned must be chosen. The possible structures which come to mind are a triparite structure; a structure where the exporting and importing groups hold equal shares; or a structure where exporting countries could have the majority, a proposal they have already made, at the Dakar Conference early in 1975. In each case, the Common Fund would be supplemented by capital loans from official sources in importing countries and petroleum-producing countries or from official international and regional organizations. Subsequently, the Common Fund could rely more on market resources.

Table 6-2 presents three capital structures from among the different combinations possible. First, we notice that in all three cases there is a 2:1 debt-equity ratio. This is similar to the ratio characterizing the capital structure of the International Bank for Reconstruction and Development, and other international institutions. However, we must not forget that—although this ratio follows the current practices of international institutions making medium- or long-term loans—here, we are concerned with financing short-term buffer stocks. Consequently, lenders will only tolerate such a ratio if the US $1 billion of capital available for contingencies is a hard fact and not just an agreement in principle.

Table 6-2
Common Fund: Examples of Capital Structure
(*US millions of $*)

System	Sum Paid in	Sum Available in Case of Need	Total
A: Tripartite structure			
Capital	1000	1000	2000
Exporting countries Importing countries } Petroleum exporting countries	1000	1000	2000
Loans from	2000	2000	4000
Importing countries } Petroleum exporting countries	1755	1755	3510
International and regional institutions and exporting countries	245	245	490
Total resources	3000	3000	6000
B: Exporting and importing countries— equal capital shares for each group			
Capital	1000	1000	2000
Exporting countries	500	500	1000
Importing countries	500	500	1000
Loans from	2000	2000	4000
Importing countries	938	938	1875
Petroleum exporting countries	817	817	1635
International and regional institutions and exporting countries	245	245	490
Total resources	3000	3000	6000
C: Exporting and importing countries— exporting countries hold majority share of capital			
Capital	1000	1000	2000
Exporting countries	527	527	1055
Importing countries	473	473	945
Loans from	2000	2000	4000
Importing countries	695	695	1390
Petroleum exporting countries	1005	1005	2010
International and regional institutions and exporting countries	300	300	600
Total Resources	3000	3000	6000

Source: UNCTAD, *A Common Fund for the Financing of Commodity Stocks: Amounts, Terms and Prospective Sources of Finances,* Geneva, 1975, TD/B/C.1/184, pp. 17-18. Reprinted with permission.

Second, it is important to notice that whatever debt-equity ratio is chosen, negotiations on capital structure are likely to be long. In fact, if importing countries are called upon to subscribe heavily to the fund's capital, they will prefer a debt-equity ratio higher than that favored by commodity exporting countries. There are also differences of views between the two groups as concerns the uses of the fund. Developing countries want sums paid in to be loaned to the buffer stocks, while industrial countries suggest they be used as guarantees for Common Fund loans. Negotiations will become very tough when the time comes to determine each country's subscription to the Common Fund capital. What criterion should be used in carrying out this distribution? Should it be a country's share in the trade of all ten core commodities? The share of selected groups in the trade for each product? The criterion of equality by which all countries would contribute the same amount regardless of economic strength? The capacity to pay estimated according to the gross national product, per capita GNP, level of international reserves, share in world trade? Even if negotiations finally end in a compromise formula (which will surely be strongly influenced by the IMF's method of calculating subscriptions), we fear the compromise sought will accord more importance to political considerations than to economic efficiency criteria.

Some other difficulties must be smoothed out to make way for the establishment of a common fund: choice of the terms and conditions according to which Common Fund loans are to be made to the various international commodity agreements; position of developed countries concerning their aid policies (whether or not their subscription to a Common Fund will be to the detriment of other forms of aid); and the form of guarantees to be given to potential lenders.[12]

The Common Fund's Organization and Operation

The UNCTAD Secretariat envisages the Common Fund as a new entity within the UN. On this ground, its organization will resemble that of other international financial institutions generally having three main agencies: a Board of Governors or a General Assembly, a Board of Directors and an executive director. The General Assembly meets once a year to examine general policy and set the organization's future orientation; all members, regardless of economic standing, participate. The Board of Directors is elected by the Board of Governors or by the General Assembly. In addition to approving each financial transaction, its main task is the supervision of operations. The executive director is elected by the Board of Directors for a certain length of time. His or her principal role is to preside over the board (but without voting power) and to take responsibility for administrative personnel.

The only difficulty likely to slow down negotiations at this point concerns the system to be established for the allotment of votes on the board of directors. There are three possibilities open to consideration: an equal allotment of votes between the importing and exporting groups (method adopted by those agreements based on chapter 6 of the Havana Charter); a weighted system of vote allotment where the larger countries have the right to name their directors and the smaller form coalitions to elect theirs (method used by the IMF); or an allotment system based on capital subscriptions.

The formula for equal vote allotment, as it has been applied in the past by International Commodity Agreements, hardly seems acceptable because of the large number of commodities the Common Fund will have to manage. Since one country may be both an exporter of some of the core commodities on the Nairobi list and an importer of others, the defining of groups becomes difficult. Moreover, it is hard to see how a country's relative trading strength (and thus its vote percentage) is to be determined on a ten-product basis. The difficulties encountered in setting such percentages for sugar, coffee, and tin would be increased tenfold.

The weighted system of vote allotment which the UNCTAD Secretariat seems to prefer implies an apportioning of votes among those groups having participated in negotiations for the ICP—the Group of 77, industrial countries with market economies, Eastern European countries and petroleum-exporting countries. This formula would also prove difficult to negotiate, not only for lack of any direct connection between the way the groups break down and their respective interests in the commodity debate but also because of wide variations in the number and relative international importance of the countries composing each group.

The system of alloting votes according to each group's capital subscription to the Common Fund poses other kinds of problems. The countries exporting the ten core commodities will find, to the extent that industrial countries subscribe the largest share of capital, that this proposition does not adequately reflect their interests. In order to assemble the elements of the three proposed systems, a compromise formula will once again have to be invented, at the risk of putting political persuasion over economic realities.

We close this section with a presentation of how the UNCTAD Secretariat views the Common Fund's relations to other organizations concerned with commodities. The secretariat proposes that these relations may be envisaged according to one of two rules: a regime based on separation (where the fund would be administered separately, intervening only at the request of organizations and lending only at fixed rates) or, an integrated regime (where each organization, as a member of the board of directors, would actively participate in administering the fund; not only would the fund lend at fixed interest but would also hold shares in each stock). Although the regimes are proposed as alternatives, the secretariat seems clearly to prefer the second since an integrated regime would allow the needs and experience of each commodity market to reverberate on the fund's operations. The board of directors being composed of representatives from both countries and organizations concerned with commodity products, the preoccupations of national politics and commercial considerations could have a fruitful association. Having this form, the board, in applying its policy, could give proper consideration to the interests of countries concerning each commodity. (It would still have to be decided how many votes should be granted to directors representing "commodities" as opposed to those representing "countries.") In fact, the UNCTAD proposal goes even further, suggesting that the Common Fund not only grant loans at fixed rates to other commodity organizations but that it also be entitled to hold shares in the commodity stocks controlled by these organizations.[13] According to the secretariat, the fund could thus, directly and automatically, share the risks of commercial transactions: it would receive profits in proportion to its share holdings and be equally responsible for losses.

The advantages of an integrated regime are twofold: the use of existing expertise, and reduction of this new bureaucratic structure's operating costs. Although there are these two advantages in having the participation of commodity representatives on the Board of Directors, we do not believe it essential they be accorded voting rights beyond those already ascribed to the member countries of these organizations. This would be a useless complication of the decision-making process and would slow down the intervention necessary for stabilizing prices.

Notes

1. United Nations Conference on Trade and Development, *Resolution Adopted by the Conference: Integrated Programme for Commodities.* (Adopted without dissent, May 30, 1976).

2. Ibid.

3. Barnouin, J.P., *IMF Survey*, International Monetary Fund, vol. 6, no. 13, July 4, 1977, p. 220. Reprinted with permission.

4. Commodities Research Unit Ltd., "A Common Fund—Financial Organisation, Operations and Management," p. 12. Reprinted with permission.

5. Barnouin, *IMF Survey*, pp. 222-223. Reprinted with permission.

6. The most important are: J.R. Behrman, *Intenational Commodity Agreements: An Evaluation of the UNCTAD Integrated Commodity Programme*; Commonwealth Secretariat, *Some of the Principal Issues in the Negotiation for a Common Fund*; Commonwealth Secretariat, *The Evolution of Proposals on the Constituent Elements of the Common Fund*; Commonwealth Secretariat, *The Progress of Negotiations on the Common Fund*; Commonwealth Secretariat, *The Common Fund: Report of the Commonwealth Technical Group*; Commodities Research Unit Ltd., "A Common Fund: Financial Organization, Opera-

tions and Management"; Congress of the United States, *Commodity Initiatives of Less Developed Countries: U.S. Responses and Costs*; Carlos F. Diaz-Alejandro, *North-South Relations: The Economic Component*; R.H. Green, *The Common Fund: Prolegomena to Cost/Benefit Estimation*; N. Kaldor, "Inflation and Recession in the World Economy," *Economic Journal*, vol. 86, 1976; G.K. Sarkar, "The UNCTAD Integrated Programme and Macro-Economic Considerations."

7. Walter C. Labys, and Yves Perrin, "Multivariate Analysis of Price Aspects of Commodity Stabilization," pp. 556–564.

8. United Nations Conference on Trade and Development, *A Common Fund for the Financing of Commodity Stocks: Amounts, Terms and Prospective Sources of Finances*, p. 13.

9. The UNCTAD Secretariat gives an example in indicating that if the commodity is stocked for eighteen months, if storage expenses are at 1% a year and the funds required to buy this commodity are borrowed at an annual 10% rate, total expenses will be at 17% when the product is sold. Such is the required margin (gap) between purchase and sales price if losses are to be avoided. According to the secretariat, this margin is in no way excessive and falls far below the normal recorded fluctuations on nonregulated commodity markets. But if the product must be stocked for three years, if storage expenses reach 4% a year and if interest rates stay at 10% a year, accumulated expenses will amount to 48%, a figure incompatible with stabilization. The interested reader is referred to United Nations Conference on Trade and Development, *A Common Fund for the Financing of Commodity Stocks: Amounts, Terms and Prospective Sources of Finances*, p. 11.

10. According to UNCTAD Secretariat, these payments could be reduced in the following ways: (1) A portion of the funds could be provided by participating governments through nonfixed remuneration in the form of subscribed social capital. Existing regional and international organisms of finance, recognized as serving the public interest, are based on this principle. Usually, the governments do not require distribution of dividends on capital paid up, allowing the organisms to enlarge their base and build up reserves. (2) The Common Fund could have the right to borrow, at favorable rates, another portion of funds from aid organizations in participant importing countries. In 1972-73, the average interest rate on Public Aid to Development (PAD) loan pledges applied for by member countries of the Committee on Aid to Development (CAD) was 2.7%. Loan conditions offered by the petroleum exporting countries are not known, except that they are on the average the same as PADs. (3) The Common Fund could have the right to borrow from governments and other regional and international organisms of finance at rates comparable to those for other loans granted, that is between 7 and 8% interest. (4) By carefully choosing the moment for floating a loan, the average cost of real interest could be reduced. Short-term interest rates tend to decrease sharply in periods of industrial recession; this is exactly when funds are needed to support

commodity prices. (5) The Common Fund could be authorized to sell its commodity stock holdings, which would give buyers the right to receive a share of profits rather than a fixed interest rate. (6) The IMF mechanism for financing buffer stocks would offer a relatively cheap source of funds. Its interest rates hover around 5 percent.

Thus, if a third of funds are secured by capital subscription (that is, by using a fixed interest rate equal to zero); the second third on conditions like those offered by PAD (for example, a rate falling between 3 and 4%) and the remaining third at 7-8%, the average real expenses on fixed interest payments will be 3.6% a year. The interested reader is referred to United Nations Conference on Trade and Development, *A Common Fund for the Financing of Commodity Stocks: Amounts, Terms and Prospective Sources of Finance*, pp. 11-14.

11. As explained by E.M. Brook, and E.R. Grilli, "Commodity Price Stabilization and the Developing World."

12. This gives rise to some interesting practical problems.

Stock warrants represent well tried and widely acceptable collateral for buffer stock stabilization but excessive borrowing against such warrants would make buffers vulnerable to bear speculation. Moderation in warrants-backed borrowing and in the ratio of total debt to equity should meet this difficulty. However, an important practical difficulty about the use of warrants needs to be faced. Unless buffer stocks are owned by a Common Fund, banks and other *lenders might prove reluctant* to lend to a Common Fund against warrants for stock owned by another party, that is, an individual buffer. The other side of this practical problem is that if a way is found by which banks and other lenders are willing to advance funds directly to a Common Fund, mechanisms would need to be designed to give buffer managers rapid and uncomplicated access to their financial entitlements from a Common Fund at times of heavy market intervention. Another question to be faced is that where ICOs draw on a Common Fund against the security of the stock warrants, *the Common Fund may not be able to use such warrants as collateral* for market borrowing of its own, since such warrants would not be considered as the Common Fund's property to be pledged.

Commodities Research Unit Ltd., "A Common Fund—Financial Organisation, Operations and Management," p. 10. Reprinted with permission.

13. United Nations Conference on Trade and Development, *A Common Fund for the Financing of Commodity Stocks: Amounts, Terms and Prospective Sources of Finances*, p. 23.

7

CIPEC and the International Copper Market

During the years from 1964 to 1978, the world not only witnessed the pursuit of international agreements (for tin, wheat, coffee, sugar, cocoa and other important commodities) and negotiations to set up an ambitious integrated program (financed by a Common Fund and covering several commodities), but also saw the establishment of formal cartels for copper, petroleum, bauxite, iron ore and mercury. In the next four chapters, we will attempt to analyze the structure of those markets which have been the object of various controls instituted by governments of producing countries since the mid-sixties.

The international copper market represents one of these markets with a rather long history of controls. Both private producers and speculators have tried to restrict the supply of this metal and so influence its international market price. The interventions of the French financier, Pierre Secretan (1886-1889), the Amalgamated Copper Company (1890-1901), the Association of Copper Exporters (1918-1923), Copper Exporters Inc. (1926-1932) and the International Copper Cartel (1935-1939) are all examples of such attempts.[1]

The role of governments in this market became particularly noticeable after June 8, 1967. It was on this date that the political authorities of Chile, Zaire, Peru, and Zambia established an advisory body, Conseil Intergouvernemental des Pays Exportateurs de Cuivre (CIPEC). Known in English as the Intergovernmental Council of Copper Exporting Countries, it was founded in recognition of the importance of copper in each country's economy; in consideration of the need to prevent excessive price fluctuations; and in the belief that their situation could be improved through increased cooperation and concerted action.

The member countries of CIPEC—a body composed of a Conference of Ministers, a Governing Board, a Copper Information Bureau and an Executive Committee—quickly realized that they could not influence the market through export quotas unless this common action were prefaced by increased control of the local mining industry.[2] They therefore decided to follow Zaire's example and nationalize the subsidiaries of multinational firms operating within their boundaries. Imitating Zaire's 1966 nationalization of the Société Générale des Minerais (subsidiary of Belgium's Union Minière du Haut Katanga), in 1970 Zambia raised to 51% its share of capital stock in the subsidiary of American Metal Climax (Roan Selection Trust) and of the Anglo-American Corporation of South Africa (Zambian Anglo-American). Between 1967 and 1972, the Government of Chile took over the subsidiaries of the American companies

Kennecott, Anaconda and Cerro, while increasing its control of the subsidiary of the French company, Le Nickel. Also, in 1974, Peru nationalized Cerro de Pasco.[3]

Eight years after the creation of CIPEC, its member countries, holding the majority control of their mining and refining industries, decided to intervene on the international copper market. On November 19, 1974, CIPEC announced that, for the six months following December 1, 1974, its member countries would reduce monthly exports by 10% from earlier 1974 levels. The effects of this first intervention by CIPEC on the international scene were very modest. We notice from table 7-1 that the average price of copper, which stood at US 78.8¢/lb. in 1973 on the London market, climbed to US 90.4¢/lb. in 1974 before falling back to US 53.2¢/lb. in 1975. This 70% drop occurred despite the fact that in April 1975 CIPEC raised the quota applied by member countries to 15%.

Although Indonesia has joined the ranks of regular CIPEC members and Australia, Mauritania, and Papua New Guinea have become associate members, available statistical data seem to indicate that this body's interventions have little influence on the international copper market. What are the main reasons for this? What are the traits of the international copper market limiting CIPEC's influence on price, production, and the inflow of foreign exchange? What are the future prospects of such a cartel? In order to answer such questions, some knowledge (even elementary) of the international copper market's basic characteristics seems essential.[4]

Since the beginning of the 1930s, the international copper market has been divided in two parts: the American market where transactions are made at "U.S. producer prices", and the rest of the world market where transactions are mainly influenced by London Metal Exchange prices (LME). The general operation of the American market is characterized by the following traits. Copper production is highly concentrated. It is in fact estimated that in 1969 Anaconda, Phelps Dodge, Kennecott and American Smelting and Mining held clsoe to 65% of American production capacity.[5] Given this small number of big producers and the discipline they show, price-fixing by one or more of these leaders seems to be the current practice.

How does one go about setting price levels in such a situation? According to the Fisher-Cootner-Baily model, a reasonable price is set taking into account recent stock variations, negotiations with specific consumers and economic forecasts.[6] Based on this price, considered as stable in the medium term, American producers decide how much copper to produce, thus determining the market's supply of primary copper. Copper consumers consider this price an economic fact because they, being so numerous and individually of so little weight in total consumption, cannot change it. Those consumers who find the price acceptable will buy the quantities desired. The others can import from the other market at LME prices (which seldom happens, since the LME price is

Table 7-1
Average Annual Price of Copper and Aluminum on the American Market (EMJ price), and Price of Copper on the Rest of the World Market (LME price): 1951-1977.
(US ¢/lb.)

Year	Copper EMJ[a]	Copper LME	Aluminum EMJ
1951	24.2	26.3	19.0
1952	24.2	31.7	19.4
1953	28.8	30.8	20.9
1954	29.7	29.9	21.8
1955	37.5	39.1	23.7
1956	41.8	40.4	24.0
1957	29.6	27.2	25.4
1958	25.7	24.1	24.8
1959	31.2	28.9	24.7
1960	32.0	29.9	26.0
1961	29.9	27.9	25.5
1962	30.6	28.5	23.9
1963	30.6	28.4	22.6
1964	31.9	30.9	23.7
1965	35.0	35.6	24.5
1966	36.2	49.5	24.5
1967	38.2	47.2	24.9
1968	41.8	50.3	25.6
1969	47.5	61.9	27.2
1970	57.7	62.7	28.7
1971	51.4	47.8	29.0
1972	50.6	46.5	26.4
1973	58.8	78.8	25.0
1974	76.6	90.4	34.1
1975	63.5	53.2	39.8
1976	68.8	62.6	44.3
1977	66.2	58.6	51.3
1978	63.6[b]		53.0[b]

Sources: Derived from *Engineering and Mining Journal,* McGraw-Hill Publications, New York, March 1976 and March 1977; *Metal Statistics,* American Metal Market Publications, New York, 1976; *Metals Week,* McGraw-Hill Publications, New York, various issues.

[a]The Engineering and Mining Journal price approximates the U.S. producer price. It is a weighted average of the U.S. producer price (95%) and the LME price.

[b]Average of daily prices from January 1 to February 28, 1978.

usually higher than the American, and long-term contracts are common) or buy on the secondary (scrap) copper market. The decisions of these two consumer groups determine total aggregate demand, which depends on variables such as

Table 7-2
World Production of Copper Ore (0) and Refined Copper (R): Selected Years

Country	1960 O	1960 R	1972 O	1972 R	1975 O	1975 R	1976 O	1976 R	1977[a] O	1977[a] R
Africa	23.3	12.4	20.0	11.7	19.5	11.6	18.7	10.0	18.8	10.2
Zaire	7.1	2.9	6.2	2.7	6.7	2.7	5.6	0.7	6.2	1.1
Zambia	13.6	8.0	10.2	7.6	9.2	7.5	9.0	7.9	8.2	7.3
Others	2.6	1.5	3.6	1.4	3.6	1.4	4.1	1.4	4.4	1.8
America	50.4	46.5	46.4	38.8	42.8	33.8	44.6	35.2	45.5	34.5
Canada	9.4	7.6	10.2	6.1	10.5	6.3	9.4	5.8	9.8	5.5
Chile	12.6	4.5	10.2	5.7	11.3	6.4	12.7	7.1	12.9	7.3
United States	23.1	32.9	21.5	25.4	17.4	19.2	18.4	19.4	17.5	18.7
Peru	4.3	–	3.2	–	2.4	–	2.8	–	4.1	–
Others	1.0	1.5	1.3	1.6	1.2	1.9	1.3	2.9	1.2	2.9
Asia	5.0	5.3	5.7	10.6	6.4	10.8	6.2	11.0	6.2	11.5
Japan	2.1	5.0	1.6	10.0	1.2	9.8	1.0	9.8	1.0	10.1
Philippines	–	–	3.0	–	3.0	–	3.0	–	3.1	–
Others	–	0.3	1.1	0.6	2.3	1.0	2.2	1.2	2.1	1.4
Europe	3.0	19.4	3.6	15.8	3.9	16.3	4.0	16.9	3.9	17.5
England	–	–	–	2.0	–	1.8	–	1.6	–	1.3
Belgium	–	–	–	3.9	–	4.0	–	4.8	–	5.7
Spain	–	–	0.6	–	0.7	–	0.6	–	0.5	–
West Germany	–	–	–	4.9	–	5.0	–	5.0	–	4.8
Sweden	–	–	0.4	–	0.6	–	0.6	–	0.5	–
Yugoslavia	–	–	1.5	1.6	1.5	1.6	1.7	1.5	1.7	1.3
Oceania	2.6	1.7	4.4	1.9	5.3	2.3	4.9	2.1	4.8	2.0
Australia	2.6	1.7	2.6	1.9	3.0	2.3	2.7	2.1	2.6	2.0
P.N.G.	–	–	1.8	–	2.3	–	2.2	–	2.2	–

Table 7-2 – *Continued.*

Country	1960 O	1960 R	1972 O	1972 R	1975 O	1975 R	1976 O	1976 R	1977[a] O	1977[a] R
Socialist Countries	14.7	16.0	19.9	21.2	22.0	25.1	21.6	24.8	20.8	24.3
Poland	—	—	1.9	1.5	3.1	3.0	3.4	3.1	3.3	3.0
USSR	—	—	14.6	15.2	15.0	17.0	14.3	16.5	13.6	16.2
Others	—	—	3.4	4.5	3.9	5.1	4.0	5.2	3.9	5.1
World[b,c]	100.0	100.0	100.0	100.0	100.0	100.0	100.0	100.0	100.0	100.0
CIPEC[d]	37.6	15.5	29.8	16.3	29.6	16.9	30.1	15.7	31.4	15.7

Source: Derived from World Bureau of Metal Statistics, *World Metal Statistics*, London, December 1976 and January 1978.

[a]January to September only.

[b]The totals do not actually add up to 100, because of rounding error.

[c]In 1972, 1975 and 1976 world copper ore production stood at 7.04, 7.36 and 7.92 million MT, respectively, while similar levels for refined copper stood at 8.09, 8.40 and 8.85 million MT.

[d]Percentages apply to the Intergovernmental Council of Copper Exporting Countries' founders: Zaire, Zambia, Peru, and Chile.

level of industrial activity, prices of primary and secondary copper, and prices of substitutes.

The supply of secondary copper depends on the quantity of primary copper produced in the past, the ease with which this past production can be gathered and sold as secondary copper, and the price of secondary copper. So, the American market's total copper supply is composed of primary and secondary supply and imports. The percentage of total supply for each stands respectively at 63, 32 and 5; these percentages have remained relatively stable since the beginning of the seventies.

The difference between aggregate American demand and the total market supply determines the periodic variations observed in American stocks. If this variation proves positive and if the average price of supply on the American market is higher than the LME price, producers, judging that the appropriate long-term price must fall below the current level, will revise their prices downward. If the reverse is the case, prices will be raised. In both cases, prices are adjusted and the process continues.

The other market responds to just about the same variables except that its producers and consumers are chiefly influenced by the London market price (LME). This latter, unlike the "administered price" of American producers, is more responsive to the play of competition and to stock variation.[7,8]

With this very general presentation of the way in which the international copper market operates, we can now ask how copper prices behave on the two markets. Do these prices evolve differently from those of aluminum, copper's main substitute? Who are the major producers of copper ore and refined copper? How important are CIPEC member countries in world production? In what regions of the world is the consumption of refined copper concentrated and how does this shape trade movements? What are the world stock levels of refined copper?

The statistical data in tables 7-1 through 7-5 go a long way toward answering these questions.

Except for the years 1955-56 when the American government started to build a million-ton strategic stock (thus raising prices), the American market proved especially stable during the 1951-64 period. Copper prices stood between 24.2 and 31.9¢/lb., a 7.7¢/lb. gap. From 1964 to 1977, the American copper market showed greater instability: prices doubled between 1964 and 1974 when they reached the record level of 76.6¢/lb. falling back by 13.6¢/lb. until the beginning of 1978.

Except for the 1955-56 period, LME prices also showed an approximate 8.0¢/lb. gap between 1951 and 1964, but after that, fluctuations in copper prices were much more marked. In fact, the LME price tripled between 1964 and 1974, reaching the unequaled level of 90.4¢/lb. It afterwards fell 70% to 53.2¢/lb. in 1975, climbed back to 62.6¢/lb. in 1976 before falling to 58.6¢/lb. in 1977. It stood at 56.2¢/lb. during the opening days of January 1978.

Table 7-3
World Consumption of Refined Copper: 1972-1977
(*percent*)

Country	1972	1973	1974	1975	1976	1977[a]
Africa	0.8	1.0	1.1	1.1	1.0	0.8
South Africa	0.6	0.7	0.8	0.9	0.7	0.6
Others	0.2	0.3	0.3	0.2	0.3	0.2
America	31.4	31.2	30.9	25.4	27.6	29.5
Brazil	1.4	1.4	2.1	2.1	2.1	2.7
Canada	2.8	2.8	3.2	2.6	2.5	2.4
United States	25.4	25.3	23.7	18.7	20.9	22.4
Others	1.8	1.7	1.9	2.0	2.1	1.9
Asia	13.3	15.3	12.1	12.8	14.4	14.2
Japan	11.9	13.7	10.5	11.0	12.3	12.2
Others	1.4	1.6	1.6	1.8	2.1	2.0
Australia	1.3	1.4	1.4	1.4	1.3	1.3
Europe	31.4	30.2	31.8	32.4	31.1	30.8
England	6.7	6.2	5.9	6.0	5.4	5.7
Belgium	1.9	1.9	2.1	2.4	2.7	3.2
France	4.9	4.6	4.9	4.9	4.3	4.3
Italy	3.5	3.4	3.7	3.9	3.8	3.5
West Germany	8.4	8.3	8.7	8.5	8.7	8.3
Others	6.0	5.8	6.5	6.7	6.2	5.8
Socialist Countries	21.8	20.9	22.6	26.8	24.5	23.4
China[b]	3.4	3.4	3.6	4.4	3.9	3.9
USSR	13.5	12.5	13.7	16.0	14.7	13.9
Others	4.9	5.0	5.3	6.4	5.9	5.6
World[c,d]	100.0	100.0	100.0	100.0	100.0	100.0

Source: Derived from World Bureau of Metal Statistics, *World Metal Statistics,* London, December 1976 and January 1978.

[a]January to September only.

[b]China and other socialist countries of Asia.

[c]The totals do not actually add up to 100, because of rounding error.

[d]From 1972 to 1976, world consumption of refined copper stood at 7.958, 8.770, 8.402, 7.485 and 8.525 million MT.

The price of aluminum—copper's main substitute—showed strong stability compared to its rival. In fact, except for 1970 and 1971, American prices held to the 8¢/lb. gap between 1951 and 1973, showing no net progression before 1974.

Table 7-4
Direct Copper Scrap Used by Manufacturers: 1972-1977
(*thousand MT*)

	1972	1973	1974	1975	1976	1977[a]
Africa	22	32	34	30	26	6
South Africa	16	23	25	23	20	4
Others	6	9	9	7	6	2
America	1,051	1,060	1,000	735	878	248
Brazil	14	17	23	18	21	7
Canada	43	36	37	20	19	9
United States	946	957	878	651	780	218
Others	48	50	62	46	58	14
Asia	397	466	493	376	413	75
Japan	360	416	443	340	359	61
Others	37	50	50	36	54	14
Australia	34	43	43	36	37	9
Europe	767	950	849	675	865	213
Belgium	29	29	31	28	25	8
France	97	151	118	94	152	39
Holland	23	23	16	14	15	4
Italy	158	183	195	144	198	45
West Germany	148	192	144	117	157	30
United Kingdom	134	178	164	124	147	40
Scandinavia	66	76	60	48	52	13
Switzerland	28	36	30	20	25	6
Yugoslavia	33	31	48	48	49	12
Others	51	51	38	33	45	16
Western World	2,271	2,551	2,419	1,852	2,219	551

Source: World Bureau of Metal Statistics, *World Metal Statistics,* London, January 1978, p. 37 (Reprinted with permission).

[a]January-March.

For the last ten years LME copper prices have tended to outstrip the price of American copper. This characteristic is particularly noticeable during periods when the international copper market is unstable.

The statistical data reveal a very marked difference between the world distribution of copper mining production and the world distribution of refined copper production, with western industrial countries and socialist countries refining more copper than warranted by their mining production. At a less aggregate level, only Japan, Chile, Australia, the USSR, and Poland recorded an increased percentage of world refined copper between 1960 and 1977, while for Zaire, the U.S. and Canada this percentage decreased considerably. As for copper

Table 7-5
World Stocks of Refined Copper, in Countries, with Producers, and on the LME Market: 1972-1977.
(*thousand MT*)

	1972	1973	1974	1975	1976	1977
Country Series						
South and South-						
west Africa[a]	2.8	1.2	5.8	1.5	4.4	11.4 (Oct)
Australia[a]	5.6	5.2	10.0	12.1	6.2	7.6 (Nov)
Canada[a]	20.6	9.4	27.2	56.1	34.8	36.5 (Nov)
United States						
Producers[c]	90.3	39.2	137.6	236.5	247.5	153.9 (Aug)
Others	70.0	65.7	131.0	136.2	135.9	172.2 (Aug)
Strategic Stocks	228.2	228.2	32.0	23.7	38.2	–
Total	388.5	333.1	300.6	396.4	421.6	326.1 (Aug)
France[b]	48.7	52.0	64.3	57.3	53.0	61.0 (Aug)
Japan						
Producers	27.1	53.1	106.7	187.8	156.1	188.6 (Sept)
Merchants	16.0	15.8	24.0	48.0	50.6	59.6 (Sept)
Consumers	22.8	33.5	41.1	62.4	50.4	76.0 (Sept)
Total	65.9	102.4	171.8	298.2	257.1	324.2 (Sept)
Peru[a]	2.2	–	–	–	–	–
West Germany						
Producers	22.8	15.8	27.5	39.4	32.4	43.8 (Sept)
Merchants	6.2	5.2	5.0	7.7	7.6	8.7 (Sept)
Consumers	53.8	36.2	50.8	61.4	64.8	65.3 (Sept)
Total	82.8	57.2	83.3	108.5	104.8	117.8 (Sept)
United Kingdom[b]	29.7	15.4	26.2	20.4	22.8	30.3 (Oct)
Zambia[a]	5.0	5.8	9.7	21.6	19.6	31.6 (Nov)
Total of Countries	651.8	581.7	698.9	972.1	924.3	935.0 (Approx.)
Producer Stocks[d]						
United States	90.3	39.2	137.6	236.5	247.5	242.6 (Nov)
Outside of U.S.	189.2	281.5	403.6	525.8	409.6	473.5 (Nov)
Total	279.5	320.7	541.2	762.3	657.1	716.1 (Nov)
Comex	52.4	5.3	39.2	90.7	182.3	171.9 (Nov)
LME Market						
Warehouses						
Belgium	2.2	1.2	2.4	31.3	43.7	43.4 (Nov)
West Germany	58.7	11.0	36.3	159.9	232.3	294.7 (Nov)
Holland	75.8	11.3	76.6	232.2	233.6	212.4 (Nov)
United Kingdom	46.3	11.3	10.6	73.6	93.9	88.2 (Nov)
Total	183.0	34.8	125.9	497.0	603.5	638.7 (Nov)

Source: World Bureau of Metal Statistics, *World Metal Statistics,* London, January 1978, p. 41. Reprinted with permission.

Note: At end of period.

(*Table notes continued on next page*)

Table 7-5 – *Continued*

[a]At producers.

[b]At consumers.

[c]Includes stocks in transit, on consignment, and New York Commodity Exchange.

[d]Includes stocks at refineries and in transit.

ore production, only Papua New Guinea (PNG) and the socialist countries showed any notable percentage gains in world production between 1960 and 1977. Between 1960 and 1972, this percentage took a particularly sharp drop for CIPEC member countries, but afterwards steadied around 30%. CIPEC members show much greater influence on the world exports of blister copper.[9]

Despite the occurrence of numerous nationalizations in this industry during the past fifteen years, it still remains well integrated and very concentrated. As a matter of fact, in 1970, eleven companies, a consortium and three government corporations controlled 81% of the West's copper ore production, while thirty-four companies and government corporations controlled 94% of world refining capacity.[10] Capital-intensive technology and fear of substitutes are among the reasons most often cited to explain this degree of concentration and vertical integration.[11]

Statistical data reveal a very heavy geographic concentration of the world consumption of refined copper in a few industrialized countries. As a matter of fact, in 1976, the U.S., Japan, and Europe (especially the EEC) were responsible for more than 64% of the consumption of refined copper, and this percentage reaches close to 80% if the USSR is included. These data also indicate that, between 1972 and 1977, consumption rates remained stable for Japan and Europe, while the U.S. percentage followed very closely the evolution of the international economic conjuncture.[12]

Besides being influenced by industrial activity and price, consumption of refined copper also depends on the price of substitutes in its main fields of use: electrical industry, construction, consumer durables, transportation, and industrial equipment. In each of these industries, refined copper is in competition with aluminum and plastics. Aluminum has increased its market share relative to copper for overhead high tension lines, composite lines, and interior electric wiring. Plastics has gained ground for transportation equipment and construction (especially plumbing). Unless this competition levels off in the next few years, it is likely to affect the growth rate of world refined copper consumption. But we have good reason to believe that these effects will only be felt in the long term because, as shown by the Fisher-Cootner-Baily model, copper's short-term cross-elasticity is relatively weak.[13] This means that the demand for refined copper is relatively insensitive to the price variations of its substitutes on a short-term basis.

That part of the copper demand involved in the production of finished products can also be satisfied by the secondary copper supply. Since 1972, secondary copper's level of use by manufacturers has fluctuated between 1.85 and 2.55 million MT. In 1976 it reached 2.22 million MT, 26% of world refined copper consumption. It is important to note that this secondary copper supply responds to variables such as the amount of primary copper produced in the past; the ease with which this production can be gathered and sold as secondary copper; and its price. Table 7-4 shows its evolution in time and space. It only includes direct scrap used by manufacturers and therefore does not take into account the production of secondary refined copper.

Since 1974 the international refined copper market has been characterized by the buildup of large stocks by producers, by countries and on the LME and COMEX markets.[14] After having fallen from 1.2 to 0.9 million MT between 1972 and 1973, the total of these stocks has continued to grow, even exceeding 2.4 million MT in the third quarter of 1977. The increase on the LME market was particularly strong, going from 34,800 MT in 1973 to 638,700 MT in November 1977. Moreover, the slight decrease recorded in Canada and the U.S. was more than counterbalanced by stock increases held in France, Japan, West Germany, Zambia, at producers and on the COMEX market. Table 7-5 offers particularly complete statistical data on this subject. Except for a slight increase during part of 1976 and first half of 1977, copper prices continued to fall between 1974 and the beginning of 1978.[15] During this latter period world stocks more than doubled in size.

The short-term prospects for any noticeable improvement in the world copper industry are rather poor. One of the economic experts in mining from the IMF's Research Department gives this assessment of the situation.

> Stocks continued to accumulate, and in November the LME spot price of copper declined to its lowest monthly average for the year— 53.6 cnets a pound. By then, consumers had worked off some of their excess stocks. After reports of Soviet purchases and announcements by three members of the Intergovernmental Council of Copper Exporting Countries—Peru, Zaire, and Zambia—of intended production cutbacks, the LME spot price recovered to an average of 57.2 cents a pound for December. Part of the recovery is attributable to a decline in value of the U.S. dollar. . .

> Prospects in 1978 for any substantial improvement in copper prices and export earnings do not seem promising, unless there is a marked unanticipated growth in the world economy. Even if demand were to improve rapidly, shortages are unlikely. Producers' stocks are at higher levels than ever; many producers are operating well below capacity.

New capacity totaling about 390,000 tons a year, of which 145,000 tons is in Iran, is scheduled to come into operation in 1978.[16]

Our analysis shows that the most important of the CIPEC member countries (Chile, Peru, Zaire, and Zambia) presently control about 30% of world copper ore production, 16% of world refined copper production, 75% of international trade in blister copper and 58% of world exports of refined copper. Considering these facts, why is it that none of the export and production quotas set by CIPEC (whether in November 1974, in April 1975, in January 1976, or in mid-1977) succeeded in reversing the trend towards lower copper prices begun in the first quarter of 1974? We believe that CIPEC's lack of influence on the international copper market can be explained by the following factors.

In the first place, CIPEC is composed of countries whose ideologies and administrations are too diverse and too unstable to permit any sustained co-operation or concerted action. We had an example of this divergence of views in 1976 when, despite a CIPEC directive setting a 15% cut in production for the first semester, there was a phenomenal 200,000 MT increase in Chilean mining production. The same phenomenon recurred in 1977 and only Zambia, Zaire, and Peru decided to cut back production. Without Chile's collaboration in the cartel's interventions, CIPEC controls less than 20% of copper mining production and scarcely 10% of world refined copper production. Moreover, since CIPEC members are developing countries, export and production restraints imply enormous sacrifices because of the unemployment created, the decrease in government receipts from export taxes, and the losses in exchange reserves.[17] Finding it impossible to reduce or slow down mining production indefinitely, these countries realized that it was preferable to stabilize this metal's price and receipts on an international scale and agreed to the establishment of UNCTAD's integrated program. We have already seen that the negotiations for this program are likely to be long.

Second, we find it erroneous to believe that, since CIPEC has either direct or indirect control over 60% of world exports in blister or refined copper, it can have a determining influence on this product's international market. We believe rather that it is the control, not just of exports but of production which determines a cartel's monopolistic power. In actual fact, a reduction of copper shipments by all CIPEC members can cause increased production and exports by nonmember countries (responsible for 70% of world production); an increased use of secondary copper; a cut in primary copper consumption due to price increases; and its eventual replacement by substitutes. The obvious possibility that consumers and nonmember producers could make these adjustments makes the world demand of CIPEC copper very elastic, implying that the decrease in demand will be greater than the increase in prices, thus reducing export receipts.[18] Demand elasticity would be much weaker if the control of world copper production were comparable to that enjoyed by OPEC. In this case, economic agents can only make long-term adjustments to a price hike.

Third, it is important to note that international consumers have access to secondary copper and to substitutes, such as aluminum and plastics, to satisfy their demands for the manufacture of finished products. Although the degree of short-term substitution has often been exaggerated, the long-term importance of copper substitutes is much larger than that detected for other metals.[19] Moreover, secondary copper consumption has since 1972 accounted for more than 30% of American consumption and close to 35% of consumption in the rest of the world. The demand for secondary copper is sensitive to price variations for primary copper and any move to increase primary copper prices by voluntary production restraints will be hobbled by the importance of copper scrap. It is estimated that about 60% of all copper consumed in the United States is eventually used as secondary copper, thus guaranteeing the world's largest consumer with continued supplies for a great number of years to come.

Finally, identified copper reserves were estimated at 450 million short tons in 1975 when world production rose to 7.85 million tons. Copper's reserve production ratio thus stands at 57, a level higher than that calculated for tin (46), lead (42) and zinc (24); only bauxite (250), among the nonferrous ores, shows a ratio higher than copper's. This ratio approaches 200 if hypothetical copper resources are taken into account.

> There are about 480 million tons of identified copper resources. An additional 320 million tons are assigned to areas not yet prospected and at least 800 million tons of copper are presumed to exist in sub-economic deposits, with about half of this quantity assigned to deep sea nodules.[20]

These reserves, 63% of which are located in non-CIPEC countries, limit this body's present and future action and afford it a much less strategic and monopolistic position than that held by OPEC. As a matter of fact, each restriction of supply causes a price rise, encourages prospecting for new lodes, favors production growth in nonmember countries, and makes the enormous quantities of inferior copper ore economically profitable.

Furthermore, these repeated market interventions lead to the concentration of exploration and new mineral investments in "politically reliable" countries, a trend which started with the first nationalizations. The following sums up rather well the causes and consequences of such a structural upheaval:

> The 15-year record of nationalization of existing projects in Zaire, Zambia, Peru, and Chile in the case of copper, . . . , plus the attitude of "sovereign-take-all" on the part of many countries, had entirely predictable results . . . One result was that "political risk analysis" came to supplement—and in many cases was now conceived to surpass

in importance—the usual "economic risk analysis" involved in making new investment decisions. . . .

. . . By the early '70s, a preponderant share of exploration and new mineral investment in the non-Communist world was going into four areas: the United States, Canada, Australia, and South Africa. . . .

. . . The shift of interest away from the Third World began almost as soon as the challenge to established methods of financing development became apparent. During the 1960s, each major nationalization in the developing world brought a reevaluation of the relative attractiveness of other sources of minerals. For example, the nationalization of copper industries in Zaire, Chile and Zambia 5 to 15 years ago encouraged the development of deposits containing lower grades of copper in North America. The relative attractiveness of higher-grade ores in outlying parts of the world was altered in favor of the higher political attractiveness—and overall profitability—of lower grade deposits elsewhere which rated better with investors. . . .

. . . It cannot be too much stressed that this shift in emphasis of development of new supplies has been under way from the beginning of the new political trends. Already, hundreds of millions of dollars, billions even, of capital that might have flowed to the Third World have been invested in developing alternative supplies in areas where the financial outcome is more predictable and the profitability more assured. And, the competitiveness of these alternative supplies has been enhanced by substantial increases in the cost of Third World output, as many of the developing countries that took over control of mineral operations have not maintained the former efficiencies of production. At the same time, the cost economies of *very* large-scale operations of the lower-grade deposits shifted the competitive balance in favor of this type of mining.

Perhaps even more important for its long-range implications for mineral development is the effect of recent trends in discouraging new exploration in the Third World. Exploration is the essential seedcorn of new investment . . . . The effect of the recent shift of exploration activity away from areas considered too exposed to various security risks will probably show up in the early or mid-'80s.[21]

Although the author's interpretations of Third World desires for more control over the economic levers of their development need to be clarified and more balanced, these important shifts of new mining activity can, in effect, be verified.

What can be the future of this cartel or of any other body attempting to stabilize copper prices and export receipts? Perusal of the latest press releases leaves this question largely unanswered. In fact, on December 7, 1977 CIPEC delegates could not agree on emergency measures to harden world copper prices. Moreover, UNCTAD negotiations, within the Copper Group and the Intergovernmental Experts Group, could reach no international agreement on setting up a buffer stock or even on creating an International Copper Council to centralize the collection and exchange of economic information on copper.

Notes

1. The reader interested in the history of private controls for this market is referred to the excellent study by Harry G. Cordero, and Leslie H. Tarring, *Babylon to Birmingham*.

2. The Conference of Ministers is CIPEC's highest body. Composed of the ministers of mines from each member country, it has been meeting annually since 1974. Voting rights are equally divided among member countries. Decisions on important questions require a unanimous vote while those of lesser importance need only a simple majority. The Conference of Ministers itself determines the degree of importance of each item on its agenda.

The Governing Board is composed of two representatives from each member country. Responsible to the Conference of Ministers, the Governing Board meets twice a year. It is supposed to propose and coordinate individual and collective measures aimed at influencing the international copper market and at modifying production process, exports, consumption or any other measure decided on by the Conference of Ministers. Finally, this body is also responsible for the Copper Information Bureau.

This bureau is charged with collecting and disseminating all available statistical and technical information dealing with supply, demand, marketing, mining, work conflicts, transportation, and international agreements likely to influence the sales of copper and its derivatives. This Bureau is governed by an Executive Director (Mr. Sacha Gueronick has held this post for many years); the director decides what tasks the bureau must undertake; supervises their execution, and distributes their conclusions to interested governments and the information media.

The Executive Committee was created in 1974 during the Lusaka Conference. All indications are that its role is primarily financial: collecting funds to finance a possible buffer stock and coordinate its presence on international capital markets alongside other associations of producing countries.

3. The chronology, compensation fees, and levels of the new ownership controls can be found in Kenneth W. Clarfield et al., *Eight Mineral Cartels* pp. 85-87.

4. Readers interested in a more detailed presentation of this market's economic and institutional characteristics are referred to the following works: Ferdinand E. Banks, *The World Copper Market: An Economic Analysis;* F.M. Fisher; P.H. Cootner; and M.N. Baily, "An Econometric Model of the World Copper Industry"; and R.H. Lisemann, "Copper-The Long, Slow Road Back."

5. Banks, *The World Copper Market*, p. 27.

6. Fisher, Cootner, and Baily, "An Econometric Model of the World Copper Industry."

7. On this market, total supply equals the sum of primary copper supply in producing countries, secondary copper supply, copper imports from the U.S. minus exports towards the U.S. The difference between total supply and demand motivates stock variations and the direction of the price movement.

8. Although little copper is physically exchanged on the LME market (less than 20,000 MT a month at the beginning of the seventies) it has much greater importance as a forward market. In fact, it is estimated that in 1968, when the world consumption of refined copper reached 7 million MT, approximately 2 million MT were sold in forward trading on the LME.

9. Although the U.S., the USSR, Chile, Canada and Zambia represent in descending order the principal producers of copper ore and concentrates, these countries do not all turn out to be the major exporters of this ore. In fact, in 1976 the major exporting countries were (in descending order) Canada, 308,900 MT; the Philippines, 236,800 MT; Papua New Guinea, 179,100 MT; Chile, 156,200 MT; and Indonesia, 66,800 MT. As for blister copper exports, the five largest exporting countries in 1975 were Zaire, 315,500 MT; Chile, 231,000 MT; South Africa, 106,000 MT; Peru, 45,800 MT and West Germany, 38,900 MT. Japan and West Germany remain the principal importers of copper ore and concentrates, while Belgium and West Germany are the chief importers of blister copper. Notice that both the U.S. and Russia are absent from the scene of world trade in nonmanufactured copper, while CIPEC member countries have a much larger role in world trade of blister copper (75% of total) than in world production of copper ore (30%).

10. In descending order, the most important companies are: Anaconda, Anglo-American, Kennecott, American Metal Climax, Ascaro, Phelps Dodge, Noranda Mines, Newmont Mining, Union Miniere, International Nickel, Norddeutsche Affinerie, Mitsuibishi and Nippon Mining. The reader interested in knowing more about the control of the copper industry is referred to Banks, *The World Copper Market*, chapter 2.

11. In fact, vertical integration allows for better control of input costs in the production process and reduces the impact that variations in certain production factor prices have on the price of the output. By controlling these variations, it is possible to better control the price of the final product and provide some protection against competition from substitutes on markets where copper is most in demand. Fear of substitutes also explains the horizontal integration practised increasingly in the nonferrous metal industry.

12. As concerns international trade in refined copper, here is the 1976 list of the principal exporting and importing countries, in descending order. The most important exporters turn out to be: Zambia, 712,400 MT; Chile, 594,700 MT; Canada, 313,200 MT or 60% of its refined copper production;

Belgium, 307,500 MT; Peru, 122,100 MT; U.S., 102,300 MT; Australia, 76,200 MT and Zaire, 74,000 MT. So we notice that in 1976 the four founding countries of CIPEC were responsible for 57.4% of world exports of refined copper. The 1976 list of the major importing countries for refined copper shows the following decreasing order: West Germany, 409,700 MT; the United Kingdom, 367,900 MT; the U.S., 346,100 MT; France, 338,100 MT; Belgium, 302,200 MT; Italy, 288,300 MT and Japan, 200,500 MT. In 1976 five EEC countries absorbed more than 65% of the refined copper imported internationally.

13. Fisher, Cootner, and Baily, "An Econometric Model of the World Copper Industry."

14. The Commodity Exchange (COMEX) is a commodity market situated in New York. Although less copper is traded on this market than in London and it is less oriented to the international market, COMEX offers commercial agents a larger variety of metals. Moreover, it is estimated that most of the copper bought and sold in the U.S. by merchants is transacted for at COMEX prices, different from those of U.S. producers.

15. The price increase during the first half of 1977 can be explained by the buildup of stocks by consumers against the possibility of a long strike in the American copper industry where a large number of collective agreements were to expire in July 1977 and would have to be renegotiated. As the threat of a strike faded, the price of available copper started to slide; producer stocks, already large and still increasing, prevented any possible recovery.

16. G.I. Brown, *IMF Survey*, International Monetary Fund, vol. 7, no. 3, February 6, 1978, p. 35. Reprinted with permission.

17. Approximately 75% of Chile's export receipts and 60% of Zaire's come from their international copper shipments. The percentage is even higher for Zambia. Moreover, their copper industry employs such a large portion of the local workforce that production cutbacks can cause a politically unacceptable increase in unemployment.

18. A study by Charles River Associates evaluates this elasticity at −2.81 for an adjustment period of six to ten years and at −1.4 for an adjustment period of a single year; this implies that a 10% price increase by CIPEC (following a cut in their exports) would provoke a long-term net decrease of 28.1% in international demand. Charles River Associates Inc., *Economic Issues Underlying Supply Access Agreements: a General Analysis and Prospects in Ten Mineral Markets*. p. IV-11.

19. As a metal, copper is malleable, resistant, relatively noncorrosive and a good conductor of heat and electricity. Although it has no perfect substitutes, it can be replaced by aluminum for electrical wiring, while steel, various alloys, or plastics can be considered as substitutes by current users looking for corrosion-resistant materials. From another viewpoint, the importance of these substitutes must not be exaggerated since their use is still limited by their current and forecasted prices; the existence of long-term contracts, and the

enormous investments required to modify production techniques. Just the same we would point out that given the nature of these obstacles to change, once begun, substitution becomes irreversible and tends to increase cross-elasticity in the long run. This characteristic has been tested by the econometric models of Fisher-Cootner-Baily and Banks; these models are based on various periods going from 1948 to 1968.

20. British-North American Committee, *Mineral Development in the Eighties: Prospects and Problems*, p. 39. Reprinted with permission.

21. Ibid., pp. 12, 14, 15. Reprinted with permission.

8

IBA and the International Bauxite Market

In its commercial meaning, the term "bauxite" refers to an ore, containing a minimum of 40% alumina and a maximum of 10% silica, which can be used economically to produce alumina and aluminum.[1] Bauxite is thus the raw ore from which alumina is extracted by use of the Bayer process; the alumina is subsequently reduced to aluminum following an electrolytic process discovered by Charles Hall.[2] Although there exists several variations of the Bayer process to convert low-grade bauxite into alumina, (the most important being the soda-lime sinter process and that using serial, parallel, and modified combination process) notice that they raise investment costs by 30% to 70% compared with the American or European Bayer process and can be used only to supply captive markets.[3]

The bauxite-alumina-aluminum industry is highly concentrated and vertically integrated on the international level. This has been occasioned by the size of investments related to bauxite mining; the necessity of establishing an economic infrastructure in countries producing this ore; the level of transportation costs; and the necessity of converting bauxite into alumina, and this powder into aluminum, by means of a captial- and energy-intensive process. Table 8-4 indicates that before nationalizations and the establishment of a cartel of producing countries, six multinational companies (Alcan, Alcoa, Alusuisse, Kaiser, Pechiney-Ugine-Kuhlmann and Reynolds) controlled 57.3% of bauxite production capacity and about 70.0% of alumina and aluminum production. Up until the beginning of the sixties, the transformation of ore into alumina or aluminum took place largely in industrial countries but rising transportation costs encouraged companies to transform bauxite locally before importing the alumina to the U.S., Canada, Europe, and Japan. Since 2.22 tons of bauxite are needed to obtain a ton of alumina, this structural change in fact permitted the reduction of shipping and transportation costs by half. So, the percentage of alumina production in developing countries as compared to world production moved from 10% in 1960 to 25% in 1970; in 1975 it stood at 34%.

Producing countries found this increase clearly insufficient and demanded not only a larger share in converting bauxite into alumina, but also an increase in the local transformation of alumina into aluminum. Their arguments were based on the fact that more than 80% of bauxite extraction was carried in their countries while they were responsible for only 5% of West's aluminum production. Also, if these countries intend to increase government receipts from profit and export taxes, it is in their interest to encourage plants with highly value-added activity since:

> The economics of the aluminum industry are such that the more basic the process, the less value is added to the product. For example, in April 1974, one ton of Jamaican bauxite was considered to be worth about $2.50 in the ground and $11 mined. However, converted into alumina, that same ton of bauxite was worth about $40. As aluminum ingot, it was worth about $125 at the list price and $200 at the free market price. Fabricated into sheet, plate, or foil, it was worth still more.[4]

Finding it impossible to reconcile producing countries' demands and the offers of multinational companies, Guyana and Jamaica launched the idea of creating an international bauxite cartel to control the price of ore (as early as 1971, Guyana nationalized the Alcan subsidiary's mine and alumina plant, placing them under the direction of the government agency, Guybau). Jamaica encountered little difficulty in convincing other West Indian producing countries to participate in the cartel and increase their control over the foreign companies operating on their territory. She pointed out that the region's bauxite was characterized by high levels of alumina, that Caribbean countries were very close to the American market (giving them a cost advantage over other bauxite sources), and that OPEC furnished a good example of what could be gained when producing countries cooperated to determine prices. Countries which remained reluctant were convinced by a crushing argument: petroleum price increases begun in 1973 had caused enormous deficits in their balance of payments; these could now be wiped out through increasing bauxite prices.

After a few preliminary meetings, a meeting was called on March 8, 1974 at Conakry, Guinea, to lay the foundation of an International Bauxite Association (IBA). Australia, Guinea, Guyana, Jamaica, Sierra Leone, Surinam, and Yugoslavia accepted the 28-article text defining the objectives and internal regulations of this new organization. When a few months later, this group was joined by Indonesia, Ghana, Haiti, and the Dominican Republic, IBA member countries could be shown to control 71% of world bauxite production. IBA objectives resembled those stipulated by Nairobi resolution 93(IV): to promote the rational and orderly development of the bauxite industry and to guarantee member countries that the exploitation, transformation, and marketing of bauxite will assure them a "just and reasonable" real income. After having decided that the offices of the new association would be in Kingston, Jamaica and provided with a Council of Ministers, an Executive Board and a Secretariat, the delegates agreed to reconvene in Georgetown, Guyana on November 4-8, 1974.[5]

These objectives are general enough to allow each member country to make the interventions it judges appropriate. In fact, during the eight months separating IBA's first two meetings, a large number of member countries modified their mining policy and tax structure.

On May 15, 1974, Jamaica levied a uniform royalty of US $0.55 on each long ton of bauxite mined on its territory (before that date royalties stood at $0.29 for exported bauxite and $0.55 for bauxite refined into alumina on the domestic market). What is more, Jamaica imposed a variable production levy on the quantity of bauxite extracted by aluminum companies. This levy is related to the average price brought by an aluminum ingot when sold by Alcoa, Reynolds and Kaiser on the American market. The relationship is established according to the following formula: $VBPL = MLP \cdot ALP/4.3$, where VBPL stands for the variable bauxite production levy collected by the Jamaican government per long dry ton (LDT) of bauxite; MLP indicates the maximum levy percentage specified in the 1974 Jamaican Bauxite Act and retroactive to January 1, 1974 (the act established this percentage at 7.5% from January 1, 1974 to March 31, 1975, at 8% from April 1, 1975 to March 31, 1976 and at 8.5% from April 1, 1976 to March 31, 1977); ALP stands for the list price of a short ton of refined aluminum on the American market and 4.3 indicates that the production levy is per LDT of bauxite (since 4.3 LDT of Jamaican bauxite are needed to produce a short ton of aluminum).

Therefore, since May 15, 1974, the tax collected by the Jamaican government and the ingot price obtained by companies on the American market vary at the same rate.[6] Now, since the tax is levied on production and not profits or revenues, companies could avoid it by reducing their Jamaican production and increasing it in non-IBA countries such as Brazil. To avoid such substitution, new legislation assigns each company a minimum quarterly amount of bauxite to be produced in Jamaica. By fixing this minimum at about 90% of production capacity, government receipts are stabilized through the minimum quarterly payments to be made by each aluminum company operating within the country. Finally, we point out that this fiscal reform raised the total taxes collected by the Jamaican government on each ton of bauxite from $1.77 to $15.08, an increase of 752%.

In November 1974 the government of Surinam increased its bauxite mining related revenues by 340% by means of a 6% retroactive tax on production. From a study by Charles River Associates we learn that these two countries have since been imitated by Guyana, Haiti, the Dominican Republic, and, to a smaller degree, by Australia.[7]

The second IBA meeting was held in Georgetown, Guyana on November 4-8, 1974. Several administrative questions were then approached: nomination of a secretary-general and judicial, technical, and scientific advisors; admission of new members (Dominican Republic, Ghana, and Haiti); pursuit of talks with potential members (Greece, India, Indonesia, and other producing countries), and other matters. Even if the participants, judging that the time was not ripe, showed little interest in discussing the principle of a uniform price, they did emphasize their interest in the future establishment of a floor price, and took note of the fiscal reforms in the mining sector initiated by Jamaica and Surinam.

A few months later, imitating these unilateral moves, they brought about an almost complete equalization of bauxite prices on the American market. This second IBA meeting also left aside discussions concerning the establishment of a common policy on nationalizations. All interventions in this field were left up to the discretion of each member country, with the IBA acting only to coordinate their individual actions and furnish the technical support necessary to allow each country to increase its participation in mining and refining operations.

We would do well to take a closer look at the methods used by principal IBA members since the beginning of 1975 to concentrate high value-added operations in producing countries.

After having taken over the Alcan subsidiary mine and alumina works in 1971, Guyana nationalized the Reynolds company bauxite mine in January 1975 and placed it under control of Berbice Mines. In 1977 Berbice and Guybau were exploiting mines with an annual 4.2 million MT capacity. The Guyana Bauxite Co. (Guybau) also operates this country's only alumina plant with a 315,000 MT annual production.[8] The government is studying projects which would raise alumina production to 630,000 MT in 1980. The production of primary aluminum is not foreseen before 1981. Guyana has created a national company (Guybulk) for the transportation of its bauxite and alumina and is requiring that its services be used for a growing share of the exportation of these products.

In order to profit from export taxes Jamaica did not nationalize all the bauxite mines, whose operational capacity is evaluated at 16.4 million MT. The major companies, such as Alcan, Alcoa, and Reynolds operate most of their mines "freely" while the Jamaican government controls 51% of Kaiser Jamaica Bauxite Co. and of Revere Jamaican Alumina. Jamaican alumina production stands at 3 million MT a year, 33% of which is government-controlled. The realization of projects currently under study (like Jamex) would give Jamaica an annual capacity of 3.8 million MT tons by 1980. For lack of adequate energy resources, Jamaica cannot launch any projects for the production of primary aluminum. The government has also created a maritime company (Jamaica Merchant Marine) in order to handle a growing percentage of bauxite and alumina exports and thus increase its foreign exchange inflow.[9]

Australia is the world's largest producer of bauxite. The installed capacity of its mines is evaluated at 23 million MT, with the largest share under foreign control. In 1975 Australia was producing an estimated 6 million MT of alumina annually (1.3 million by Alcoa, 1 million by Alusuisse and 2.4 million by a consortium composed of Kaiser, Alcan, PUK, Comalco and CRA). The realization of current projects would raise annual alumina production to 10.4 million MT in 1980. Unlike the other members of IBA, Australia produced about 237,000 MT of primary aluminum in 1976 (96,000 MT by Comalco; 91,000 MT by Alcoa and 50,000 MT by the Alcan subsidiary at Kurri Kurri). With these characteristics Australia holds an important strategic position in the determination of all common policies by IBA members.

In 1976 Surinam was the world's fifth largest bauxite producer. Its mines have a 7 million MT capacity and are 100% controlled by Alcoa (4.5 million MT) and Royal Dutch Shell (2.5 million MT). While the Dutch company exports the totality of its mined bauxite, Alcoa uses its for the local production of alumina (1.3 million MT in 1977) and aluminum (66,000 MT). The government is planning construction of an alumina plant at Bakhuis which will be producing about 200,000 MT of alumina by the beginning of the eighties. Although the government does not seem interested in nationalizing or expropriating aluminum companies, it has often expressed the desire to see a larger proportion of the bauxite and alumina now exported, refined in Surinam.

Guinea produced about 11.3 million MT of bauxite in 1976, thus becoming the second largest world producer. The extraction was carried out by two consortiums in which the government holds a 49% interest; the Guinea Bauxite Company (Alcan, 13.8%, Alcoa, 13.8%, Pechiney-Ugine-Kuhlmann, 5.1%, Martin Marietta, 10.2%, VAW, 5.1%, Montedison, 3.1%, Guinean government, 49%) and Friguia (Alusuisse, 5.1%, Pechiney-Ugine-Kuhlmann, 18.6%, Noranda, 19.6%, VAW, 2.6%, British Aluminium, 5.1%, the Guinean government, 49%). Friguia also owns alumina plants with a 700,000 MT capacity forecasted for 1977. A project under study, involving the government and Energoinvest (a Yugoslavian firm), will add 508,000 MT of alumina to the current capacity by 1980. Unlike other members of IBA who levied taxes on the ingot price of primary aluminum, Guinea's are based on the alumina content of the bauxite. Since January 1975, these taxes, which are added to the price of bauxite, vary between 50% (for a 45% or less alumina content) and 75% (for a 56% and more alumina content) of the bauxite price.

Among the other interventions which have influenced the international structure of the bauxite-alumina-aluminum industry since 1975, we should mention IBA's first common action: in December 1977 its members announced agreement on a minimum price of US $24.00 per ton of bauxite headed for the North American market. Although this action proved important in principle, it would have little short-term effect; prices actually charged by all the suppliers of this market are higher than that figure.

Since March 1974, what influence has the IBA exercised over the price of bauxite, government receipts, and producing countries' share of ownership in mining and refining activities? What predictions can be made for the future? The data in tables 8-1 through 8-8 will help to answer these questions.

In 1976, IBA countries were responsible for 72.7% of world bauxite production. If the production by communist countries is excluded, this percentage climbs to 84.6%. These proportions are sufficient to influence the international price of bauxite. Moreover, these ratios have become larger since the creation

Table 8-1
World Bauxite Production: 1974-77
(*million MT*)

	1974	1975	1976	1977[a]
Europe				
France	2.95	2.56	2.31	1.53
Greece	2.78	3.00	2.75	1.71
Italy	0.03	0.03	0.02	0.02
Spain	0.01	0.01	0.01	0.01
Yugoslavia	2.37[b]	2.31	2.03	1.57
Total	8.15	7.92	7.13	4.82
Africa				
Guinea	7.60	8.41	11.32	8.49
Ghana	0.36	0.33	0.27	0.19
Sierra Leone	0.67	0.72	0.66	0.50
Total	8.64	9.46	12.25	9.18
Asia				
India	1.27	1.27	1.44	1.00
Indonesia	1.29	0.99	0.94	0.93
Malaysia	0.95	0.70	0.66	0.43
Turkey	0.67	0.63	0.46	0.34
Total	4.18	3.60	3.50	2.70
Australia	19.99	20.96	24.09	19.90
America				
Brazil	0.86	0.97	1.00	0.75
Dominican Republic	1.20	0.79	0.52	0.39
Guyana	3.61	3.83	3.11	2.40
Haiti	0.66	0.52	0.66	0.48
Jamaica	15.33	11.57	10.31	8.23
Surinam	6.89	4.75	4.59	2.03
United States	1.98	1.83	1.99	1.65
Total	30.52	24.26	22.17	16.00
Total	71.47	66.19	69.13	52.60
Other Countries				
People's Republic of China	0.70	0.80	0.85	0.65
Hungary	2.75	2.89	2.92	2.27
Rumania	0.86	0.78	0.89	0.67
USSR	8.40	6.60	6.70	5.04
Total	12.71	11.07	11.36	8.60
World Total	84.18	77.26	80.49	61.20
IBA	59.97	55.18	58.50	45.11
	(83.9)[c]	(83.3)	(84.6)	(85.7)
	(71.2)[d]	(71.4)	(72.7)	(73.7)

Source: World Bureau of Metal Statistics, *World Metal Statistics,* London, January 1978,
p. 8. Reprinted with permission.

Table 8-1 – *Continued*

Note: Bauxite production is expressed in gross weight and so does not account for differences by country in content and composition.

[a]January-September.

[b]Totals do not correspond exactly, due to rounding error.

[c]Percentage of world production of noncommunist countries.

[d]Percentage of total world production.

of IBA in 1974, implying that price rises have not yet provoked a notable increase of production in nonmember countries. Despite the association's overall performance during a period of decreasing demand, we call attention to the fact that in 1976 West Indian-produced bauxite provided only 24% of world production, compared to 33% in 1974. If IBA managed a slight increase in its international market share, it was thanks to Australia and Guinea (20.5% and 49% increase, respectively) where bauxite production growth more than counterbalanced the drop in Surinam (−33.4%), Jamaica (−32.7%) and Guyana (−14.0%). This shift in world production can be largely explained by the increase in export taxes levied by Jamaica and Surinam; the Guyana nationalizations; Australia's relative liberal attitude (especially in the western province) and the discovery of very large lodes in Guinea (and in Brazil).

From table 8-2 we find that only Australia, Ghana, Surinam and Yugoslavia produce aluminum, implying that the IBA can exercise effective control over 4.77% of this production (6.11% if communist countries are excluded). This percentage has remained relatively stable since 1974. This kind of variable is little affected by the creation of a bauxite producers' cartel since bauxite accounts on the average for less than 10% of the price of aluminum. As for alumina, a recent survey shows that production capacity in 6 IBA countries (Australia, 5.9 million MT, Jamaica, 3.01 million MT, Surinam, 1.3 million MT, Yugoslavia, 0.91 million MT, Guinea, 0.7 million MT and Guyana, 0.315 million MT) totaled 12.135 million MT in 1975, or 34% of world alumina production capacity.[10] Even if it is still too soon to evaluate IBA's effect on the installation of alumina plants in member countries, we would point out that this percentage stood at 25% in 1970.

The price of bauxite increased 88% from 1965 to 1973, going from US $32.20/MT to US $60.68/MT. Since the cost of bauxite represented only a small percentage of the price of aluminum produced in North America, the price of this metal increased by a scant 11%, going from US 24.50¢/lb. in 1965 to US 27.20¢/lb. in 1973. The fiscal reform encouraged by IBA modified the evolution of both these prices. Given that the variable tax on West Indian bauxite production is based on the ingot price of aluminum, since it went into

Table 8-2
World Primary Aluminum Production: 1974-1977
(*thousand MT*)

	1974	1975	1976	1977[a]
Europe				
Austria	91.6	89.1	88.7	45.4
France	393.3	382.6	385.1	198.1
West Germany	688.9	677.6	697.1	367.1
Greece	149.0	136.0	134.0	57.4
Iceland	69.6	61.8	65.3	36.0
Italy	212.2	190.1	206.5	126.9
Holland	247.4	257.6	248.9	123.3
Norway	648.2	594.9	620.9	316.0
Spain	191.3	210.4	209.0	107.1
Sweden	82.2	78.0	81.4	41.1
Switzerland	87.2	79.0	78.2	39.4
United Kingdom	293.1	308.3	334.5	179.4
Yugoslavia	147.1	168.3	197.7	97.3
Total	3,301.1	3,233.7	3,347.3	1,734.5
Africa				
Cameroon	46.8	51.9	48.7	30.0
Egypt	–	2.0	59.0	30.0
Ghana	157.2	143.3	151.1	81.1
South Africa	75.0	75.9	78.4	38.3
Total	279.0	273.1	337.2	179.4
Asia				
Bahrain	118.0	116.3	122.1	65.0
India	128.8	167.1	211.8	92.3
Iran	49.0	51.0	30.6	10.0
Japan	1,118.4	1,013.3	919.4	579.4
South Korea	17.7	17.6	17.6	10.0
Taiwan	31.3	28.1	25.7	16.5
Turkey	–	16.5	37.4	25.5
Total	1,463.3	1,409.9	1,364.6	798.7
America				
Canada	1,020.9	886.8	633.4	464.5
United States	4,448.3	3,519.1	3,856.8	2,043.8
Argentina	1.1	24.1	43.1	20.0
Brazil	113.6	121.4	139.2	85.0
Mexico	41.1	39.9	42.4	20.0
Surinam	57.0	42.0	44.8	24.4
Venezuela	39.2	49.7	46.5	22.5
Total	5,721.2	4,683.0	4,806.2	2,680.2
Oceania				
Australia	219.1	214.2	231.3	117.7
New Zealand	110.3	108.6	139.8	71.2
Total	329.4	322.8	371.1	188.9
Eastern Countries				
Czechoslovakia	49.8	43.3	40.0	20.0
East Germany	60.0	60.0	60.0	30.0

Table 8-2 — *Continued*

	1974	*1975*	*1976*	*1977*[a]
Hungary	69.0	70.2	70.5	35.4
Poland	102.0	102.9	103.0	52.0
Rumania	187.0	204.2	203.0	105.0
USSR	2,100.0	2,150.0	2,200.0	1,100.0
China	160.0	180.0	180.0	90.0
Total	2,727.8	2,810.6	2,856.5	1,432.4
World Total	13,821.7	12,733.1	13,082.9	7,014.1
IBA (Australia, Ghana,	580.4	567.8	624.9	320.5
Surinam, Yugoslavia)	(4.20%)[b]	(4.46%)	(4.77%)	(4.57%)
	(5.23%)[c]	(5.72%)	(6.11%)	(5.74%)

Source: World Bureau of Metal Statistics, *World Metal Statistics,* London, January 1978, p. 9. Reprinted with permission.

[a]January-June.

[b]Percentages of total world production.

[c]Percentages of world production of noncommunist countries.

effect input and output prices have had parallel fluctuations. In fact, while a set of variables (such as the industrial production index and the evolution of the stocks/consumption ratio) pushed the price of aluminum up by 120% between 1973 and February 1978, the price of bauxite recorded a 128% increase—this slightly greater increase for bauxite being due to increased royalties (fixed royalties). Finally, we note that although the cost of bauxite went from US $42.39/MT in 1970 to US $138.42/MT in February 1978, this US $96/MT increase caused, according to table 8-6, an increase of US 2.0¢/lb. of aluminum produced by an integrated plant and of US 4.5¢/lb. if bauxite was imported from Jamaica.

In 1971, the bauxite-alumina-aluminum industry was characterized by heavy vertical integration. In fact, the "six giants" (Alcan, Alcoa, Reynolds, Pechiney-Ugine-Kuhlmann, Kaiser and Alusuisse) controlled 57.3% of international bauxite production capacity and 70% of the alumina and aluminum production capacity. The control exercised by the six giants over bauxite mining has been modified by the majority shares held by Ghana (55% financial interest in the British Aluminium Co. subsidiary at Awaso) and Jamaica (51% financial interest in Revere Jamaica Alumina, Kaiser Jamaica Bauxite Co., and others); Guyana's nationalization of the Alcan and Reynolds mines; and the minority share (49%) of the Guinean government in the consortiums Friguia and Guinea Bauxite Company. In 1976 this control stood at no more than 48.3%, the various interventions having assured producing countries direct control over a production capacity of about 12 million MT.[11] Calculations using Metal Bulletin

Table 8-3

Bauxite and Aluminum Prices: 1960-1978

Year	Bauxite Price (US $/MT Guyana to Baltimore)	Aluminum Price (US ¢/lb. Canada to United Kingdom)
1960		23.30
1961		23.30
1962		22.60
1963		22.60
1964		23.90
1965	$ 32.20	24.50
1966	36.25	24.50
1967	42.00	24.50
1968	43.05	25.10
1969	42.39	26.70
1970	42.39	27.90
1971	49.53	28.40
1972	53.30	26.80
1973	60.68	27.20
1974	71.91	34.70
1975	105.31	39.40
1976	117.28	40.40
1977	134.82	51.90
1978	138.42[a]	59.70[a]
	138.42[b]	59.90[b]

Source: Derived from International Monetary Fund, *International Financial Statistics*, Washington, D.C., various issues.

[a]January.

[b]February.

statistical data allow us to conclude that the six giants' control of alumina production capacity went from 70% in 1971 to 58% in 1976; for aluminum, it stood at only 63%.[12] These modifications are not all the results of IBA's sustained action to encourage increased control of value-added activities by bauxite producing countries. They also reflect the entrance of some tenacious new competitors on the international aluminum market, such as: Amax, Anaconda, Martin Marietta, Noranda, Vereingte Aluminium Werke AG (VAW), Empresa Nacional del Aluminio S.A. (Endesa) and Ardal og Sunndal Verk (ASV).

Table 8-5 informs us that in 1975 identified bauxite reserves stood at about 17 billion long tons, 72% of which were in IBA countries. The Australian, Guinean and Jamaican reserves alone account for 60% of world reserves and 83% of IBA reserves. These are especially impressive data, if one considers that the identified reserves/production ratio stands at 230—much larger than those for nickel (72), copper (57), tin (46), lead (42) and zinc (24). The sum of

Table 8-4

Principal Bauxite, Alumina and Aluminum Producing Companies: 1971

(*percent of World Total*)

Bauxite	
1. Alcoa (United States)	16.5
2. Kaiser (United States)	15.6
3. Reynolds (United States)	10.4
4. Guybau (Guyana)	7.3
5. Alcan (Canada)	6.6
6. Conzinc Rio Tinto (Australia)	5.3
7. Pechiney-Ugine-Kuhlmann (France)	4.9
8. Billiton (Surinam)	4.9
9. Alusuisse (Switzerland)	3.3
	74.8

Alumina	
1. Alcoa (United States)	20.6
2. Alcan (Canada)	14.2
3. Kaiser (United States)	11.7
4. Reynolds (United States)	10.6
5. Pechiney-Ugine-Kuhlmann (France)	10.0
6. Sumitomo (Japan)	3.3
7. VAW (West Germany)	3.2
8. Alusuisse (Switzerland)	3.1
	76.5

Aluminum	
1. Alcoa (United States)	19.0
2. Alcan (Canada)	17.0
3. Reynolds (United States)	11.0
4. Pechiney-Ugine-Kuhlmann (France)	9.6
5. Kaiser (United States)	8.0
6. Alusuisse (Switzerland)	5.0
7. VAW (West Germany)	2.4
8. Showa Denko (Japan)	2.1
9. Anaconda (United States)	1.2
	75.3

Source: H. Nicolas, "L'aluminium," *La Revue Economique de la Banque Nationale de Paris,* No 33, January 1975, p. 7. Reprinted with permission.

hypothetical and identified reserves varies between 25 and 35 billion long tons while nonbauxite resources with a variable alumina content are not only located in industrial aluminum producing countries but are also almost inexhaustible. Size of reserves may limit, in the short and medium-term, the IBA's action; for even if only 28% are situated in nonmember countries this would suffice to

Table 8-5
Identified Bauxite Reserves: 1975

Country	million LT	percent of world reserves
Australia	4,590	27.0
Guinea	4,590	27.0
Jamaica	1,020	6.0
Greece	680	4.0
Countries with centrally planned economies	680	4.0
Surinam	510	3.0
Indonesia	510	3.0
Ghana	340	2.0
Yugoslavia	255	1.5
Guyana	220	1.3
India	135	0.8
Sierra Leone	125	0.8
Dominican Republic	70	0.4
United States	50	0.3
Haiti	35	0.2
World reserves (I)	17,000	100.0
IBA reserves (II)	12,265	72.2
Reserves of non-IBA Countries (III)	4,735	27.8
World Production, 1976 (IV)	74	
Ratio I/IV	230	
Ratio II/IV	166	
Ratio III/IV	64	

Source: Derived from British-North American Committee, *Mineral Development in the Eighties: Prospects and Problems,* British-North American Research Association, National Planning Association, C.D. Howe Research Institute, London-Washington-Montreal, 1976, p. 36; Clarfield, K.W. et al. *Eight Mineral Cartels: the New Challenge to Industrialized Nations,* Metals Week, McGraw-Hill Publications Company. 1975, p. 129.

supply alumina plants for another sixty-four years at the 1976 production rate. Its action is also hobbled by the possibility Australia might withdraw from the association or else refuse to agree to the establishment of a common price; by the concentration of exploration investments in nonmember countries such as Brazil and, finally, in the long run, by recourse to nonbauxite sources of alumina.

In order to better evaluate IBA's past effects and future prospects, we will take a closer look at this industry's structure of production costs by studying the operating costs for a new integrated primary aluminum 150,000-ton plant working at 100% capacity. Table 8-6 shows that aluminum production is capital-intensive since between 1970 and 1977 costs related to depreciation and interest payments represented, on the average, 17% of total costs.[13] The average cost of transforming bauxite into alumina (20.2%) is on a level with capital

Table 8-6

Operating Cost of a New Integrated Primary Aluminum Plant at 100 Percent Capacity

(*totals cumulative*)

	1970		1977 (estimate)	
	US¢/lb.	*Percent of total*	*US¢/lb.*	*Percent of total*
Bauxite	0.85	4.1	2.93[c]	7.7
Value added	2.92	14.1	10.05	26.3
Total alumina cost (1.93 tons)	3.77	18.2	12.98	34.0
Power cost (6.8 kwh/lb.)	2.72[a]	13.1	8.16[b]	21.3
Raw materials (carbon of anodes, fluorspar, fuel oil, etc.	5.00	24.2	4.50	11.8
Labor	2.00	9.7	3.48	9.1
Total direct metal costs	13.49	65.2	29.12	76.2
Selling and administrative costs	3.00	14.5	2.00	5.2
Capital cost (depreciation, interest expense)	3.96	19.1	5.72	14.9
Transportation	0.25	1.2	1.40	3.7
Total cost	20.70	100.0	38.24	100.0

Source: The cost structure estimate for 1977 is from Oppenheimer & Co., *Aluminum Industry Report: Mid-Year Survey of Free World Primary Aluminum Capacity: 1974-1979*, Metals Review, New York, September 1974, p. 21. Reprinted with permission. The cost structure for 1970 is derived from Oppenheimer & Co., *Aluminum Industry Report: Mid-Year Survey of Free World Primary Aluminum Cpaacity: 1969-1974*, Metals Review, New York, July 1970, pp. 5-6.

Note: 150,000-ton plant; assumes 20 years life; 20% scrap value; 5% per year depreciation.

[a]Implies 4.0 m/k, the unit cost of power per kilowatt/hour in .001¢.

[b]Implies 12.0 m/k, the unit cost of power per kilowatt/hour in .001¢.

[c]Because of the variable production levy, the same bauxite would have cost 5.32¢ if imported from Jamaica, or 14% of the price of aluminum.

costs. The aluminum industry is also characterized by heavy energy consumption since in 1977 power cost represented about 21% of total costs.[14] Other important production factors include: raw materials such as carbon of anodes, fluorspar, fuel oil, and other requisites (18%); selling and administrative costs (10%); labor (an average of 9.4% of total cost, a percentage roughly comparable to that of most nonferrous metals); bauxite (6%); and transport costs (2.5%).

Between 1970 and 1977, this cost structure underwent a change. Capital cost increased 44%, going from US 3.96¢/lb. to US 5.72¢/lb. and it now accounts for about 15% of total cost.[15] The increase in production taxes and other input costs pushed bauxite unit cost from US 0.85¢/lb. to US 2.93¢/lb., thus accounting for 7.7% of total costs, a percentage almost equal to that for labor. (The bauxite imported from Jamaica is estimated to cost, in 1977,

Table 8-7
Distribution of Primary Aluminum Production by Country and Energy Source
(*thousands MT*)

	Hydroelectric Energy		Coal		Petroleum		Natural Gas		Nuclear Energy		Other		Present and Planned Primary Aluminum Production	
	1974	1980	1974	1980	1974	1980	1974	1980	1974	1980	1974	1980	1974	1980
Germany	75	74	461	533	44ᵃ	49ᵃ			109	164			689	820
France	98	112	43	47	90	99	146	142	12	26	4	4	393	430
Italy	81	74			131	198		48					212	320
Holland													252	
United Kingdom	33	38	103	120					157	208			293	366
Austria													92	
Spain													181	
Greece													147	
Iceland													70	
Norway	649	700											649	700
Sweden													83	
Switzerland	69	72			15	4			3	14			87	90
Turkey	.7	20	.7	40	.8	1							2	61
Canada	1,030	1,107											1,030	1,107
United States	1,681	1,751	1,633	1,946	102	243	912	730	120	195			4,448	4,865
Japan	150		76		795		97						1,118	
Australia	89	131	130	204									219	335
New Zealand													100	
Yugoslavia													147	

Source: Organization for Economic Cooperation and Development, *Industrial Adaptation in the Primary Aluminum Industry*. Paris, 1976, p. 13. Reprinted with permission.

ᵃPetroleum and natural gas

Table 8-8

Interarea Seaborne Trade in Bauxite (B) and Alumina (A): 1974 (million MT)

| | From | | | | | | | | | | | | | | | |
| Toward: | West Indies | | South America | | West Africa | | Asia | | Australia | | Southern Europe | | Others | | World Total | |
	B	A	B	A	B	A	B	A	B	A	B	A	B	A	B	A
North America	9.3	1.01	5.25	0.48	3.42	—	0.04	—	—	2.43	—	—	—	0.12	18.01	4.03
United States	9.3	0.82	3.62	0.44	2.08	—	—	—	—	2.00	—	—	—	0.02	15.00	3.27
Canada	—	0.19	1.63	0.04	1.34	—	0.04	—	—	0.43	—	—	—	0.10	3.01	0.76
Europe	—	1.76	0.39	0.77	1.31	0.35	0.03	—	4.36	0.29	2.99	0.58	0.04	0.18	9.13	3.92
Scandinavia	—	0.96	—	0.34	—	0.15	—	—	—	0.13	0.07	—	—	—	0.07	1.57
Other Western Europe	—	0.55	0.38	0.35	1.31	0.20	0.03	—	4.17	0.16	1.07	0.44	0.04	0.18	7.01	1.88
Eastern Europe	—	0.25	0.01	0.08	—	—	—	—	0.19	—	1.85	0.14	—	—	2.05	0.47
Asia	—	0.09	0.06	0.06	—	—	2.16	0.05	3.16	1.20	0.01	—	—	0.08	5.38	1.49
Japan	—	—	0.06	—	—	—	2.09	—	3.16	0.63	0.01	—	—	—	5.31	0.64
Other Asia	—	0.09	—	0.06	—	—	0.07	0.05	—	0.57	—	—	—	0.08	0.07	0.85
Others	—	0.25	—	0.09	—	0.17	—	—	—	—	—	—	—	0.10	—	0.60
World	9.30	3.11	5.70	1.38	4.73	0.52	2.23	0.05	7.52	3.92	3.00	0.58	0.04	0.48	32.52	10.04

Source: H.P. Drewry (shipping consultants) Ltd, *Ocean Shipping of Bauxite and Alumina*. no. 43, London, March 1976, pp. 29 and 40. Reprinted with permission.

US 5.32¢/lb. of aluminum or 14% of total cost.) The costs related to alumina production and electricity increased by 244% and 200%, respectively. From this information we are convinced that the fiscal reform undertaken individually by most of the IBA countries does not represent the major cause for the 85% aluminum price increase observed between 1970 and 1977. Rather, there was coincidence between the creation of this body and a period when the aluminum industry was feeling the consequences of a set of structural changes such as sustained growth of energy (and consequently transportation) costs; alumina production and capital cost increase; search for new environmental protection norms, and the like. However, the fear of more severe variable levies on bauxite production and exportation has strongly encouraged the search for substitutes. The tangible results of this research will come at the beginning of the eighties and may have a long-term effect on the growth rate of export receipts for IBA countries. The vice-president of Kaiser Aluminum and Chemical Corporation assesses the situation thus:

> In the area of raw material, we are likely to see continued emphasis on changing the traditional method of producing alumina. If recently adopted bauxite production taxes and levies become more severe, the potential cost of alumina must also increase, a trend which would tend to minimise some of bauxite's natural advantages. There is no shortage of bauxite, but, as noted previously, it seems likely that new mines will become more remote and possibly of lower quality than current reserves. The combination will obviously increase the cost of alumina production.
>
> These concerns have prompted an active search for a new domestic raw material source for the industry. Since the USA has very little bauxite, most of the materials under consideration are non-bauxite in nature. A number of materials and processes are currently being evaluated under a project being jointly sponsored by government and industry and coordinated by the US Bureau of Mines. The present phase of this work is concentrating on selecting the most competitive domestic ores and processes from among the many alternatives available. The ores have been identified and process technology and overall economics are currently under study. This work will proceed to the feasibility study stage, and ultimately on through construction and operation of a demonstration facility. It seems both possible and practical for this work to reach a successful conclusion during the early 1980s.
>
> In Europe, Pechiney, working in conjunction with Alcan, recently began operating a 20-tpd plant near Marseilles which produces alumina from clays and shales.
>
> Even with successful completion of the work on non-bauxite ore, however, it still seems unlikely that existing facilities could be modified to use a substitute raw material. Nor, in view of the industry's capital-intensive nature, is it likely that existing plants would be

replaced. Rather, it is more likely that domestic ores will be used as a basis for a portion of future expansion needs. . . .

In summary then, although bauxite will continue to serve as a major source for alumina, work will continue on non-bauxite ores, and it seems probable that an alternative ore process will be proven during the 1980s. However, because the industry is unlikely to concentrate all its resources on a new ore process, the portion of the world's alumina produced from non-bauxite materials will grow slowly at first, accelerating as the industry gains confidence or as bauxite levies are increased.[16]

What are the consequences of increased energy costs? The importance of this factor of production will increasingly favor the transformation of raw materials in countries with abundant and cheap hydro- , thermo- and petroelectric resources. This new structural change which will be affecting the international aluminum industry during the next few years is well illustrated by the location (and planned location) of smelting facilities in countries "rich in energy" and "poor in bauxite", such as: Abu Dhabi (300,000 MT primary aluminum capacity foreseen for 1980); Algeria (127,000 MT), Bahrain (120,000 MT); Brazil (170,000 MT in 1976 and between 500,000 and 730,000 MT at the beginning of the 1980s); Canada (production capacity is expected to increase from 1.06 million MT to 1.9 million MT during the eighties); Dubai (planned 135,000 MT capacity); Iran (45,000 MT); Iraq (150,000 MT); Kuwait; Libya; Mexico (70,000 MT); Norway (683,000 MT); Qatar; Saudi Arabia (200,000 MT planned for beginning of next decade) and Venezuela (120,000 MT).[17] This trend also shows that IBA member countries will no longer be alone in wanting high value-added plants installed on their domestic markets. The staff of the IBA Secretariat is very aware of the impact of these new developments.

In these cases, the inflow of foreign capital to develop the downstream industries is related to the availability of cheaper energy, coupled with less stringent environmental protection requirements than those prevailing in the developed world. These factors, and especially the energy component, will be the major determinants as to whether the IBA members will, in fact, make a significant impact on the market at a tertiary production level.[18]

In closing we may point out that the energy crisis will have no uniform effect on the distribution by country of primary aluminum production. Table 8-7 in fact illustrates that the aluminum industry depends less on petroelectric than hydroelectric energy and that the crisis will be an added motivation for the industry to maintain and improve the use of hydroelectric power. In 1974, more than 39% of world aluminum production was carried out using hydroelectric power; percentages for other energy sources stood at 24% for coal, 11.5% for petroleum, 11.3% for natural gas and 4% for nuclear energy. Data available for planned primary aluminum production by energy source show that, in the 1980s, hydroelectric energy and coal will have even greater importance.[19]

Regarding international trade in bauxite and alumina, table 8-8 shows that the West Indies (9.3 million MT or their total exports) represent the major supplier for the North American market, followed by South America (5.25 million MT) and West Africa (3.42 million MT). This dependence is explained by the quality of bauxite produced (trihydrated bauxite or a mixture of mono- and trihydrated) which requires treatment by the American Bayer process. The North American market shows up as the major importer of African bauxite, while Australia and Southern Europe ship all their bauxite exports toward European and Asian markets. Interzone alumina shipments are less subject to technological constraints and therefore reflect greater market diversification. So it is that the West Indies export more alumina toward Europe than toward North America, while the reverse is true for Australia. Unlike bauxite, the alumina produced in South America and West Africa is mainly sent to European markets.

The 1985 estimates for international trade in bauxite and alumina indicate a very strong growth in international alumina shipments, a relatively slow growth in bauxite shipments and a serious decline in the West Indies' and, to a lower degree, South America's share in the international trade of these two products.[20] The nationalizations, share holdings and joint ventures imposed by the governments of bauxite producing countries; the new locations of aluminum plants due to transportation costs and the energy crisis, and IBA's potential policies impact—these are the main variables explaining the changes foreseen.

Such is our view of the principal characteristics of the international bauxite-alumina-aluminum industry. They lead us to conclude that, despite the lack of common action by IBA members,[21] the interventions carried out individually by most member countries did have the following successes: increase of bauxite prices and government receipts; acceleration of the installation on domestic markets of high value-added operations such as the transformation of ore into alumina (movement begun in the first part of the sixties); an increasing percentage of control over alumina production capacity; and the development of transportation for bauxite and alumina. All of this was made possible by the comparative advantages held by these countries over other sources of supply. The IBA Secretariat is very aware of these advantages and views the future optimistically.

> Furthermore, IBA members still hold the key of being able to exert the greatest influence on the way the market develops by virtue of their combined productive and negotiating strength, the already existing investments made in plants and infrastructure within those countries which have a significant cost advantage over greenfield ventures, the greatest ease with which mining can be done in many of these countries and the strategic geographic position with respect to major markets that many countries in the group enjoy....

Overall, it may be reasonably expected that 1974 production levels will be once again attained by 1977, with continued growth up to 1980. Although some non-IBA members will increase their production over this period, it is not expected that IBA members will suffer any serious setbacks on the market as a result. The truth is that the new capital needed to be invested in new regions in order to make serious impressions on IBA's trading strength will just not be available. Furthermore, IBA countries are still and will continue to be for a long time the most economical locations in which to mine bauxite.[22]

Although we believe that IBA countries will go on enjoying their successes for a few more years, we do not share the optimism of Brown and Cornish concerning the length of time they may continue, at least for certain members. As a matter of fact, our analysis has shown adverse factors. The bauxite produced in the West Indies, Guyana and Surinam accounted for only 24% of world production in 1976 (21% for the first half of 1977) compared to 33% in 1974; in Jamaica and Surinam this production has fallen by 33%. Although only 28% of identified bauxite reserves are located in nonmember countries, these are sufficient to feed alumina plants for another sixty years or so at 1976 production rates. The increase in bauxite prices (or the fear of more severe levies) has encouraged the search for substitutes and there will be tangible results toward the beginning of the eighties. The importance of energy costs will increasingly favor the refining of raw materials in countries where electric power is cheap and plentiful (not true of all IBA members). A marked decline in the West Indian and, to a lower degree, South American share in international bauxite and alumina trade is foreseen. There is no assurance that Australia, the world's largest bauxite producer, will remain a member of this organization or conform to the policies suggested by smaller and more interventionist countries. The IBA Secretariat does not accord enough attention to these elements in its evaluation of this association's future. It enumerates the successes obtained by the IBA as a whole without mentioning the future price certain members will perhaps have to pay.

Notes

1. Although there are several types of bauxite, they can be divided into three distinct groups, corresponding to three types of technological treatment: monohydrated bauxite found in France, Hungary, Italy, Yugoslavia, Greece, Turkey, and the Soviet Union (treated with the European Bayer process); trihydrated bauxite found in Guyana, Surinam, Guinea, Ghana, Sierra Leone, and Australia, (treated with the American Bayer process) and bauxite characterized by a mixture of the two types found in Jamaica, Haiti, and the Dominican Republic (treated with a combination of the two processes).

2. The classic Bayer process contains the following phases: grinding of

bauxite (at this stage the ore is treated with soda); digestion (depending on the plant, pressure may vary from 1 to 40 atmospheres and temperature from 100° to 290°C); dilution of solution after digestion; separation of red mud residue by settling, washing and filtration; clarification of saturated solution by filtration; cooling and crystallization in the presence of "seed"; calcination of alumina at 1100° − 1200°C.

The differences in quality of bauxite have led to a certain number of variations in the use of the Bayer process. Thus, we find the American Bayer process, adapted to the treatment of trihydrated bauxite and suitable for bauxites containing a certain percentage of silica in the form of quartz. Although this process requires a weak concentration of calcified soda, relatively low temperatures (100° − 150°C) and, since it deals with a simpler material, investments less than those required for other processes, it also has its disadvantages. These have to do with the fact that pure trihydrated bauxite reserves are limited and that, depending on the ore's levels of monohydrated bauxite, temperature and concentration must be increased and the material design adapted. The European Bayer process uses higher temperatures (180° − 250°C) and requires a heavier concentration of caustic soda. On the other hand, it is adaptable to both monohydrated and trihydrated bauxites, except that the latter must contain at least 10 to 15% monohydrated bauxite and be free of quartz. Moreover, it permits production of higher quality alumina and requires lower levels of energy consumption. Finally, it should be noted that four tons of bauxite produce a little less than two tons of alumina, which produces about a ton of aluminum.

3. Research in this field has been strongly stimulated by the energy crisis; the 1974 creation of the International Bauxite Association; the availability of low-grade bauxite; and the desire to use other ores containing alumina in countries without bauxite. This research has come up with methods of extracting alumina from clays and not bauxite (processes worth pointing out are the potassium-alumina process, the nitric acid process, the soda-lime sinter process and the sulphurous acid-sulphuric acid process) and has also found the means of producing aluminum directly (the Toth process). Although technically feasible, processes involving the production of alumina from clays have proved unprofitable and furnish lower quality output. As concerns the Toth process which involves the direct production of aluminum from raw materials, skipping the intermediate phase of alumina production, we note that although it considerably reduces capital costs, uses much less energy, and cuts out pollution by recycling inputs, aluminum companies have not yet adopted it for a certain number of technical and commercial reasons. The reader interested in further study of processes for producing aluminum from nonbauxite sources is referred to E.W. Greig, and M.J. Adams, "Non-bauxite sources of alumina," *World Aluminium Survey*, Metal Bulletin Ltd., London, 1977, pp. 73-82.

4. Kenneth W. Clarfield et al., *Eight Mineral Cartels,* p. 117. Reprinted with permission.

5. The Council of Ministers is IBA's highest body. Composed of a representative from each member country, its role consists of defining that association's general strategy and policy, approving its budget, studying the candidacies of possible members, naming the secretary-general, and the like. Important decisions (such as common price policy) require a unanimous vote while less important policies need only a two-thirds majority. The Executive Board proposes precise policies, coordinates members' interventions, studies budgets and supervises the secretariat's activities. The Secretariat is composed of a secretary-general nominated by the Council of Ministers (Mr. Henri Guda of Surinam was the first to hold this post) and of engineers, technicians, and economists. Its role is to collect and disseminate information concerning bauxite's supply and demand and the existence of agreements, commercial practices, and technological changes likely to influence the bauxite-alumina-aluminum industry on the international level.

6. If we suppose a list price of US $1,000 per short ton of aluminum (or US 50.0¢/lb.) and a levy percentage of 8%, the *VBPL* would then be: 0.08/4.3 ($1,000) = $18.60. By adding the fixed uniform royalty of $0.55, we obtain the total tax revenue collected by Jamaica on each long dry ton (LDT) of bauxite, in our example, US $19.15.

7. Following Jamaica's tax increases most of the other members of the IBA took similar action. Guyana recently passed new tax legislation featuring a production levy formula nearly identical to the Jamaican formula. The new law raises the tax rate per LDT of bauxite to equality with Jamaica's. Moreover, Guyana has nationalized the Guyanan subsidiaries of both Alcan and Reynolds and now controls 100 percent of its bauxite industry. In December 1974 "American Metal Market" reported that Surinam and the Dominican Republic had raised their bauxite export taxes to $10 per ton and that Haiti's tax was $9.33 per ton. The Dominican Republic apparently imposed production minimums but Surinam and Haiti did not. Finally, in 1975 Guinea imposed taxes of $6.49 per ton on bauxite exports and $8.60 per ton on alumina.

The only major bauxite and alumina exporting country that has not made major changes in its bauxite and alumina taxes since 1974 is Australia. The state of Queensland in Australia did raise its bauxite levy from $0.10 to $1.50 per ton and its tax on alumina exports to $0.50 per ton. However, the state of Western Australia has refused to make any change in its mining tax policies and its liberal premier, Court, has been outspokenly critical of the national government decision to join the IBA.

Quoted from Charles River Associates Inc., *Economic Issues Underlying Supply Access Agreements*, p. I-12. Reprinted with permission.

8. Information concerning the names of companies; present and forecasted ore, alumina and aluminum production; as well as property ties, was gathered from Metal Bulletin Ltd., *World Aluminium Survey*, 1977, pp. 93–123.

9. A Metals Week publication considers the economic and political philosophy of the Jamaican government as more pragmatic than that revealed for

Guyana. It explains that faced with a possible economic crisis caused by sky-rocketing oil prices, the Jamaican government undertook its fiscal reform to solve its immediate financial problems. Also, the government wanted to establish with the companies a new relationship which would put both of them on a more or less equal footing. The Metals Week publication adds that the Jamaican government never gave the impression that it would expropriate properties or put an embargo on bauxite exports. The interested reader is referred to Clarfield et al., *Eight Mineral Cartels*, p. 134.

10. Metal Bulletin Ltd, *World Aluminium Survey*, 1977, pp. 101-107.

11. Base data from Metal Bulletin Ltd., pp. 93-99.

12. Since 1971 the ranking of the largest aluminum companies in terms of production capacity has changed slightly. In the mid-seventies the ranking was: Alcan (17.0% of production capacity), Alcoa (15.4%), Reynolds (9.8%), Pechiney-Ugine-Kuhlmann (9.4%), Kaiser (8.3%) and Alusuisse (3.2%).

13. A classic plant requires a workshop to produce carbon anodes; alumina works for the electrolytic conversion of alumina; equipment to treat and re-cuperate fluorine and other gases; a foundry to pour metal aluminum; work-shops for maintaining equipment and machinery; administrative offices and, sometimes, even a hydroelectric or thermoelectric station. Purchase of such equipment involves enormous costs. Since they may vary from plant to plant it would be unrealistic and arbitrary to attempt to make an exact evaluation of capital cost per ton. The reader should consider percentages of table 8-6 to be very approximate.

14. Between 60 and 64% of total energy is consumed in converting the alumina to aluminum (Hall process), while the energy used to produce alumina (Bayer process) represents 16-20% of total energy. The mining, treatment and transportation of bauxite require 2% of energy consumed, while the manu-facture of finished products demands 12-15%. The interested reader is referred to "Conference on Energy Conservation and Recycling in the Aluminum In-dustry."

15. The increase of fixed capital cost is directly related to inflation (which more than doubled the construction costs of a new aluminum plant as compared with those of the sixties) and to the need for new antipollution equipment. It should be pointed out that smelting facilities are that part of the production process most heavily contributing to the increase of costs, representing a 50% increase between 1973 and 1975. For the same period, the fixed costs for power stations saw a 44% increase while those involved in alumina conversion rose 43%. There was less cost increase in the fixed capital required to mine bauxite, only 25%.

16. A.S. Hutchcraft, Jr., "Developments in Alumina: 1970-80", *World Aluminium Survey*, Metal Bulletin Ltd., 1977, pp. 25-27. Reprinted with per-mission.

17. Data from Metal Bulletin Ltd., *World Aluminium Survey*, 1977, pp. 109-123.

18. Garnet Brown and John Cornish, (IBA Secretariat), "Bauxite production and marketing", *World Aluminium Survey*, p. 16. Reprinted with permission.

19. The aluminum industry's efforts to reduce the importance of the energy factor resulted in a noticeable increase of productivity. While in 1939 aluminum production required 12 kwh/lb., today only 8 kwh/lb., and in some cases only 6.5 kwh/lb. are needed. This industry has therefore justly deserved an honorable mention in the field of energy conservation. The reader more particularly interested in these questions is referred to Organization for Economic Cooperation and Development, *Industrial Adaptation in the Primary Aluminum Industry*.

20. H.P. Drewry (Shipping Consultants) Ltd. *Ocean Shipping of Bauxite and Alumina*, pp. 57-58.

21. The December 1977 announcement of a minimum c.i.f. price of US $24.00/ton of bauxite for the North American market represents a policy with very minimal short-term effects. Major suppliers of this market charged prices far higher than the one announced.

22. Brown and Cornish, (IBA Secretariat), "Bauxite Production and Marketing," *World Aluminium Survey*, pp. 19-20. Reprinted with permission.

AIEC and the International Iron Ore Market

Iron ore, with identified reserves estimated at more than 260 billion long tons, is reputed to be one of the most abundant elements in the earth's crust. Although iron is found in various quantities and qualities in most countries, it is the iron oxides which are the most economically suitable for extraction. International demand thus proves especially strong for oxides such as magnetite (72.4% iron content), hematite (69.9% iron content) and limonite (62% iron content).

Before the second world war, there was little world trade in iron ore. The availability of resources in most industrialized countries and the high cost of transporting the ore meant that scarcely 15% of world production entered into world trade. Moreover, since extraction of this ore was characterized by high capital intensity, prospecting investments were mainly concentrated in the U.S., Western Europe and the USSR. The second world conflict completely altered this situation. In fact, in industrialized countries, demand was strongly stimulated by the need to reconstruct economic infrastructures destroyed in the war and the search for new mineral resources to produce goods related to those industries (automobile, aeronautic, electronic, and so on) which had most benefited from the technological development stimulated by the war effort. Also, the highly intensive nature of the capital needed to transform iron ore into cast iron and steel, was calling for large-scale production and therefore long-term adequate supplies to secure the profitability of the enormous investments.

From 1945 on, the iron reserves of industrialized countries, considered adequate on the basis of prewar production, became clearly insufficient to respond to projected demand. International trade was also stimulated by the availability in developing countries of deposits rich in iron content. Through economies of scale, the maritime transport of immense tonnages of ore from these countries counterbalanced the higher costs occasioned by their distance from the main centers of world steel production.

Thus, the percentage of world iron ore production involved in international trade went from 17% in 1950 to 55% in 1974. It is estimated that this percentage will increase to 70% between now and 1985. A report from the Department of Energy, Mines and Resources (Canada) gives the following summary of the reasons responsible for such a development.

While annual growth in iron ore production has been about four per cent over the past 15 years (from 1960 to 1974), world iron ore trade has been increasing at an annual rate of about seven per cent. This strong growth in iron ore trade has been, in part, carried by:

the rising world demand for steel from 270 million net tons in 1955 to 710 million tons in 1974, to an International Iron and Steel Institute (IISI) projected 939 million tons in 1980;

the exploitability of ore deposits with higher iron content (the average grade of ores entering international trade was 51 per cent Fe in 1950, 53 per cent in 1960 and an estimated 59 per cent in 1975), which are remote from the main centres of world steel production (the index denoting average distance of sea transport of iron ore has risen from 100 in 1960 to 133 in 1965 and 185 in 1973);

the economies of scale in ocean transportation through availability of larger ore carriers;

the emergence of Japan as one of the world's principal steel producers and its almost total dependence on imported iron ore (19 million metric tons of ore imported in 1964, 135 million tons in 1973);

the depletion of some of the traditional European ore deposits, as well as the high cost of processing many existing low quality European ores;

the improvement in blast furnace technology, the effectiveness of which depends on high quality feedstock in terms of high Fe content and improved physical and chemical characteristics;

and the technological achievements in the beneficiation of certain lower grade ores, notably taconites.[1]

Faced with this unprecedented growth of iron ore demand in the industrialized countries, Western steel companies began developing (at the beginning of the fifties) production centers in Brazil, Chile, Liberia, Mauritania, Peru, Venezuela, and elsewhere, to assure themselves long-term iron ore supplies. They were provided this assurance through signing long-term contracts of guarantee for large tonnages with developing countries; by vertical integration of mines or the f.o.b. purchase of iron ore, allowing for capitalization on maritime transport economies. Although the rush to discover new deposits provoked a noticeable price rise in the beginning of the fifties, this situation favorable to producing countries was not long-lasting. Even before the beginning of the sixties the international iron ore market was characterized by excess supply and sliding prices. In fact, the 1952 price of Brazilian iron ore (US $22.30/MT) was exceeded only in 1957 (US $22.45/MT) and 1975 (US $22.80/MT).

Given the continual fall in their export receipts, some Third World producing countries tried to form an association to help member countries receive "fair and remunerative" returns from the mining, processing and marketing of iron ore. A first meeting was held at Caracas in August-September 1968. At this meeting, representatives from Algeria, Brazil, Chile, Gabon, India, Liberia, Mauritania, Peru, the Philippines, and Venezuela discussed the problem of low prices, excess iron ore supplies, and solutions capable of correcting what was judged an unjust situation. Even if no concrete decision was taken by the "Caracas group," their deliberations opened the way to establishing the Association of Iron Ore Exporting Countries (AIEC) seven years later. The countries mentioned held a second meeting in Geneva in 1969. This was the year in which the United Nations suggested to the United Nations Conference on Trade and Development (UNCTAD) that it harmonize the efforts of these countries in their search for correctives to the situation of excess supply characterizing the international iron ore market. In order to promote an international agreement on this ore, UNCTAD called an ad hoc meeting (bringing together twenty-five producing and consuming countries) in January 1970. Although it was decided at this meeting to gather statistical and technical information on the production and marketing of iron ore, there was total disagreement between producing countries (wishing to improve profit margins on exported ore) and consuming countries (clearly preferring the status quo). UNCTAD organized a second meeting on February 24-25, 1972. As the position of the two parties proved irreconcilable, some of the producing countries decided to form an association independent of the United Nations. This association (from which consuming countries would be absent) would see to it that the producing countries' interests in the industry of iron ore were safeguarded. The group, composed mainly of developing countries, met on February 20-23, 1973. After requesting that experts from all large iron ore-producing countries meet in order to consider possible solutions to the market's problems, they invited Australia, Canada, and Sweden to join the group as full members or participating observers. The three industrial countries having preferred observer status, no fewer than nineteen exporting countries were invited to meet at Geneva in November 1974 to study a proposal (prepared mainly by Algeria, India, and Venezuela[2]) aimed at setting up an Association of Iron Ore Exporting Countries. Australia, Brazil, and Canada would reject the proposal, declaring that although iron ore prices did not follow the evolution shown by coal and steel, the interests of consuming countries had to be represented on the same footing as those of exporting countries. Given the importance of these three countries in world iron ore trade, the proposal was withdrawn and a committee was charged with reformulating it so as to make it acceptable to all parties present. (The idea was then conceived of a system of periodic consultations with consuming countries concerning their steel mill expansion programs and the fixing of prices for iron ore, other inputs, and steel). The committee met in January 1975 in New Delhi and worked out a text to be submitted to a ministerial meeting planned for April of the same year.

The proposal was accepted by the following countries: Algeria, Australia, Chile, India, Mauritania, Peru, Sierra Leone, Sweden, Tunisia, and Venezuela.

Liberia and the Philippines refused to make an immediate commitment, while Canada declared that it would not sign the agreement so long as consuming countries could not become association members. Canada also indicated its clear preference for a solution to trade problems on the basis of cooperation between producers and consumers. Although Australia did become a member of the AIEC, it warned the other signatories of its opposition to all attempts to control production and exportation. Finally, Brazil refused membership in the group for fear of compromising the very ambitious expansion plans projected for its iron mines and which were to be financed with funds from consuming countries such as the United States, the United Kingdom, and Japan.

What are the objectives of the AIEC which in 1977 counted a total of eleven members (Algeria, Australia, Chile, India, Liberia, Mauritania, Peru, Sierra Leone, Sweden, Tunisia, and Venezuela)? The major objectives of the association are:

> to promote close cooperation among member countries with a view of safeguarding their interests in relation to the iron ore export industry;
>
> to ensure an orderly and healthy growth of the export trade in iron ore;
>
> to assist member countries to secure fair and remunerative returns from the exploitation, processing and marketing of iron ore with a view to improving their export earnings and terms of trade;
>
> to contribute to the economic and social development of the member countries and in particular to encourage further processing of iron ore in member countries including iron and steel; and
>
> to provide a forum for the exchange of information and effective and meaningful consultations on problems relating to the iron ore export industry with a view to enabling member countries to take appropriate action.[3]

Although these seem to us very praiseworthy objectives, the means chosen by AIEC to attain them have proven very limited.[4]

> Under the draft charter, AIEC will not take collective actions or impose directives upon its members. Independent governmental decisions, presumably taking into account AIEC advice, will be the key. AIEC will not fix iron ore floor prices, export quotas or maintain buffer stocks.
>
> The preparatory committee has noted that AIEC would not really be capable of setting prices because of widespread variances in the physical and chemical characteristics of ores as well as differences in freight and port conditions.[5]

We thus notice that AIEC does not represent a true cartel since it does not wish to control (nor can it control) prices by restricting production and world trade. Also, its charter foresees no mechanism permitting the unilateral imposition of collective decisions on its members.[6] This association wishes essentially to be a center for the diffusion of the economic and technical information capable of helping member countries make investments in the local iron ore industry or negotiate export contracts more successfully.

How can AIEC's inability to hold a more effective role in international iron ore trade be explained? What are this market's economic characteristics and to what extent do they limit the effects of all interventionist action (whether brought to bear by AIEC or other international institutions) on iron ore prices, production and trade? Tables 9-1 through 9-8 provide some elements of the response to these questions.

A large number of prices exist for iron ore traded on the international level; each price reflects the ore's specific content and the distance separating the producing from the consuming country. Table 9-1 presents us with the evolution (between 1950 and 1977) of three of the market's most representative prices: the price of Brazilian ore (average iron content 68%) including transportation costs, insurance, and freight to North Sea ports; the domestic/export price of American ore (average content 51.5%) shipped out by Great Lakes ports and the price of Swedish ore, c.i.f. Rotterdam. Despite their difference in level, these prices all peaked in 1957, afterward to show a continual decline and drop to their lowest postwar level in 1969. Although the seventies permitted a certain recovery for iron ore prices, Brazilian and Swedish 1977 prices remained below those recorded in 1957.

What about steel prices? The evolution of steel prices is clearly distinguishable from that shown by its input. In fact, despite a few slight cyclical slumps, steel prices have continually increased since mid-century, 1977 American and German prices showing respective increases of 262% and 491% compared with those of 1950. These divergencies in growth rates and the mediocre performance of iron ore prices explain in large part the legitimate concerns of producing countries (especially developing ones). These countries, faced with a marked deterioration of their terms of trade, held a first meeting in Caracas in 1968 to discuss the means to be used in correcting such a situation. Tables 9-2 to 9-8 attempt to explain the depressed state of this market and the reasons why all attempts at intervention seem doomed to failure.

World production has responded very well to the increase in iron ore demand which took place after the second world war, growing by 390% between 1948 and 1974 (an annual 15% growth rate).[7] This production increase was mostly concentrated in countries which did not appear on the 1948 list of leading producers. While American, French, English, and German production

Table 9-1

Price Evolution of Iron Ore and Steel: 1950-1978

Year	Brazilian Iron Ore[a] (US$/MT)	U.S. Iron Ore[b] (US$/LT)	Swedish Iron Ore[c] (US$/MT)	U.S. Steel[d] (US$/MT)	German Steel[e] (US$/MT)
1950	–	10.4	–	89.1	54.1
1951	–	11.0	–	93.0	66.7
1952	22.30	11.0	–	95.0	91.7
1953	20.05	11.4	–	100.8	95.5
1954	17.10	10.3	12.3	103.4	92.1
1955	18.20	10.5	13.0	105.2	93.3
1956	21.36	10.4	14.4	111.8	95.7
1957	22.45	11.6	15.1	120.2	100.2
1958	21.48	11.6	14.5	125.0	104.3
1959	17.08	11.6	11.5	127.0	104.3
1960	17.08	11.6	11.5	126.8	104.3
1961	17.79	11.6	11.5	119.7	108.2
1962	16.75	10.9	10.8	118.6	109.5
1963	15.69	10.8	10.1	119.9	109.5
1964	15.69	10.6	10.1	124.1	109.5
1965	15.69	10.6	10.1	124.1	107.3
1966	15.25	10.6	9.9	124.1	109.3
1967	13.50	10.6	8.7	124.1	102.0
1968	12.63	10.6	8.4	130.5	94.5
1969	11.68	10.6	8.4	141.5	100.5
1970	15.22	10.8	9.3	151.9	124.9
1971	13.46	11.2	10.5	n.a.	137.1
1972	12.79	11.2	10.8	179.7	157.4
1973	17.13	11.8	10.1	187.2	207.9
1974	18.97	13.9	12.8	255.5	250.0
1975	22.80	17.8	19.3	290.1	300.8
1976	22.00	19.4	16.1	295.7	329.5
1977	21.67	20.9	13.4	322.6	320.0
1978	22.80[f]	–	12.6[f]	352.9[f]	376.7[f]

Sources: Derived from International Monetary Fund, *International Financial Statistics,* vol. XXX, no. 5, and vol. XXXI, no. 2, Washington, May 1977 and February 1978; United Nations, *Statistical Yearbook,* New York, various issues; World Bank, *Commodity Trade and Price Trends (1978 edition),* Report No EC-166/78, Washington, August 1978, pp. 108-109 and 114-115.

[a]Brazilian 65%, c.i.f. North Sea ports; before 1975, Brazilian 68%.

[b]Domestic/Export Price delivered lower lake ports Mesabi, regular-unscreened; before 1964, Domestic/Export Price delivered lower lake ports, Mesabi Bessemer with 51.5% iron.

[c]Kiruna D, c.i.f. Rotterdam.

[d]Carbon plates, f.o.b. at most midwestern points; before 1972, export price f.o.b. Pittsburgh, hot rolled plates.

[e]Bessemer Bars, Domestic/Export Price, delivered Oberhausen basis.

[f]January to June 1978.

Table 9-2
World Production of Iron Ore (Fe Content): Selected Years
(*million MT*)

Country	1948	1960	1970	1974	1976
South Africa	0.70	1.96	5.89	7.22	9.80
Algeria[a]	1.02	1.79	1.55	2.06	1.73[b]
Angola	–	0.41	3.75	3.10	3.50[b]
Australia[a]	1.36	2.86	28.68	57.80	59.31
Brazil	1.07	6.35	24.74	41.21	45.62
Canada[c]	1.46	10.75	29.19	29.13	34.17
Chile[a]	1.68	3.80	6.94	6.36	6.33
China	n.a.	30.25	24.00	34.50	n.a.
Korea, Democratic Peoples' Republic	n.a.	n.a.	4.01	3.76	n.a.
Spain	0.77	2.80	3.51	4.56	3.80
United States[e]	50.89	47.87	53.31	51.13	49.13
France	7.56	21.74	17.76	16.71	13.55
India[a]	1.49	10.13	19.65	22.10	26.87
Japan	0.30	1.57	0.92	0.44	0.41
Liberia[a]	–	2.19	15.81	24.46	18.47[b]
Malaysia[d]	–	3.21	2.52	0.27	0.17
Mauritania[a]	–	–	5.92	7.58	5.65[b]
Mexico	0.23	0.52	2.61	3.34	3.65
Norway	0.13	1.06	2.62	2.55	2.55
Peru[a]	–	3.95	7.93	6.20	4.58[b]
Philippines	0.01	0.64	1.17	1.00	0.84
German Federal Republic	1.79	4.56	1.77	1.41	0.72
United Kingdom	3.99	4.69	3.37	0.94	1.19
Sierra Leone[a]	0.57	0.88	1.38	1.50	0.87[b]
Swaziland	–	–	1.50	1.31	1.22
Sweden[a]	8.20	13.01	19.80	22.86	19.08
Tunisia[a]	0.38	0.56	0.42	0.43	0.26
Turkey	0.12	0.44	1.66	1.27	1.93
USSR	16.23	61.42	106.06	123.16	143.40
(Ukraine)	(7.05)	(34.26)	(60.74)	(67.23)	n.a.
Venezuela[a]	–	12.47	14.08	16.71	15.43[b]
Yugoslavia	0.31	0.79	1.30	1.81	1.49
AIEC (*I*)	14.70	51.64	122.16	168.06	158.58
World (*II*)	103.50	262.45	424.10	507.50	n.a.
Non-communist world (*III*)	87.27	170.78	290.03	346.08	–
I/II (percent)	14.20	19.67	28.80	33.11	–
I/III (percent)	16.84	30.24	42.12	48.56	–

Source: Derived from United Nations, *Statistical Yearbook*, New York, various issues.

Note: Data usually refer to iron contained in extracted marketable ore, including manganiferous ore but not pyrites. These data are very broad estimates obtained by applying a fixed percentage to raw ore production.

[a]Members of the Association of Iron Ore Exporting Countries (AIEC).

[b]Data corresponding to 1975 production.

[c]Shipments from mines.

[d]These data refer only to western Malaysia.

[e]Shipments of useable iron ore, not including manganiferous iron ore containing 5% or more of manganese.

Table 9-3
Crude Steel Production (P) and Apparent Consumption (C) Expressed in Crude Steel Equivalents: Selected Years
(million MT)

	1948	1950-52	1960		1970		1974		1976
	P	C	P	C	P	C	P	C	P
South Africa	.6	1.5	2.1	2.2	4.7	4.8	5.8	6.5	—
Algeria[a]	—	.2	—	.6	—	.7	.2	1.5	—
Argentina	.1	1.0	.3	1.6	1.9	3.3	2.2	4.2	2.4
Australia[a]	1.2	2.3	3.8	4.1	6.9	6.1	7.7	7.5	7.9
Austria	.6	.9	3.2	1.9	4.1	2.9	4.7	3.4	5.0
Belgium-Luxembourg	6.4	2.3	11.3	2.6	18.0	4.8	22.7	5.3	16.7
Brazil	.5	1.2	1.8	2.7	5.4	6.1	7.5	12.8	9.1
Canada	2.1	4.8	5.3	5.5	11.2	11.1	13.6	15.6	13.1
Chile[a]	—	.2	.4	.5	.5	.8	.6	.8	.5
China	—	1.2	18.4	19.2	18.0	22.5	27.0	30.8	
Spain	.6	.9	1.9	1.9	7.4	8.5	11.5	12.1	10.9
United States	80.4	87.2	90.1	90.5	119.3	127.3	132.2	144.1	116.3
France	7.2	8.4	17.3	13.9	23.8	23.2	27.0	24.1	23.2
India[a]	1.3	1.8	3.3	4.6	6.3	6.4	6.7	8.4	9.2
Italy	2.1	3.5	8.2	9.2	17.3	21.1	23.8	23.6	23.3
Japan	1.7	4.8	22.1	19.5	93.3	69.9	117.1	75.7	107.4
Mexico	.3	.9	1.5	1.7	3.8	4.2	5.0	6.1	5.2
Norway	.1	.5	.5	1.0	.9	1.9	.9	2.5	.9
Netherlands	.3	1.8	1.9	3.2	5.0	5.7	5.8	5.8	5.2
Peru[a]	—	.1	.1	.2	.1	.5	.5	.9	—
Poland	1.9	—	6.7	6.3	11.8	11.7	14.2	17.4	
German Federal Republic	6.8	11.9	34.1	29.2	45.0	40.6	53.2	42.1	42.4
United Kingdom	15.1	14.7	24.7	22.2	28.3	25.5	22.4	23.1	22.2
Sweden[a]	1.3	2.3	3.2	4.1	5.5	5.9	6.0	6.3	5.2
Czechoslovakia	2.6	—	6.8	6.5	11.5	8.8	13.6	10.3	14.7
Tunisia[a]	—	.1	—	.1	.1	.2	.1	.3	—
Turkey	.1	.3	.3	.6	1.3	1.8	1.5	1.9	1.6

Table 9-3 – Continued

	1948	1950-52	1960		1970		1974		1976
	P	C	P	C	P	C	P	C	P
USSR	18.5	—	65.3	63.5	115.9	110.2	136.2	137.5	145.0
(Ukraine)	(4.5)	(—)	(26.2)	(—)	(46.6)	(—)	(52.4)	(—)	(—)
Venezuela[a]	—	.4	.1	.5	.9	1.6	1.0	2.7	.9
Yugoslavia	.4	.6	1.4	1.7	2.2	3.4	2.8	4.2	2.7
AIEC (I)	3.8	7.4	10.9	14.7	20.3	22.2	22.8	28.4	23.7
World (II)	155.8	—	353.0	337.6	594.0	589.6	704.8	704.7	—
Non-communist world (III)	133.4	162.0	249.1	236.4	436.3	413.1	531.4	480.6	—
I/II (percent)	2.4	—	3.1	4.4	3.4	3.8	3.2	4.0	—
I/III (percent)	2.8	4.6	4.4	6.2	4.6	5.3	4.3	5.9	—

Source: Derived from United Nations, *Statistical Yearbook*, New York, various issues.

Note: Data refer to the apparent consumption of crude steel (production plus imports minus exports) and thus do not take into account annual stock variations which have been considerable in many European countries. Because of this, much more attention must be paid to the general level and trend of the data than to the order of magnitude of any specific annual datum. Foreign trade data used for iron and steel products refer to ingots and semimanufactured products; all rolled products; steel tubes and trimmings; steel wire; wheels, tires and axles for road equipment. For countries whose foreign trade statistics were not sufficiently detailed, import data have been calculated from the export statistics of steel exporting countries.

[a]Members of the Association of Iron Ore Exporting Countries (AIEC).

Table 9-4

International Iron Ore Exports by Leading Countries: 1974, 1975 (*million MT*)

Country	1974	1975
Algeria[g]		
Total	2.615	–
Australia,[a,g] toward:		
Belgium-Luxembourg	1.758	2.546
France	1.355	1.584
German Federal Republic	2.235	5.085
Italy	1.882	2.621
Japan	64.948	66.951
United Kingdom	.919	1.069
United States	.496	1.158
Total	78.265	88.123
Brazil		
Total	59.000	–
Canada,[b] toward:		
Belgium-Luxembourg	.529	.123
France	.655	.530
German Federal Republic	2.334	2.341
Italy	2.327	2.376
Japan	4.674	4.644
Netherlands	2.652	4.136
Spain	.699	.717
United Kingdom	5.327	3.396
United States	21.837	21.266
Total	41.279	39.721
Chile,[g] toward:		
Argentina	.048	
Belgium	.206	
Japan	8.459	
Netherlands	.056	
United States	.282	
Total	9.051	4.975
France, toward:		
Belgium-Luxembourg	16.187	13.301
German Federal Republic	3.659	2.711
Total	19.846	16.016
India,[c,d,g] toward:		
Belgium-Luxembourg	.146	.170
Czechoslovakia	.658	.515
German Federal Republic	.065	.302
Hungary	.134	.140
Japan	19.235	16.128
Netherlands	.061	1.243
Poland	.438	2.142
Rumania	1.890	2.142
Yugoslavia	.006	–
Total	23.748	22.295

Table 9-4 — *Continued*

Country	1974	1975
Liberia,[g] toward:		
Belgium-Luxembourg	1.868	
France	2.290	
German Federal Republic	9.822	
Italy	3.778	
Japan	1.126	
Netherlands	1.662	
United Kingdom	0.799	
United States	2.827	
Total	25.485	—
Mauritania[e,g]		
Total	11.666	—
Norway,[d] toward:		
Finland	.243	
German Federal Republic	1.217	
Poland	.281	
United Kingdom	.873	
Total	2.657	3.154
Peru[g]		
Total	9.942	—
Philippines[d]		
Total	1.508	.824[f]
Spain, toward:		
Belgium-Luxembourg	.367	.103
France	.474	.304
German Federal Republic	1.112	.918
Netherlands	.399	.333
United Kingdom	.243	.107
Total	2.962	1.960
Sweden,[g] toward:		
Belgium-Luxembourg	8.896	
Czechoslovakia	.549	
Finland	.659	
France	1.634	
German Federal Republic	8.352	
Netherlands	1.821	
Poland	1.137	
United Kingdom	2.080	
United States	.101	
Total	25.448	17.620
Tunisia[g]		
Total	.526	—
United States,[b,d] toward:		
Canada	2.032	2.783
Japan	.492	.044
Total	2.602	2.841

Table 9-4 – *Continued*

Country	1974	1975
USSR, toward:		
Austria	.634	
Bulgaria	1.962	
Czechoslovakia	11.820	
German Democratic Republic	2.628	
Hungary	3.910	
Italy	1.628	
Japan	1.008	
Poland	11.389	
Rumania	5.699	
United Kingdom	1.114	
Total	43.300	–
Venezuela[g]		
Total	26.277	–
AIEC Countries (*I*)	213.023	–
World Total (*II*)	415.000	–
Percentage *I/II*	51.32%	–

Source: Derived from Metal Bulletin Limited, *Metal Bulletin Handbook,* 9th edition, London, 1976.

[a]Exports calculated for a year ending June 30.

[b]Short tons.

[c]Exports calculated for a year ending March 31.

[d]Ore and concentrates.

[e]Long tons.

[f]January to June.

[g]Members of the Association of Iron Ore Exporting Countries (AIEC).

decreased during the period under study, Australian (4150% increase), Brazilian (3751%), Canadian (1895%), Indian (1383%), Liberian (more than 1000%), South African (931%), Russian (658%), Spanish (492%), and Chilean (279%) production reached unequaled levels.

If we consider only those countries which signed the AIEC Charter in 1975, we notice a 1,000% increase in their production for the period covered by available statistics. Their share of world production thus went from 14.2% in 1948 to 33.1% in 1974; this percentage climbs to 48.6% if we only take into account countries with market economies. Despite this performance for the association as a whole, Australian, Liberian, Swedish, and Indian production alone accounts for 75% of the total production for the eleven AIEC member

Table 9-5
International Imports of Iron Ore by Leading Countries: 1974, 1975
(*million MT*)

Country	1974	1975
Austria, from:		
Brazil	1.529	1.473
USSR	.623	.716
Total	2.800	2.578
Belgium-Luxembourg, from:		
Australia	2.212	2.270
Brazil	1.643	1.944
France	13.534	10.802
Liberia	1.964	.916
Mauritania	1.316	.921
Sweden	8.875	4.919
Total	33.430	25.520
Canada,[a] from:		
Brazil	.591	.760
United States	1.833	4.385
Total	2.572	5.338
Finland[b], from:		
Norway	.247	–
Sweden	.659	–
Total	1.035	1.057
France, from:		
Brazil	4.211	3.491
Liberia	2.078	1.994
Mauritania	2.452	2.163
Sweden	2.664	1.646
Total	15.932	13.169
Greece		
Total	1.025	.529[c]
German Federal Republic, from:		
Angola	1.335	.602
Australia	4.780	6.412
Brazil	11.980	11.023
Canada	3.976	4.065
France	3.675	2.623
Liberia	9.745	6.196
Mauritania	1.516	.603
Morocco	.287	.036
Norway	1.462	1.160
Peru	1.167	.593
Sierra Leone	.710	.614
Spain	1.056	.879
Sweden	10.586	5.762
USSR	1.039	.170
Venezuela	2.711	1.873
Total	57.720	44.322

Table 9-5 — *Continued*

Country	1974	1975
Italy, from:		
Australia	2.235	1.742^d
Brazil	3.237	2.072^d
Canada	1.998	1.248^d
Liberia	3.812	1.921^d
Mauritania	1.198	.996^d
USSR	1.675	1.245^d
Venezuela	1.836	1.649^d
Total	18.055	11.416^d
Japan, from:		
Angola	2.799	1.431
Australia	67.881	63.253
Brazil	19.523	23.460
Canada	4.504	3.900
Chile	8.571	8.057
India	17.333	16.790
North Korea	.305	.203
South Korea	.083	.062
Liberia	1.315	.528
Malaysia	.084	.121
Mauritania	2.187	.975
Peru	5.960	2.732
Philippines	1.636	1.513
South Africa	2.215	1.632
Swaziland	1.925	1.743
Sierra Leone	1.018	.907
United States	.342	—
USSR	.987	1.243
Total	141.816	131.657
Netherlands, from:		
Brazil	1.613	1.769^d
Canada	.600	.930^d
Liberia	1.595	1.082^d
Mauritania	.305	.371
Norway	—	—
Sierra Leone	.318	—
Spain	.302	.395^d
Sweden	1.856	1.537^d
Total	7.061	7.372^d
Poland		
Total	15.609	11.821
Spain, from:		
Australia	.612	.907
Brazil	1.303	1.594
Canada	.403	.742
Liberia	.469	.617
Mauritania	.678	.604
Sweden	.730	.462
Venezuela	.896	.941
Total	5.280	6.135

Table 9-5 – *Continued*

Country	1974	1975
United Kingdom, from:		
Australia	.792	.858
Brazil	3.141	2.205
Canada	4.292	3.061
Liberia	.701	.505
Mauritania	1.533	1.609
Norway	1.074	1.639
Sweden	3.924	2.242
USSR	1.091	.969
Venezuela	1.728	1.803
Total	19.675	15.783
United States,[d] from:		
Australia	.638	.803
Brazil	6.572	7.526
Canada	19.702	19.112
Chile	.296	.931
Liberia	2.730	2.496
Peru	1.810	1.551
Venezuela	15.378	13.137
Total	48.029	46.742
Yugoslavia, from:		
Brazil	.301	–
India	–	–
Total	.431	.320[c]
European Economic Community	151.873	117.582
Japan	141.816	131.627
North America	50.601	52.080

Source: Derived from Metal Bulletin Limited, *Metal Bulletin Handbook,* 9th edition, London, 1976.

[a]Short tons.

[b]Ore and concentrates.

[c]January to June.

[d]Long tons.

countries, while the production percentage for the two industrial countries (Australia and Sweden) stands at 48%. These characteristics can limit the formulation of any common policy on the association's part. Moreover, the extent of coverage of world production assured by the AIEC proves clearly inferior to that held by OPEC and IBA. This implies that any attempt to restrict production can give rise to production increases in nonmember countries such as Brazil, Canada, and the United States (countries on the 1974 list of the four leading iron ore producers of the Western world).

Table 9-6
Export Receipts of Some Iron Ore-Producing Countries: 1974-1977
(*US$ million*)

Country	1974	1975	1976	1977	Percentage Variations 1976 to 1977
Total	2,426	3,001	3,163	2,907	−8
Australia	850	980	1,019	1,034	1
Brazil	571	921	966	850	−12
Chile	73	90	86	80	−7
India	198	244	293	275	−6
Liberia	262	294	332	276	−17
Mauritania	130	142	154	127	−18
Peru	60	52	60	50	−17
Sierra Leone	15	15	−	−	−
Venezuela	267	263	253	215	−15

Source: International Monetary Fund, *IMF Survey*, vol. 7, no. 3, Washington, February 6, 1978, p. 37. Reprinted with permission.

Table 9-7
National Significance of Iron Ore: 1974
(*percentages*)

	Production as Percentage of GNP	Export as Percentage of Total Exports
Australia	1.00	5.7
Brazil	0.68	7.2
Canada	0.65	1.9
Chile	0.55	6.0
India	−	7.5
Liberia	55.00	65.0
Mauritania	35.00	73.4
Peru	0.80	5.8
Sierra Leone	3.20	10.4
Sweden	1.05	2.7
Venezuela	1.20	3.6

Source: Energy, Mines and Resources Canada, *Iron Ore,* Mineral Policies Series MR 148, Ottawa, July 1976, p. 27. Reproduced by permission of the Minister of Supply and Services Canada.

Table 9-8
World Iron Ore Reserves: 1975
(*percent*)

USSR	45
Canada	14
Brazil	11
United States	7
Australia	6
India	3
France	3
Venezuela	1
Sweden	1
Liberia	0.3
Others	8.7
World	100.0[b]
Maximum for AIEC[a]	20

Source: Derived from British-North American Committee, *Mineral Development in the Eighties: Prospects and Problems,* British-North American Research Association, National Planning Association, C.D. Howe Research Institute, London-Washington-Montreal, 1976, p. 34; Energy, Mines and Resources Canada, *Iron Ore,* Mineral Policy Series MR 148, Ottawa, July 1976, p. 25.

[a]Association of Iron Ore Exporting Countries.

[b]266,600 million MT.

We do not know exactly the growth rate of world iron ore demand, but to the extent that it parallels the growth rate of world steel consumption, we can suppose that during the period under study it stood at about 5% in comparison to an annual 15% growth rate for production (11% for the non-communist world).[8] In this case, it is not surprising to notice that Brazilian and Swedish ore prices fell 22% between 1957 and 1961, and that their 1957 level was only "temporarily" exceeded in the second half of the seventies.

The AIEC countries' share of world crude steel production in 1974 remains below 3.5% (4.3% if we exclude countries with planned economies); this percentage slips to 1.3% if we do not take into account Australian and Swedish production. Since the beginning of the sixties this ratio has proved very stable, implying that the larger portion of iron ore production continues to be oriented toward a few industrial countries where it is transformed into semimanufactured products. In fact, in 1974 the crude steel production of the United States, Japan and the EEC represented 76% of western steel production, while their consumption of this product was equivalent to 71.5% of the apparent consumption of non-communist countries. These data draw attention to a crucial trait of the iron ore industry, a trait preventing any marked price increase and limiting AIEC chances of playing a more effective role on this market. This industry is so structured that widely scattered sources of supply must respond to demand from concentrated markets, and these monopolistic elements in the demand are reinforced by organisms coordinating ore purchases in most consuming countries.

Tables 9-4 and 9-5 provide more complete information on world iron ore trade. One notices that in 1974 more than 50% of world exports were coming from AIEC member countries; this means 213 million MT—103.7 million from the association's two industrial members (Australia and Sweden) and 75.5 million from Venezuela, Liberia, and India. Australian and Indian exports are directed mainly to Japan, while Swedish and Liberian shipments feed EEC steel mills. We would also point out that nonmember countries such as Brazil (59 million MT), the USSR (43.3 million MT) and Canada (41.3 million MT) remain on the list of the five leading world exporters of iron ore. More than 50% of Canadian exports find their way to the United States, while 86% of Brazilian shipments are absorbed by the European (32 million MT) and Japanese (19.5 million MT) markets. Soviet exports are principally oriented towards Czechoslovakia, Poland, Rumania, and Hungary with Italy, the United Kingdom, and Japan importing about 4 million MT of Russian ore.

The leading world importers of iron ore remain the EEC (152 million MT in 1974), Japan (142 million MT), and the United States (48 million MT). EEC overseas imports have increased progressively during the last decade due to the depletion of ore with low iron content located in France, the United Kingdom, Spain, and West Germany, and to the increased demand for ore high in iron content and low in phosphorus. The imports of West Germany, Belgium-Luxembourg, and the United Kingdom represent 73% of EEC imports. Although Sweden appears as an important supplier of ore for the three countries mentioned, the gradual depletion of Swedish mines forced West Germany to increase progressively its imports from Brazil and Liberia, while Belgium-Luxembourg made still more intensive use of French ore. Close to 50% of the United Kingdom's imports come from Canada and Northern European countries, while Brazil, Venezuela, and Mauritania occupy an increasingly important place on the list of its iron ore suppliers. Japan's insignificant production (0.41 million MT in 1976) forces it to import all the ore necessary for its steel production from overseas. In 1974 no fewer than eighteen countries sold about 142 million MT of iron ore on the Japanese market; among these were Australia (68 million MT), Brazil (19.5 million MT), India (17.3 million MT), Chile (8.5 million MT), and Peru (6 million MT). Even if the United States is not self-sufficient for this ore, its average annual iron ore production of 50 million MT permits it to import much less than other world industrial centers. Moreover, 55% of its imports come from nonmembers of AIEC (Canada, 19.7 million MT and Brazil, 6.6 million MT).

Tables 9-6 and 9-7 provide interesting information on the importance of iron ore in the leading producing countries. One thus learns that the production value of this ore represents 55% of Liberia's gross national product (GNP) and 35% of Mauritania's. This percentage varies between 0.8% and 3.2% for the other AIEC members, while it is less than 0.68% for nonmember producing countries like Brazil and Canada. Moreover, iron ore exports, as percentage of total exports, reach 73.4% for Mauritania, 65% for Liberia, 10.4% for Sierra Leone, and 7.5% for India. These data convince us that certain of the association's countries cannot long tolerate production and export restrictions since their foreign exchange inflow and their national employment levels depend too heavily on iron ore extraction, this being especially true for the African countries. This capacity to restrict supply is also handicapped by the construction in certain consumer countries of warehouses meant to stock large quantities of iron ore and the possibility by which nonmember countries can increase their share of a market characterized by excess supply for the last twenty years.[9] Finally, we would point out the marked instability characterizing the export receipts of some large producing countries. Thus, Venezuelan receipts dwindled by 24% between 1974 and 1977, while the 1977 receipts of Chile, Liberia, Mauritania, and Peru are lower than those recorded for 1975. Only Australia has experienced a continual growth in its iron ore export receipts during recent years.

> Australia is by far the world's largest exporter of iron ore, with the bulk of its exports sold under contract. In 1977, its earnings were probably a little higher than in 1976. In aggregate, the major developing country exporters, accounting for about half of Western trade, are believed to have earned about 8 percent less than in 1976.[10]

Even if in 1974 AIEC member countries were responsible for only 33% of world iron ore production, 51% of the world exports and 3.2% of steel production, (excluding countries with planned economies, the percentages rise to 48.56%, 60% and 4.3% respectively) one may think that, in the coming years, they will be able to play a more decisive role on the world iron ore market if their collective share of identified world reserves proves substantial. But this is not the case, since compared to world reserves estimated at 266,600 million MT, it is considered that a maximum of 20% may be attributed to AIEC member countries (6% of this to Australia, 3% to India, 1% to Venezuela and Sweden and 0.3% to Liberia). Identified reserves are located mostly in nonmember countries: USSR, 45%; Canada, 14%; Brazil, 11%; United States, 7% and France, 3%. At 1974-75 production rates, world reserves are sufficient for three hundred years and even more if one considers identified resources (and not reserves).

The six major continents contain vast identified resources of iron ore that exceed 760 billion tons. Some resources could be classified as reserves after only moderate amounts of development work.[11]

Finally, even excluding Soviet reserves, the AIEC share does not exceed 35%. This percentage seems to us a clearly insufficient basis for the association's successful long-term intervention on the world iron ore market, especially considering the fact that close to half of its reserves are located in industrial member countries interested, up to now, in guaranteeing continual supplies to consuming countries.

What is the future of this association or of any other organism attempting to stabilize iron ore prices and the export receipts related to its production? We have described a set of factors limiting the long-term success which could possibly arise from a unilateral price increase or restriction of supply decreed by the AIEC. First, this industry is so structured that very scattered supply sources must respond to demand from very concentrated markets. So, one can scarcely hope that a small group of nations, controlling barely 35% of production and 20% of world reserves, can limit supply and increase prices for very long. Setting up an oligopoly to counter the oligopsony of industrial centers is also handicapped by the existence of large deposits in consuming markets (USSR, United States, EEC) and other industrial countries (Australia, Spain, Sweden).

Second, this association brings together countries whose political ideologies are too diverse to expect either sustained cooperation or concerted action from them. Even if Algeria, India, Sierra Leone, and Venezuela could find a common ground and impose quotas, it seems unlikely that Australia and Sweden would submit to such a common action, considering the possible reprisals of their main trading partners. Also, given the fact that trade restrictions must be substantial and prolonged to have a positive effect on prices and receipts, this path could not be followed indefinitely by Liberia and Mauritania where iron ore production represents, respectively, 55% and 35% of their GNP.

Third, even though we were unable to find pertinent information on the cost structure of a steel mill, a recent study evaluates at about 2.2% the increase in the American price for a ton of crude steel following a 20% increase in the price of iron ore from AIEC countries.[12] In view of such results, some will conclude that association members can increase their prices and since ore is of such minor importance in the total cost of steel, the fall in demand would be less than the increase in price, resulting in an increase in their export receipts. This statement seems inexact, since it leaves aside the market's dynamics and certain of its basic characteristics. In fact, the preceding conclusion is reached under the hypotheses that iron ore stocks are null and that production in nonmember countries cannot be easily increased to replace the output the cartel no longer wishes to release on international markets. The suppositions are also that there exists no excess capacity in steel production; that stocks of steel products are nonexistent and that consumers cannot use supplies from the scrap market. Only in this case would the demand for iron ore be inelastic and an increase in its price lead to increased export receipts. But even if these heroic hypotheses (especially for 1977-78) could prove true in the short term, they cannot be accepted over a long period.

> If AIEC countries reduced production or engaged in other price fixing activity, steel producers and others would begin to expand and develop mines in more secure areas, and in three to five years could offset much of the impact of cartel action. The result of this action would be to bring ore prices back to competitive levels, reduce the shares of the market controlled by AIEC countries, and reduce the flow of foreign investment needed to develop their deposits.

> Consequently, although restrictive actions may meet some success in the short-run, the long-run impacts upon the ore exporting countries of AIEC would be quite severe. For countries such as Venezuela who plan to use domestic ore production in the development of a domestic steel industry such a strategy may make some sense as they want to sharply decrease ore exports in future years. However, for other members of AIEC the long-run effects would be likely to more than offset short-run gains. The realization of this fact by many countries is a major factor working against any action that would limit supply or sharply raise prices.[13]

All these characteristics render the demand of industrial centers for AIEC iron ore much more elastic over a long period, especially if one takes into account the fact that Western reserves remain enormous.[14] In this case, a price increase will always prove inferior to the decrease in quantities sold, thus causing export receipts to decline.

AIEC's Conference of Ministers accepts these basic economic principles, seeing that it has formulated no common policy since its creation in 1975. Moreover, in October 1977, at UNCTAD's first preparatory meeting on iron ore, the idea of stabilizing prices by setting up a buffer stock was rejected.

> During the year, the Association of Iron Ore Exporting Countries . . . established its headquarters at Geneva and met before UNCTAD's first preparatory meeting on iron ore, held in October in the context of its Integrated Program for Commodities. At the preparatory meeting, it was generally accepted that because of its diversity in form and quality iron ore was ill suited to price stabilization through an international buffer stock agreement.[15]

Solutions to ensure the stabilization of iron ore prices and export receipts must thus be found elsewhere.

Notes

1. Canada, Department of Energy, Mines and Resources, *Iron Ore,* pp. 21-22. Reproduced by permission of the Minister of Supply and Services, Canada.

2. In 1974, the Venezuelan government nationalized the iron mines belonging to U.S. Steel and Bethlehem Steel.

3. Canada, Department of Energy, Mines and Resources, *Iron Ore,* p. 28. Reproduced by permission of the Minister of Supply and Services, Canada.

4. As concerns the objective of providing a center for the exchange of information and effective consultations, the AIEC Charter foresees that it can be reached through the supervision and diffusion of specific studies on projections of iron ore demand and supply; price evolution of iron ore compared to that of steel and of inputs such as coal; effects of iron scrap on the international trade of iron ore; marketing techniques and long-term contracts; effects of exploitation of iron mines by multinational companies; problems related to the international transport of iron ore; and other topics.

5. Kenneth W. Clarfield et al., *Eight Mineral Cartels,* pp. 142-143. Reprinted with permission.

6. At the level of institutional organization, the 1975 Charter foresees that the AIEC will be composed of a Conference of Ministers, an Executive Bureau and a Secretariat. The Conference of Ministers represents the association's highest body. It meets every two years at the head office in London. On the other hand, extraordinary sessions can be called with the consent of a two-thirds majority of member countries. An important element to remember, any collective decision capable of influencing the international iron ore market requires a "unanimous" vote by member countries. The Executive Bureau is made up of permanent representatives nominated by the members. It meets twice yearly and takes care of the AIEC's day-to-day administration. It is also responsible for the secretariat which carries out the specific studies requested by the producers. The secretariat is directed by an executive secretary, assisted by two directors elected for a three-year period by the Conference of Ministers.

7. The increase is 297% if we exclude countries with planned economies from our calculations.

8. Canada, Department of Energy, Mines and Resources, *Iron Ore,* p. 26:

> The world demand for iron ore parallels world demand for steel. World consumption of crude steel increased at a growth rate of just over 5 percent a year in the 1955 to 1974 period, and attained a level of 710 million tons in 1974. The demand for iron ore increased proportionally with this trend although there was a slower growth in actual tonnage because of the progressive increase in the iron content of the ores. The average grade of iron ores entering international trade increased from 51% in 1950 to 53% iron in 1960 to an estimated 58% in 1974.

Reproduced by permission of the Minister of Supply and Services, Canada.

9. Canada, Department of Energy, Mines and Resources, *Iron Ore,* p. 29:

Of the consuming nations, Japan is the first to seriously consider large-scale stockpiling of iron ore. One Japanese steel company—Kawasaki Steel Corporation—has begun construction of a stockyard to hold 2 million tons of iron ore products, an amount sufficient to last about one and a half months at present consumption rates. Kawasaki is currently negotiating with other Japanese steel companies concerning a plan to construct a mammoth iron ore stockpiling center at Mindanao, the Philippines. The project envisages a stockpile of 10 million tons of iron ore products from Western Australia, which amount equals twenty-five days of supply for all Japanese integrated steel mills. Present stock capacities are limited to one and a half months consumption but the Japanese want to boost this inventory to at least three months.

Reproduced by permission of the Minister of Supply and Services, Canada.

10. G.I. Brown, *IMF Survey,* International Monetary Fund, vol. 7, no. 3, February 6, 1978, p. 37. Reprinted with permission.

11. British-North American Committee, *Mineral Development in the Eighties: Prospects and Problems,* British-North American Research Association, p. 38. Reprinted with permission.

12. Charles River Associates Inc., *Economic Issues Underlying Supply Access Agreements,* p. V-11. Reprinted with permission.

13. Charles River Associates Inc., *Economic Issues Underlying Supply Access Agreements,* pp. V-20 and V-21. Reprinted with permission.

14. We have not treated here the technological and commercial characteristics influencing steel production and thus the demand for iron ore. The reader interested in these questions is referred to: W.T. Hogan, *The 1970s: Critical Years for Steel;* C.R. MacPhee, *Restrictions on International Trade in Steel;* Julian Szekely, *The Steel Industry and Energy Crisis.*

15. Brown, *IMF Survey,* p. 37. Reprinted with permission.

10 ASSIMER and the International Mercury Market

Copper, bauxite and iron ore are not the only commodities over which associations of producing countries have tried to exercise price and export receipts control. In 1975 a formal cartel for mercury was created when Algeria, Spain, Italy, Peru, Turkey, and Yugoslavia formed the International Association of Mercury Producers (ASSIMER). During the seventies an informal and private cartel supported lead prices, assuring levels above the floor price set by producers. Talks have been held within the United Nations Conference on Trade and Development (UNCTAD) concerning the establishment of an international tungsten agreement; given the relative failure of these discussions, the idea of creating an International Association of Tungsten Producing Countries may revive in the next few years. Moreover, studies have been demanded to analyze the possibilities of intervention on the world markets for chrome, cobalt, manganese, phosphate, platinum, potassium, uranium, and zinc. The complex nature of these markets and the scarcity of pertinent statistical data prevent us, for the moment, from evaluating the types of controls used for this set of commodities. Our analysis, therefore, will be brief and limited to the only market for which a formal and publicized cartel has been created to control prices: the international mercury market.

Mercury, the only metal which is liquid at ordinary temperatures, is used in the electrical apparatus industry, the electrolytic preparation of chlorine and caustic soda, the construction of physics instruments and the manufacture of mildew-proofing paint. It is also used in the extraction of gold and silver, two metals with which it easily alloys.[1]

Up to the beginning of the sixties, world mercury demand was satisfied by production from Spain, Italy, the United States, Mexico, and Yugoslavia. (Tables 10-1 through 10-3). In 1960 these nations were responsible for 91% of the production from countries with market economies (the percentage is 56% for Italy and Spain alone). This production was characterized by three important traits. First, its comparative costs varied widely (the average mercury content stands at 1.5% for the Spanish ore, drops to 0.47% for the Italian ore and scarcely exceeds 0.24% for American ore). The quality of Spain's ore thus afforded this country a determining role in establishing basic mercury prices. Second, Spanish (Almaden) and Italian (especially Monte Amiata) production was dominated by a very small number of companies. This fact has allowed these companies to operate a cartel which since 1928 has not only fixed prices but divided up the world market: Monte Amiata supplied the European market

Table 10-1
Average Price of Mercury on the New York and London
Markets: 1962-1977
(dollars per flask of 76 pounds)

Year	New York	London
1962	191.27	
1963	189.93	
1964	313.08	
1965	571.19	
1966	441.82	
1967	490.47	
1968	537.69	546.80
1969	509.90	536.41
1970	418.14	411.45
1971	302.95	282.46
1972	226.76[a]	203.01[a]
1973	291.27[b]	273.54[b]
1974	291.55	267.94
1975	166.82	130.11
1976	124.25	92.02
1977	139.70	120.00
1978 (January)	143.29	
(February)	160.58	

Source: Commodity Research Bureau Inc., *Commodity Year Book
1978*, New York, 1978, pp. 224-225. Reprinted with permission.

[a]May price $170.95 (NY); $153.30 (London).

[b]January price $284.59 (NY); $260.70 (London).

while Almaden kept the North American market for itself. (In 1949 the Italian
producer made large mercury sales to the United States, a region reserved for
the Spanish producer, and the cartel disappeared. It was set up again in 1958
and controlled a good share of the world market until 1962 when it was con-
fronted with the EEC's antitrust laws.) Third, these oligopolistic practices
(in conjunction with growing demand) led to a 200% rise in mercury prices
which went from US $189.93/flask in 1963 to US $571.19/flask in 1965.
Prices remained above US $441.00/flask until the beginning of the seventies,
a level high enough to render economically profitable the low-grade deposits
in Canada, Turkey, Peru, and the Philippines while also encouraging the sale
of Chinese and Soviet mercury on western markets.

These new developments have modified the international mercury market's
structure; from 1968 on, it has been characterized by excess supply and falling
prices. In May 1972, these prices stood at US $170.95/flask on the New York
market (68% decrease) and US $153.30/flask on the London market (a 72% fall).

Table 10-2
World Mercury Production: Selected Years
(flasks of 76 pounds)

Country	1950	1960	1970	1973	1975[b]	1976[a]	1977[a]
Algeria[c]				14,000	15,000[a]	—	
Canada			24,400	12,500	14,000	—	
Chile	n.a.	—	388	798	97	—	
China[a]	—	—	20,000	26,000	26,000	26,000	
Spain[c]	51,808	53,369	45,552	62,069	47,051	44,000	40,000
United States	4,535	33,223	27,296	2,227	7,366	23,133	31,375
Italy[c]	53,346	55,492	44,470	33,504	30,400	22,278	20,000
Japan	1,312	5,791	5,170	3,742	—	—	—
Mexico	3,757	20,114	30,256	21,646	14,184	15,026	10,000
Peru[c]	—	—	3,196	3,581	3,500	—	—
Philippines	—	—	4,648	2,169	232	—	—
Tunisia	—	—	102	112	145	—	—
Turkey[c]	1	1,339	8,592	7,861	8,800	—	—
USSR[a]	—	—	48,000	52,000	55,000	55,000	—
Yugoslavia[c]	14,368	14,069	15,461	15,606	16,941	17,000	—
ASSIMER (I)			117,271	136,621	121,692		
World Total (II)	—	—	284,014	270,014	251,226	243,689	240,500
Non-communist world (III)	130,204	193,801	216,014	192,014	170,226	—	—
I/II (percent)			41.3	50.6	48.4		
I/III (percent)			54.3	71.2	71.5		

Source: Commodity Research Bureau Inc., *Commodity Year Book 1978,* New York, 1978, p. 223 (Reprinted with permission).

[a] Approximate.

[b] Preliminary.

[c] Members of the International Association of Mercury Producers (ASSIMER).

Faced with such a poor market performance, the main international producers reacted by setting a floor price. Thus, in May 1972, Almaden and Monte Amiata announced a minimum price of US $170.00/flask (price equivalent to that of New York but US $16.70/flask in excess of the London price) while the new association grouping Mexico's numerous producers agreed to defend a US $200.00/flask floor price. This intervention proved fruitful since the market price increased about 66% during the second half of 1972. The unusual growth in the industrial production index in most consuming countries was not without some effect on this improvement in mercury prices. Attracted by these unhoped-

Table 10-3
Identified Mercury Reserves: 1975
(*flasks of 76 pounds*)

Countries	Identified Reserves	Percent
Spain[a]	1,995,000	38
USSR	787,500	15
Yugoslavia[a]	787,500	15
United States	472,500	9
Algeria[a]	420,000	8
Italy[a]	420,000	8
Mexico	262,500	5
Others	105,000	2
Total	5,250,000	100
ASSIMER	3,622,500	69

Source: Derived from British-North American Committee, *Mineral Development in the Eighties: Prospects and Problems,* British-North American Research Association, National Planning Association, C.D. Howe Research Institute, London-Washington-Montreal, 1976, pp. 37 and 39.

[a]Members of the International Association of Mercury Producers (ASSIMER).

for successes, Algeria (where ore extraction was just beginning) and Yugoslavia joined with Italian, Spanish, and Mexican producers. On January 15, 1973 they proposed a uniform floor price of US $300.00/flask, US $15.00 more than the New York market price. During the first months of 1973 the current price exceeded the minimum set but since this price was not the fruit of market forces, it began to fall and dropped to US $262.50/flask in June 1973. The group was convened once again in July 1973. The goal of a minimum price of US $320.00 was then set, to be reached gradually during the six subsequent months. When, in September, producers realized that this goal could not be reached, they adjusted their aim and lowered the floor price announced by US $20.00. Although, in October 1973, Peru joined the club of producers intervening in the international mercury market, New York and London prices scarcely exceeded US $290.00/flask at year's end.

There are several reasons for the difficulties that these producers encountered in enforcing the floor prices established in 1972 and 1973, despite their control of supply. Besides the absence of the USSR, China, and Canada (three countries responsible for about 40% of world mercury production) at the ad hoc producer-held meetings and the increase of Chinese and Russian sales on Western markets, the consumption decrease due to antipollution regulations was also important.

These standards have essentially eliminated the use of mercury in many end uses in the United States, Japan and Western Europe. This reduction in demand will not be offset in the foreseeable future. Second, pollution control standards caused the obsolescence of many chlorine plants using mercury cell capacity. Each of these plants normally carries a large working inventory of mercury and these inventories are now contributing to the supply of mercury.[2]

Rather than find new uses for mercury to stimulate its demand and invite communist countries to better synchronize their sales on Western markets, the producers decided to manipulate prices. At the beginning of May 1974, representatives of Algeria, Italy, Mexico, Spain, Turkey, and Yugoslavia agreed on a minimum uniform price of US $350.00/flask despite a current monthly price of US $274.40/flask on the London market. The panic among consumers, the intervention from speculators, and the general price increases observed for most nonferrous metals at that time provoked a sudden 16% rise in mercury prices. But since this price was artificial and not a result either of increased international demand or of a serious reduction of supply, it remained above US $300.00/flask for scarcely two months. From August 1974 on, the price of mercury began to decrease at an alarming rate. At year's end it was at US $194.40/flask on the London market, wiping out in a few months the gains recorded since 1972. In May 1975 it stood at US $137.06/flask, exactly half the level reached twelve months before.

An emergency meeting was called at Ankara, Turkey in May 1975 in order to check the fall in prices. Producers from Algeria, Spain, Italy, Peru, Turkey, and Yugoslavia then formed the International Association of Mercury Producers (ASSIMER). Although one of the declared aims of this cartel was the promotion of new uses for mercury, its members launched the publicity campaign by announcing their firm intention of not selling mercury below US $350.00/flask. These producers did not seem to understand that their situation is quite different from that of OPEC and that it matters little what floor price is desired, it cannot be defended if demand declines, stocks pile up, and supply does not decrease. In 1976 the annual average price stood at US $124.25/flask and US $92.02/flask on the American and European markets respectively. This price will start to climb again the day when supply decreases sufficiently to link up with demand. The 1976 market prices permitted a first adjustment of the international mercury market.

World production of mercury declined about 3 percent to 242,300 flasks. Producers in Italy, Spain, and the U.S.S.R. reportedly discontinued sales of mercury in international markets during part of 1976. Italian and Mexican producers sharply curtailed or completely shut down mercury mining operations. Canadian mining operations, suspended in 1975 because of low prices, did not reopen in 1976. The international association of mercury producers, centered in Geneva, reportedly met during the year to review the price situation.[3]

What are ASSIMER's chances to succeed in its attempts to assure its members "more remunerative" prices and "more stable" export receipts? We feel that it will be difficult to reach these goals before the middle of the eighties. Several of the market's characteristics support this conclusion. First, laws and regulations on environmental protection will continue to limit mercury consumption in the production of paint, agricultural and pharmaceutical products and in the chlorine industry. Mercury demand will also be slowed by the recycling of mercury formerly discharged into waterways. Second, prices observed in the mid-sixties, repeated producer interventions and consumer desire for assured continuous supplies have all encouraged the discovery of substitutes.[4] Their progressive use and directives concerning environmental protection lead us to believe that world mercury demand will be stagnant before the beginning of the eighties. Third, identified mercury reserves stand at 5.25 million flasks, 70% of which are located in ASSIMER member countries. Although these reserves prove sufficient to meet current world demand for only twenty years, we should point out that world resources remain almost inexhaustible. In fact, the most recent estimates by J.W. Brinck and L. Van Wambeke establish world mercury resources at 3.2 million MT for a price of US $270/flask.[5] With a hypothetical price of US $550/flask, this level reaches 60 million MT, deposits permitting current consumption rates for more than two hundred fifty years. Fourth, since 1968 the international mercury market has been characterized by excess supply, causing the accumulation of large stocks in producing (90,000 flasks in Italy) as well as consuming (30,000 flasks in the United States) countries. The depressive effect of these stocks on prices will continue to be felt. This seems especially true when one considers that American strategic stocks stood at 191,407 flasks in 1976, three times the level of annual consumption in this country which is the main customer for Algerian, Mexican, and Yugoslavian mercury.

Finally, we should point out the political and economic considerations rendering world supply inelastic to price decreases.

Most mercury producers are government-owned, and for political reasons the owner-governments are understandably loathe to close marginal operations or lay off workers. Also, mercury sales are substantial contributors to the foreign exchange earnings of Algeria, Italy, Mexico, Spain and Yugoslavia. . . . the mercury producers are not particularly rich, and the poorer ones are inclined to short the market to raise cash rather than turn to the other producers for short-term financing. This, of course, depresses the market.[6]

Notes

1. American mercury consumption was distributed as follows in 1976: electrical apparatus, 40%; electrolytic preparation of chlorine and caustic soda, 24%; mildew-proofing paint, 11%; industrial and control instruments, 7%; and other uses, 18%. The interested reader may consult Commodity Research Bureau Inc., *Commodity Year Book,* various issues.

2. Charles River Associates Inc., *Economic Issues Underlying Supply Access Agreements,* p. VII-7 and p. VII-8. Reprinted with permission.

3. Reprinted with permission from the 1977 Commodity Year Book, published by Commodity Research Bureau Inc., New York.

4. Examples are solid state devices for control instruments; nickel-cadmium battery systems for electrical apparatus; diaphragm cells for mercury cells in the chlor-alkali industry and organotin compounds in paints.

5. J.W. Brinck and L. Van Wambeke, "World Resources of Mercury," *Congreso Internacional del Mercurio,* 1974.

6. Kenneth W. Clarfield et al., *Eight Mineral Cartels,* p. 166. Reprinted with permission.

11 Summary and Conclusion

In the late 1960s a study of the evolution and effects of controls on international commodity markets would have had a limited public, consisting primarily of a few specialists and academicians. Small wonder: the oil tankers were docking as scheduled. Ore ships spilled forth their increasingly heavy loads. Newspaper readers learned that enormous quantities of coffee and wheat were being burned or otherwise destroyed. But, most important, commodity prices of that time appeared generally to be "steady to low."

The fact is that in 1968 the average price index for foodstuffs and tropical beverages, vegetable oils and seeds, and agricultural raw materials was lower than in 1960. The increase for ores and metals had been only about 30% in nine years.

Fears raised by the Korean War and the Suez Canal conflict had been successfully quieted by a sort of economic opulence. Of course, the nationalizations taking place in some Third World iron ore- and copper-producing countries brought comment. However, self-congratulatory notice was taken of the failure of international commodity agreements (the exceptional tin agreement, it was hastily decided, only confirmed the rule). Most economic agents were still convinced that the situation of excess supply would last for some time to come. Even more, they had grown accustomed to believing not only that the scarcities observed on some markets were cyclical and thus transitory but that this problem could be solved by the production of synthetics or other substitutes, as in the case of natural rubber.

This state of psychological security was to be shaken by a number of occurences during the early 1970s. The most noteworthy was the 6.5% annual growth rate for industrial production during the 1972-1973 period (1.5% above the trend of the preceding decade). Today there can no longer be any doubt that this abnormal growth in world production and demand was one of the major causes for the spectacular rise in commodity prices. But even if growth can be accounted the takeoff point for rising prices, one must look elsewhere for the factors of acceleration.

Thus in the case of foodstuffs and tropical beverages (wheat, corn, rice, sugar, coffee, cocoa, tea, beef, and bananas) we must look to factors such as the increase of Chinese wheat purchases on Western markets, large-scale destruction of Brazil's coffee production capacity due to frost, poor weather in Colombia and the drastic drop in sugar's stock-consumption ratio. These, and an array of other variables, whose effects on commodity supplies coincided with the spectacular rise in demand, were the cause of runaway price increases.

As concerns ores and metals, even more precise events come into play. Investments in the extraction and refining sectors had been slowed down by new environment protection norms and by uncertainty stemming from the property disputes and nationalizations of the preceding decade. Thus in the 1972-73 period the mineral-producing industry found its production capacity could not meet the sudden rise in demand. Since there is inevitably a delay factor in the installation of supplementary production capacity, most ore and metal prices then shot up to still-unequaled highs.

Finally, the fear of future price increases also stimulated demand, as did speculation on foreign exchange markets where metals were observed to be increasingly preferred in replacement of currency. And, of course, on the subject of bituminous substances, there is no forgetting the role played by OPEC. This organization rode the tide of an expanding world economy, a highly inelastic short-term demand for petroleum products, the absence of appropriate substitutes, and a certain degree of cohesion and discipline among its members.

During the 1974-75 recession the fall of commodity prices was as sudden, sharp, and spectacular as had been their ascent a few years earlier. This sudden drop can be largely explained by a slowdown in the growth of the industrial production index, a sustained high level of supply stimulated by the preceding period's high prices, stockpiling and various other economic and technological factors.

It was this feverish and uncertain economic context which saw the appearance of the first formal associations of producing countries for bauxite (IBA), iron ore (AIEC), and mercury (ASSIMER). Informal cartels for lead, phosphate, uranium and other metals also came onto the scene at this point. And, although created in 1967, CIPEC announced its first copper export restrictions toward the end of 1974. Seizing upon these circumstances, the United Nations Conference on Trade and Development (UNCTAD) called meetings to negotiate an integrated commodity program. The program was to include a common fund of about $7 billion to finance an international network of buffer stocks for ten "core" products: coffee, cocoa, tea, sugar, cotton, rubber, jute, hard fibres, copper, and tin; appropriate measures were suggested for meat, bananas, wool, iron ore, bauxite, cereal, and rice as well.

Following upon this rapid series of events, the press increased coverage of questions related to the instability of commodity prices, to government and private controls of commodity markets and to the depletion of nonrenewable resources. Attention was focused on Third World demands for a redistribution of world wealth. Encouraged by the successes of OPEC and IBA, several countries dropped the international agreement formula sanctioned by the UN after World War II in favor of creating associations through which producing countries could control the international markets for their commodities.

It was especially in the first half of the seventies that we were brutally brought to realize that "sufficient" and "accessible" were not synonymous terms. Now (using the latest statistics on evolution of world production) firms, governments, financiers, and consumers are attentive not only to the availability of identified reserves and hypothetical resources but also to the international political situation and the ever-increasing cost of substitutes. These economic agents fear the creation of new producer cartels as obstacles to the control of world inflation. Moreover, economists are concerned about the reactions of industrial countries to these modifications in the economic environment. Will they be led to favor bilateral trade? Would they shelve the nondiscrimination clause in tariff negotiations, reduce or slow down international transfers of capital or even give in to the pressures of local producers and erect tariff and nontariff barriers? Some of these economists hypothesize that we are witnessing a shift from a buyer's to a seller's market and wonder just how much such a transition will modify economic and political relations among countries.

The proliferation of controls has raised the hopes of developing countries and brought fear to industrialized countries. Are these hopes and fears justified? There is the fact that, by means of legislation, associations of producing countries have taken measures to control their mineral deposits: they have taken over mining and primary processing; established public agencies for international marketing and, finally, regulated the price and production rates of their natural resources. But what about the past, present, and future performance of these associations? And, as for UNCTAD's integrated program, what are the specific bones of contention in current negotiations? What future lies ahead for the post-1947 agreements on wheat, tin, coffee, sugar, and cocoa? What bearing have these agreements on the current debate over North-South relations?

These are not new questions. In the course of our study we have tried to put them in historical perspective and thus furnish some elements of an answer. It is in fact our belief that this historical perspective is too often absent in the current debate. Far too many economic agents still believe that the history of controls over international commodity markets begins with OPEC or that producing countries have only to exercise their political will to obtain the "reasonable" prices they demand.

What are the main conclusions to be drawn from our study? What evolution is to be foreseen for the integrated program, for international agreements and associations of producing countries? When analyzing the effects of controls on international commodity markets, does there exist a difference in methodology obstructing the progress of North-South negotiations? We shall attempt to answer, in part.

International Commodity Agreements

In some measure, the recent proliferation of producer country associations as well as UNCTAD's 1976 proposition for an integrated commodity program may be explained by the disenchantment manifested by both consumer and producer countries (but especially the latter) for the so-called "international commodity agreements" formula. This formula had been accepted on March 28, 1947 by the United Nations Economic and Social Council (Resolution 30(IV)). This sanction by international authorities for production, consumption and marketing controls on commodities was granted upon the following conditions. Consumer countries would sit on the boards administering control, thus moderating producer country demands. Commodity supplies governed by international agreements would come from the most efficient sources. Boards were to discourage production in countries with high relative costs. The international agreements were to be short-term, susceptible of termination whenever the United Nations judged the problems of excess supply have been solved.

Our study has shown that these conditions have been as much honored in the breach as in the observance by the international agreements signed between 1947 and 1978 for wheat, coffee, sugar, cocoa, and tin (the only mineral having come under this sort of control).

Enlarging the administrative control boards to allow the equal participation of importing countries has been of small effect. Their moderating role has been made a mockery by the oligopolistic character of producer countries. In the case of wheat one clearly sees how very little international agreements have contributed to price stability when compared to the small group of producer countries which, through massive stockpiling, kept prices near the ceiling set by multilateral contracts.

The moderating role of importing countries has also been weakened by the level of monopsony in certain consumer countries, preventing prices from finding their own equilibrium level. A good illustration of this would be the first international coffee agreement signed in 1962. There, for reasons of political strategy, the United States encouraged the other consuming countries to ratify the agreement even if, considering stock levels, the proposed minimum price was well above the long-term equilibrium price. This remark also holds true for the international sugar market where ideological considerations often overrode economic factors. We have only to think of the United States in 1966, guaranteeing producers a 7.0¢/lb. price when the world price was a 1.5¢/lb., or of Russia, purchasing Cuban sugar at 6.0¢/lb. despite a much lower world price.

By putting off necessary economic adjustments, international agreements have often increased the price instability already characterizing commodity markets. Moreover, as illustrated by the evolution of the coffee and sugar markets, the inclusion of importing countries on control boards has not always been to the benefit of the final consumer.

What of the condition stipulating that the supply of controlled commodities come from the most efficient sources? This condition has not in general been respected. The Tin Council has in fact taken no specific measures to discourage production in countries with high relative costs such as Bolivia and

Zaire. And although buffer stocks have presented the advantage of not freezing the industrial structure, as would have quotas based on past commercial performance, they have not managed to keep prices within preestablished brackets. If, at various periods, tin prices have recorded a certain stability, this is due largely to General Services Administration (GSA) sales. The commercial sales of that organism (80,000 LT between 1964 and 1968 and 47,000 LT between 1973 and 1976) have contributed more than the Tin Council's buffer stock to prevent current prices from rising too far above this metal's price ceiling. In the case of wheat, Canadian and American policies of stockpiling have accorded producers artificially high prices, thereby occasioning transfers of human and physical resources far in excess of those called for by the long-term equilibrium price of wheat. This poor allocation of resources stemming from the refusal to link up product price and production costs has characterized the international coffee market as well. The imposition of export quotas and the council's mid-sixties commitment to set the floor price at 1962 levels encouraged producers to grow coffee instead of food crops; this move also stalled production in countries with low relative costs and jammed international transmission of technological discoveries in this sector.

According to resolution 30(IV), international agreements were supposed to be short-term and susceptible of termination at the United Nations discretion. However, not only have these agreements been continuously renegotiated but, much to the chagrin of consuming countries, their form and objectives have been so modified since 1947 as to render negotiations increasingly difficult. Since the mid-sixties, international agreements have been seen not only as appropriate means to stabilize commodity prices and producer receipts and to ensure consuming countries uninterrupted supplies but also as a legitimate means of transferring resources from rich to poor countries. To the consuming country's microeconomic concern for efficient allocation of resources have been added the producing country's macroeconomic preoccupations with development and level of foreign exchange.

These double objectives have often proved incompatible, making negotiations of international agreements very difficult and often impossible. The compromises reached touched less and less frequently on economic questions. The international wheat agreement is a good example: since 1971 it has been a purely administrative arrangement. Even when provisions of an economic interest have been successfully negotiated and ratified, they have not always been applied. Thus the Tin Council was unable to keep the current market price at ceiling level, its buffer stock having already been depleted by January 1977.

In the case of the international coffee market, between September 1972 and November 1975 there was no international agreement at all. Producing countries had disagreed among themselves concerning the allotment of export rights and the quota grid. Consuming and producing countries could reach no agreement concerning ceiling and floor price levels. And, in any case, climatic conditions in Brazil and Colombia had so reduced production as to render controls useless. The 1975 coffee agreement again provided for a system of export quotas but, since it was to become operative only if prices fell below the 1975 level, the clause was never applied. Similarly, the November 1975 cocoa agreement remains practically inapplicable since the April 1977 market price was about triple that of the ceiling price set by the agreement.

So apparently the international cocoa, coffee, and tin agreements are, for various reasons, currently inoperative. As for wheat, this agreement does not yet have economic provisions for setting a price bracket or regulating supply. Furthermore, we note that only a few commodities have been covered by international agreements and that the effect of these agreements on the international markets concerned has been generally rather modest. The high prices of recent years result from factors having little to do with these agreements.

In our opinion, there will be little future use of international agreements— at least in their current form—as a method of control ensuring stability of prices and export receipts for producing countries and uninterrupted supplies to consuming countries. Third World producers of raw materials and foodstuffs have in fact declared that a product by product study of stabilization is bound to fail. They insist that this question be discussed within the framework of a global and integrated program. Their criticism rests on the fact that negotiations of international commodity agreements are too time-consuming and that the presence of importing countries on each administrative board restricts the choice of means of intervention. Finally, drawing attention to the limited number and success of the agreements negotiated so far, they contend that this method of control cannot succeed in restructuring the international economic order.

Most consumer countries still continue to prefer the status quo, even while they criticize international agreements for not ensuring continuous supplies at "lowest price" and for replacing their microeconomic concerns for efficient resource allocation with the macroeconomic concern for development. Accordingly, their claim is that any global solution to problems related to commodity markets must take into account the specific characteristics of each product. The two groups now hold such differing positions that there can be little hope for change in the form or content of future international agreements.

UNCTAD's Integrated Commodity Program

In the debate opposing industrialized countries and the Group of 77, the United Nations has taken a stand; faced with the phenomenon of "new automatic majorities" within its midst, this international body has sided with the developing countries. Thus in 1974 resolutions were adopted, preparing the way for a global integrated program which would mean more stable markets and prices for a wide array of commodities vital to the export trade of developing countries. At Nairobi in 1976, during its fourth session, UNCTAD ratified resolution 93(IV) which defined the objectives, means, procedures, and timetable for an integrated commodity program.

The Nairobi resolution's primary recommendation concerned the establishment of a vast international network of buffer stocks financed by a common fund of about US $6 billion (1976 estimate). The fund would be applicable at first to ten so-called "core" commodities including two minerals, copper and tin. UNCTAD apparently judges the failure of international agreements for individual commodities to have been largely due to inadequate financing of stocks. This problem could be met by a common fund of US $5-6 billion. Such a fund would offer greater borrowing capacity and require less financial support than several individual funds since prices of the various products stocked are unlikely to move simultaneously in the same direction.

In addition to the buffer stock network, the Nairobi resolution recommends an arsenal of measures (compensatory finance, multilateral contracts, international aid to diversify exports, opening of industrial markets to Third World products, and others) to be applied to seven "other" commodities. These include two minerals: iron ore and bauxite (with manganese and phosphate to be added eventually). In sum, these measures apply to commodities whose market problems cannot be solved by stocking. The cost of this last set of measures is estimated at about US $1.5 billion.

The integrated program negotiations are currently at a standstill. The difference of opinion which arose between industrialized countries and the Group of 77 during the November 1977 Geneva Conference seem far from being resolved. What precisely are the points of conflict snarling current negotiations? Besides the problems involving the fund's capital structure, organization, and institutional operation, the following points deserve notice.

First the Nairobi resolution foresees not only the creation of a common fund financing buffer stocks but also separate and parallel discussions and negotiations involving international agreements for specific commodities. Industrial countries take this to mean the legitimacy of stabilization techniques other than buffer stocks and means of finance other than the common fund. The Group of 77 sees the proposition as an official consecration of the common fund as the program's central and integral element.

Second, there is persistent and almost complete disagreement concerning the form and structure of the common fund to be established. If the Group of 77 has its way the fund will include two separate accounts: a general account (around US $5-6 billion) for the short-term financing of buffer stocks and a special account to finance long-term projects for the improvement of productivity and export diversification (about US $1-1.5 billion). Industrial countries contend that the fund should finance only buffer stocks and that to use its resources for other activities would conflict with the principle according to which the fund is not to be an organization for aid.

More important, industrial countries are careful to point out that they have made no commitment involving the exact type of common fund to be set up. It is their feeling that the common fund could take several different forms. It could be a principal source of funds lending to Individual Commodity Organizations (ICOs). Its structure might resemble that of a pool of finance or a clearing house. Finally, the fund could be considered a guarantor of loans or be given a hybrid structure characterized by several of these elements. The Group of 77, on the other hand, would have the fund be purely and simply a principal source of funds. Quite obviously all these problems (type of fund, funds for activities other than buffer stocks, and the importance to be accorded ICOs within the integrated program) remain completely unsolved. Since the London summit there is agreement on the necessity for a common fund but none concerning the exact form it should take.

Third, representatives from industrialized countries and the Group of 77 cannot come to terms on the total cost of the various measures foreseen by the integrated program. This is not surprising since the two parties formulate such divergent hypotheses as to the program's mode of operation. The exact level of expenditures implied will depend, in the final analysis, on the set of hypotheses adopted. These hypotheses concern the number and size of "other measures" to be financed, overall evolution of prices, length of price cycle, price covariation, storage expenses, cost of financing loans, gap between floor and ceiling prices, existence and efficiency of a supply-limiting mechanism in case of overproduction, number of commodities retained, volume of commodities stocked, and the degree of substitution among these commodities. Considering the number of hypotheses to be sifted on the buffer stocks' mode of operation, considering also that the "other measures" may easily cost more than foreseen, we take the US $6-7 billion requested to be grossly approximative. Industrial countries tend to propose a US $10-12 billion figure while the Group of 77 calculates that the program's actual expenditures will fall below UNCTAD estimates.

In our opinion the size of the sums involved requires that the integrated program's cost be compared to other possible programs promoting the stabilization of Third World export receipts. This objective, accepted by the international community both at the London summit and during the North-South Dialogue, can also be attained by measures such as a slightly more ambitious version of the IMF's present program of compensatory finance or greater trade liberalization in favor of developing countries. It is essential to know the cost-benefit ratio of these other measures if one hopes to choose a national stabilization policy. Refusing to consider the whole range of alternatives represents, it seems to us, one of the chief reasons for the failure of the second round of common fund negotiations held at Geneva from November 7 to December 2, 1977.

Notwithstanding their seriousness, the difficulties stated are not insurmountable. Other negotiations will be held; the number of buffer stocks to be financed by the common fund will eventually be reduced; the "other measures" may possibly be redefined and some compromise formula thus worked out. However, we fear that, in the search for such a compromise, political considerations will outweigh criteria of economic efficiency.

Associations of Producing Countries

The performance of international agreements has been largely disenchanting. Negotiations for an integrated program drag on. It can, therefore, scarcely be surprising that some developing countries have felt so attracted to associations of producing countries. And so the 1964-1978 period has also seen the creation of formal cartels for petroleum, copper, bauxite, iron ore, and mercury while informal associations of producing countries or companies were set up for lead, phosphate, uranium, and other ores and metals. The national governments participating in these associations set about regulating the production, price, and marketing of the commodities mentioned. They have legislated control of mineral deposits, taking charge of mining and primary refining. Although effected without the consent of consuming countries or UN organisms, the objectives of these controls are quite similar to those set forth in 1947 and 1976 by resolutions 30(IV) and 93(IV) respectively: improve the commodity-producing countries' terms of trade, counter the effexts of inflation on their real incomes by increasing prices, eliminate the economic disparities between producing and consuming countries, and balance the influence of multinational firms on price determination and the inflow of foreign exchange.

Our study has centered on the history, performance, and structure of the international markets where producer country associations have formed to influence price, production, marketing, and various other economic variables. This approach has allowed us to evaluate the effects of CIPEC (copper), IBA (bauxite), AIEC (iron ore), and ASSIMER (mercury) on their respective markets.

Comparing the performance of these associations with that of OPEC, it is obvious that the effects of their policies have generally proven more modest. Why is this? What conditions contribute to the success of producer country associations or cartels in their attempt to influence commodity prices and production receipts?

From the story of OPEC and from economic theory we know that a producers' association can have a prolonged influence on the international market if some very specific conditions are met. We would like to mention the most important of these.

1. Association members must be responsible for a large percentage of world production or of that portion of production engaged in international

trade. This assures the association that international consumers cannot turn for supplies to nonmembers following price increases, imposition of export quotas or some other association move.

2. The international demand for the controlled commodity must be characterized by both short- and medium-term price inelasticity. This implies that, for a given commodity, the percentage variation for decreasing demand (movement forecasted when a producer increases his selling price) must be less than the percentage variation for increasing price. If this condition is met, producer receipts are sure to enjoy both short- and medium-term increases. If not, producers will witness a decrease in total revenue, the receipt increase due to higher prices having been counterbalanced by a decrease in receipts due to lower demand.

3. There should be no short- or medium-term appropriate substitutes for the commodity under controls. This would mean that the association's price increases and supply restraints could not be countered by favoring substitution of its commodity by other products which would satisfy demand at equal or lower prices.

4. Association members must give evidence of cohesion and discipline in the methods used to appropriate the economic rent, whether this is to be done through the increase of royalties, taxes, or fees. If member countries are numerous and differ markedly in economic scale or political ideology, this condition will not be easily met. So there would be greater risk of a price war and dismemberment of the association. This risk is particularly high when, for a given country, the controlled commodity accounts for such a large percentage of national production or provides employment for such a large portion of the labor force that prolonged production quotas would be unbearable.

5. Identified reserves and subeconomic resources must be largely located in association member countries. If this were not the case, association production and export restrictions would simply stimulate these activities in nonmember countries. Furthermore, price increases would intensify exploration in nonmember countries and transform subeconomic resources into identified reserves.

This does not represent an exhaustive list of the conditions for success. The success or failure of the policies adopted by an association also depends on the member's comparative advantages; the growth rate of international demand for the commodity when controls are applied; the size of the secondary market; the possibilities for recycling; the association's control of the input costs in producing the commodity. There are still other contributing factors such as the percentage accounted for by the commodity in the total cost of the manufactured or semimanufactured products in which it is used; elasticity of the international demand for such products; identified resources-forecasted demand ratio; commercial and strategic stock levels in consuming countries and an array of other factors as much related to technology; transport and international politics as to the economic structure of member countries.

Those producer associations for which the greatest number of these conditions come together will be the most effective on their respective markets. For some, this will mean a decade of power to raise prices and redistribute world wealth. For others the time of victory will be more ephemeral. Still others will go down in spectacular and sometimes irreversible defeat.

Having analyzed the international markets for copper, iron ore, and mercury we feel safe in concluding that CIPEC, AIEC, and ASSIMER are powerless to exert any tangible influence on their markets in the foreseeable future. The case of IBA, on the other hand, deserves a more balanced verdict.

Analysis of the salient characteristics of the international bauxite-alumina-aluminum industry indicates that, despite lack of common action among IBA members, most of the interventions made by individual member countries have had their impact.[1] They have succeeded in increasing bauxite prices and government receipts, accelerating the implantation of high value-added operations on the domestic market and controlling an increasing percentage of alumina production capacity.[2] All this has been possible because these countries hold comparative advantages over other sources of supply. IBA's Secretariat is well aware of these advantages and regards the future with optimism.

While we believe IBA member countries will continue to enjoy the success described for a few years to come, we do not share the secretariat's optimism that it will endure, at least not for certain of the countries involved. Our analysis has, in fact, brought out the following points.

1. Bauxite produced in the Caribbean, Guyana and Surinam represented (in 1976) only 24% of world production compared to 33% at the time of IBA's creation in 1974[3].

2. Although only 28% of identified bauxite reserves are located in non-member countries, they would be sufficient to keep up with the 1976 production rates of alumina for another sixty years.

3. The rise in bauxite prices has strongly encouraged the search for substitutes and the results of this search will become tangible at the beginning of the eighties.

4. The high cost of energy will lead increasingly to the processing of bauxite and alumina in countries with cheap and plentiful electric resources; most IBA countries cannot offer these elements.

5. There is no guarantee that Australia, the world's leading bauxite producer, will remain in the IBA or go along with policies suggested by smaller and more interventionist countries.

The IBA Secretariat does not take sufficient account of these elements in evaluating this association's future. IBA's global successes are enumerated without any mention of the future price certain member countries will have to pay.

P.L. Eckbo, in his analysis of fifty-one commodity-producing country associations, also comes to the conclusion that there are few commodities likely to afford these associations the kind of success OPEC has obtained.[4] This study estimates the average life expectancy of these associations to be 5.4 years (4.3 if we eliminate one association from the sample), with a median expectancy of 2.5 years. The evidence from economic history shows that more recent associations such as World Coffee, the Association of Natural Rubber Producing Countries and the Union of Banana Exporting Countries offer no exception to this rule. Given the relative failure of international agreements and of commodity-producing country associations, these countries will henceforth place their strongest hopes in the UNCTAD negotiations for an Integrated Program. On the other hand, UNCTAD must show that there are important potential gains for both producing and consuming countries from the proposed integrated commodity program.[5]

The North-South Dialogue: Conflicting Analytical Methods

A general conclusion can be drawn from our historical survey. Based upon microeconomic criteria related to resource allocation, the majority of governments and analysts from industrial or consuming countries conclude that interventions on commodity markets usually fail for the following reasons.

First, by guaranteeing producers artifically high prices, these interventions lead to an inordinate transfer of human and physical resources toward the controlled commodity's sector, a transfer whose proportions are unwarranted by the long-term equilibrium price.

Second, the higher prices of agricultural products destined for international markets and subject to controls encourage local producers to concentrate their resources on the production of these goods offering artificially high profits to the detriment of food crops. This impedes the diversification of national production.

Third, to the extent that quotas and other supply-control techniques push commodity prices above levels which would have prevailed without controls, these interventions feed inflation in importing countries. This cost increase is subsequently reflected in the price of manufactured goods exported to the commodity-producing countries. It is by this kind of chain reaction that developing countries find their temporary gains in terms of trade annulled.

Fourth, using the same criteria, economists show that in some cases price stabilization can have unfavorable consequences for developing countries.[6] They demonstrate that if we are in a supply shift market (the case of most agricultural products), price stabilization will increase the level of total receipts and the welfare of commodity-exporting countries. However, this scenario may also give rise to receipt instability if demand is elastic in relation to prices within given limits. Alternatively, if the stabilization policy is applied on a demand shift market (the case of most mineral markets), price stabilization will reduce the exporting country's total receipts and general welfare. But, in this case, the exporting country's export receipts will be stabilized if demand remains elastic as related to prices within certain limits.

The governments and analysts of Third World commodity-producing countries remain generally impervious to these kinds of arguments drawn mostly from classical microeconomic theory. According to this theory, product prices must be tied to production costs if the economy is to make efficient use of its scarce resources. But what counts for these governments and analysts is not efficient resource allocation but rather the macroeconomic effects to be expected from use of controls.

In response to the fear that price increases may retard diversification of their national production, Third World analysts reply that such increases would facilitate diversification. In their view, the additional income generated by increased prices can be tapped by local governments through fiscal measures or marketing boards and used to promote other production activities.

In response to the argument that price stabilization is not always in the interest of producer countries since it can sometimes destabilize receipts or even reduce them, Third World government representatives reply that these negative effects are relatively unimportant compared to more global benefits. These benefits include opportunity to rationalize and stabilize investments, improvement of the competitive position of commodities, and maintaining employment levels in mining-related sectors.

To the various reservations expressed concerning price stabilization, Third World economists reply that reduction of fluctuations in commodity prices is as much in the interest of consuming countries as of producing countries. To the latter, this stabilization provides better knowledge of future prices and receipts, contributes to sounder productive investment plans, and affords more precise indication of needs in human and physical resources and in foreign exchange. Such stabilization would also improve the competitive position of their commodities as compared to synthetic products. Industrial countries would also benefit, since stabilization reduces the risks of inflationary surges due to commodity price jumps and holds Third World demands for manufactured imports steady.

Finally, Third World economic advisors give this reply to those who fear the inflationary impact of control-related price rises. Inflation is caused by sudden sharp increases in commodity prices; these increases are amplified by the practice of "administered prices" in industrial countries. Price stabilization through buffer stocks or other techniques would prevent such excessive fluctuations and therefore be advantageous to industrial countries. In any case, developing countries are well aware that producer associations cannot increase prices unduly because of the presence of substitutes. This same remark applies to international agreements where consumer countries can always temper any exaggerated demands made by producing countries.

This debate between industrial and developing countries is likely to be a long-drawn-out affair because of the fundamental difference in their analytical approaches to the problem of commodities in international economic relations. The two groups of countries do not speak the same language, for they do not have the same perspective on what they nevertheless presume to be a common reality.

In our view, the recognition that there exists such a difference is essential if North-South negotiations are to be reopened and accelerated. In this connection, we often hear talk of the need for a new economic order, for new relations or a new marriage between industrial and developing countries. The allusion here must surely be to one of those marriages of convenience where the partners—unable because of their differences to make a love match—are still intelligent enough to see beyond these differences and appreciate the mutual advantages offered by their union.

Notes

1. The only attempt at joint action was announced in December 1977. This was to fix a minimum US $24 c.i.f. price on each ton of bauxite destined for the American market. The short-term effects of this policy were minimal since the prices of the market's main suppliers were far in excess of the announced figure.

2. Transformation of bauxite into alumina (started in the early sixties) and transport of these products are illustrations of these activities.

3. Bauxite production has decreased by 30% in Jamaica and Surinam between 1974 and 1976.

4. P.L. Eckbo, "OPEC and the Experience of Previous International Commodity Cartels."

5. In a recent simulation work, Jere R. Behrman has estimated that, under conservative assumptions, the stabilization of commodity prices could have resulted in economic gains (the "prevented" unemployment and GNP loss) amounting to a total present discounted value of about $15 billion over a decade, in the United States alone. The interested reader is referred to J.R. Behrman, *International Commodity Agreements.*

6. An example of this can be found in the study by E.H. Brook, and E.R. Grilli, "Commodity Price Stabilization and the Developing World," pp. 8-11.

Bibliography

Adams, Francis G., and Behrman, Jere R. *Econometric Models of World Agricultural Commodity Markets: Cocoa, Coffee, Tea, Wool, Cotton, Sugar, Wheat, Rice.* Cambridge, Mass.: Ballinger Publishing Co., 1976.

Banks, Ferdinand E. *The World Copper Market: An Economic Analysis.* Cambridge, Mass.: Ballinger Publishing Co., 1974.

Behrman, Jere R. *International Commodity Agreements: An Evaluation of the UNCTAD Integrated Commodity Programme.* Overseas Development Council, NIEO Series, Monograph no. 9, Washington, D.C., October 1977.

Brinck, J.W., and Van Wambeke, L. "World Resources of Mercury." *Congreso Internacional del Mercurio* I, 1974.

British-North American Committee. *Mineral Development in the Eighties: Prospects and Problems.* London: British-North American Research Association, 1976. (Publication BN-19).

Brook, Ezriel M., and Grilli, Enzo R. "Commodity Price Stabilization and the Developing World." *Finance and Development* 14 (March 1977): 8-11.

Brookings Institution. *Trade in Primary Commodities: Conflict or Cooperation?* Washington: Brookings Institution, 1974.

Canada. Department of Energy, Mines & Resources. *Iron Ore.* Ottawa: Minister of Supply and Services Canada, 1976. (Mineral Policy Series, MR 148).

Charles River Associates. *Economic Issues Underlying Supply Access Agreements: A General Analysis and Prospects in Ten Mineral Markets.* Cambridge, Mass.: Charles River Associates, 1975. Prepared for U.S. Department of Labor Bureau of International Labor Affairs.

Clarfield, Kenneth W.; Jackson, S.; Keeffe, J.; Noble, M.A.; and Ryan, A.P. *Eight Mineral Cartels: The New Challenge to Industrialized Nations.* New York: Metals Week, 1975.

Commodities Research Unit Ltd. "A Common Fund—Financial Organization, Operations and Management." *The Common Fund*, vol. 1: Papers prepared by Consultants for Commonwealth Technical Group. London: Commonwealth Secretariat, 1977. pp. 3-45. (Commonwealth Economic Papers, no. 8).

Commodity Research Bureau. *Commodity Year Book.* New York: Commodity Research Bureau, Inc., 1964, 1975, 1977.

Commonwealth Secretariat. *The Evolution of Proposals on the Constituent Elements of the Common Fund.* London: Commonwealth Secretariat, 1977. (Publication no. GFTG/B.4).

Commonwealth Secretariat. *The Progress of Negotiations on the Common Fund.* London: Commonwealth Secretariat, 1977. (Publication no. CFTG/B.5).

Commonwealth Secretariat. *Some of the Principal Issues in the Negotiation for a Common Fund.* London: Commonwealth Secretariat, 1977. (Publication no. CFTG/B.3).

Commonwealth Secretariat. *The Common Fund: Report of the Commonwealth Technical Group.* London: Commonwealth Secretariat, 1977.

Conference on Energy Conservation and Recycling in the Aluminium Industry. Cambridge, England: 1974. *Aluminium Magazine,* February 1975.

Congress of the United States. Congressional Budget Office. *Commodity Initiatives of Less Developed Countries: U.S. Responses and Costs.* Washington, D.C.: U.S. Government Printing Office, 1977.

Cordero, Harry George, and Tarring, Leslie Herbert. *Babylon to Birmingham: An Historical Survey of the Development of the World's Non-ferrous Metal and Iron and Steel Industries and of the Commerce in Metals since the Earliest Times.* London: Quin Press, 1960.

Diaz-Alejandro, Carlos Federico. *North-South Relations: The Economic Component.* Yale University Economic Growth Centre, 1974. (Centre Discussion Paper no. 200).

Drewry (H.P.) (Shipping Consultants) Limited. *Ocean Shipping of Bauxite and Alumina.* London, 1976. (Economic Study no. 43).

Eckbo, Paul Leo. "OPEC and the Experience of Previous International Commodity Cartels." Cambridge, Mass.: MIT Energy Laboratory Working Paper no 75-008WP, 1975.

Engineering and Mining Journal. New York: McGraw-Hill, March 1977.

Far-Eastern Economic Review. Hong Kong. Various issues.

Fisher, F.M.; Cootner, P.H.; and Baily, M.N. "An Econometric Model of the World Copper Industry." *Bell Journal of Economics and Management Science* 3 (Autumn 1972): 568-609.

Food and Agriculture Organization of the United Nations. *FAO Commodity Review and Outlook 1976-1977.* (Social Development Series, no. 4), 1977.

Food and Agriculture Organization of the United Nations. *Production Yearbook.* 1964-1975.

Food and Agriculture Organization of the United Nations. *Trade Yearbook.* 1948, 1952, 1954-55, 1957-59, 1961, 1965-66, 1971, 1975.

Fox, William A. *Tin: The Working of a Commodity Agreement.* London: Mining Journal Books Ltd., 1974.

General Agreement on Tariffs and Trade. *International Trade in 1976-77.* 1977.

Green, R.H. *The Common Fund: Prolegomena to Cost/Benefit Estimation.* Vienna Institute for Development, 1977. (Occasional Paper 77/3).

Hogan, William Thomas. *The 1970s: Critical Years for Steel.* Lexington, Mass.: D.C. Heath and Co., Lexington Books, 1972.

International Bank for Reconstruction and Development. *Commodity Trade and Price Trends.* 1976 ed., Washington, 1976. (Report no. EC/166/76).

International Bank for Reconstruction and Development. *Report of the International Bank for Reconstruction and Development (World Bank) and the International Development Association (I.D.A.).* Washington, 1977.

International Monetary Fund. *IMF Survey*. Washington, various issues.

International Monetary Fund. *International Financial Statistics*. Washington: International Monetary Fund, v. XXX, no 5; v. XXXI, no 2; May 1977 and February 1978.

International Tin Council. *Tin Statistics: 1964-1974.* London.

International Tin Council. *Statistical Supplement: 1963.* London.

International Wheat Council. *World Wheat Statistics: 1977.* London.

Kaldor, Nicholas L. "Inflation and Recession in the World Economy." *Economic Journal* 86 (December 1976): 703-714.

Kravis, Irving B. "International Commodity Agreements to Promote Aid and Efficiency: The Case of Coffee." *Canadian Journal of Economics* 1 (May 1968): 295-317.

Labys, Walter C., and Perrin, Yves. "Multivariate Analysis of Price Aspects of Commodity Stabilization." *Weltwirtschaftliches Archiv* 112 (1976): 556-564.

Law, Alton D. *International Commodity Agreements: setting, performance, and prospects.* Lexington, Mass.: D.C. Heath and Co., Lexington Books, 1975.

Lisemann, R.H. "Copper—The Long, Slow Road Back." *Engineering and Mining Journal,* March 1977, pp. 73-76.

MacPhee, Carig Robert. *Restrictions on International Trade in Steel.* Lexington, Mass.: D.C. Heath and Co., Lexington Books, 1974.

Mason, Edward S. *Controlling World Trade: Cartels and Commodity Agreements.* New York and London: McGraw-Hill, 1946. (Committee for Economic Development Research Study).

The Metal Bulletin. *Metal Bulletin Handbook.* 9th ed., London, 1976.

The Metal Bulletin. *World Aluminium Survey, 1977.* London, 1977.

Metals Statistics: The Purchasing of the Metal Industries. New York: Fairchild Publications, 1976.

Metals Week. New York: McGraw-Hill, 1976-77; 1977-78.

Nappi, Carmine. "Caractéristiques économiques du marché international du cuivre." *Gestion* 2 (September 1977): 48-56.

Nicolas, Henri. "L'aluminium." *La Revue Economique de la Banque Nationale de Paris,* nos. 32 and 33, October 1974 and January 1975.

Oppenheimer & Co. *Aluminium Industry Report; Mid-Year Survey of Free World Primary Aluminium Capacity: 1974-1979.* New York, Metals Review, September 1974.

Organization for Economic Cooperation and Development. *Industrial Adaptation in the Primary Aluminium Industry.* Paris: O.E.C.D., 1976.

Pan American Coffee Bureau. *Annual Coffee Statistics, 1973.* New York, 1973. (Publication no. 36).

Rogers, C.D. "International Commodity Agreements." *Lloyds Bank Review,* no. 108, April 1973. pp. 33-47.

Rowe, John Wilkinson Foster. *Primary Commodities in International Trade.* London: Cambridge University Press, 1965.

Sarkar, G.K. "The UNCTAD Integrated Programme and Macro-Economic Considerations." *The Common Fund,* vol. 1: Papers prepared by Consultants for Commonwealth Technical Group. London: Commonwealth Secretariat, 1977. pp. 46-72. (Commonwealth Economic Papers, no. 8).

Szekely, Julian, ed. *The Steel Industry and Energy Crisis: Proceedings of the Fourth C. C. Furnas Memorial Conference.* New York: Marcel Dekker, 1975.

Thoburn, John T. *Primary Commodity Exports and Economic Development: Theory, Evidence and a Study of Malaysia.* New York: John Wiley and Sons, 1977.

United Nations. *United Nations Conference on Coffee, 1968.* New York, 1969. Articles 30-39. (Publication no. TD/Coffee).

United Nations. *United Nations Conference on Wheat, 1971.* New York, 1971. (Publication no. TD/Wheat. 5/9).

United Nations. *United Nations Conference on Sugar, 1973.* New York, 1974. (Publication no. TD/Sugar. 8/6).

United Nations. *United Nations Conference on Tin, 1975.* New York, 1976. (Publication no. TD/Tin. 5/11).

United Nations. *Monthly Bulletin of Statistics.* New York, various issues.

United Nations. *Statistical Yearbook.* New York, various issues.

United Nations Conference on Trade and Development. *Resolution Adopted by the Conference: Integrated Programme for Commodities.* Geneva, TD/RES/93(IV), 1976. (Adopted without dissent, May 30, 1976).

United Nations Conference on Trade and Development. *A Common Fund for the Financing of Commodity Stocks: Amounts, Terms and Prospective Sources of Finances.* Geneva, TD/B/C.1/184, 1975.

United Nations Conference on Trade and Development. *Handbook of International Trade and Development Statistics,* Geneva, 1976.

World Metals Statistics. Edgbaston, Birmingham, England. World Bureau of Metal Statistics, December 1976 and January 1978.

Index

About the Author

Carmine Nappi received the B.A. and Ph.D. in economics from McGill University in Montreal. He has taught at the University of Quebec and at Montreal Business School (Ecole des Hautes Etudes Commerciales) where he is presently an associate professor of international trade and economics of natural resources. He has published a book and several articles on Quebec foreign and interprovincial trade. Professor Nappi's recent writings have centered on mineral and agricultural policies of the developing world, and on econometric models of international commodity markets.